Acker & Blacker Present...

THE THRILLING ADVENTURE HOUR ™

J. Bone
Omi Remalante Jr.

Sparks Nevada, Marshal on Mars in...

MARTIAN MANHUNT

BOOM! STUDIOS

A Comic Collection
Produced in Spectacular
WORKJUICE COLOR
for a Superior Reading
Experience

WARNING:
This volume may contain two-fisted action,
full-hearted romance and spine-tingling terror.
Sometimes concurrently.
PLEASE READ
RESPONSIBLY.

DESIGNER
SCOTT NEWMAN

ORIGINAL SERIES EDITOR
NATE COSBY

COLLECTION EDITOR
CAMERON CHITTOCK

THE THRILLING ADVENTURE HOUR: MARTIAN MANHUNT, February 2019. Published by BOOM! Studios, a division of Boom Entertainment, Inc. The Thrilling Adventure Hour is ™ & © 2019 Workjuice Corp. Originally published in single magazine form as THE THRILLING ADVENTURE HOUR PRESENTS: SPARKS NEVADA: MARSHAL ON MARS No. 0-4. ™ & © 2014-2015 Workjuice Corp. All rights reserved. BOOM! Studios™ and the BOOM! Studios logo are trademarks of Boom Entertainment, Inc., registered in various countries and categories. All characters, events, and institutions depicted herein are fictional. Any similarity between any of the names, characters, persons, events, and/or institutions in this publication to actual names, characters, and persons, whether living or dead, events, and/or institutions is unintended and purely coincidental. BOOM! Studios does not read or accept unsolicited submissions of ideas, stories, or artwork.

BOOM! Studios, 5670 Wilshire Boulevard, Suite 400, Los Angeles, CA 90036-5679. Printed in China. First Printing.

ISBN: 978-1-68415-316-9, eISBN: 978-1-64144-169-8

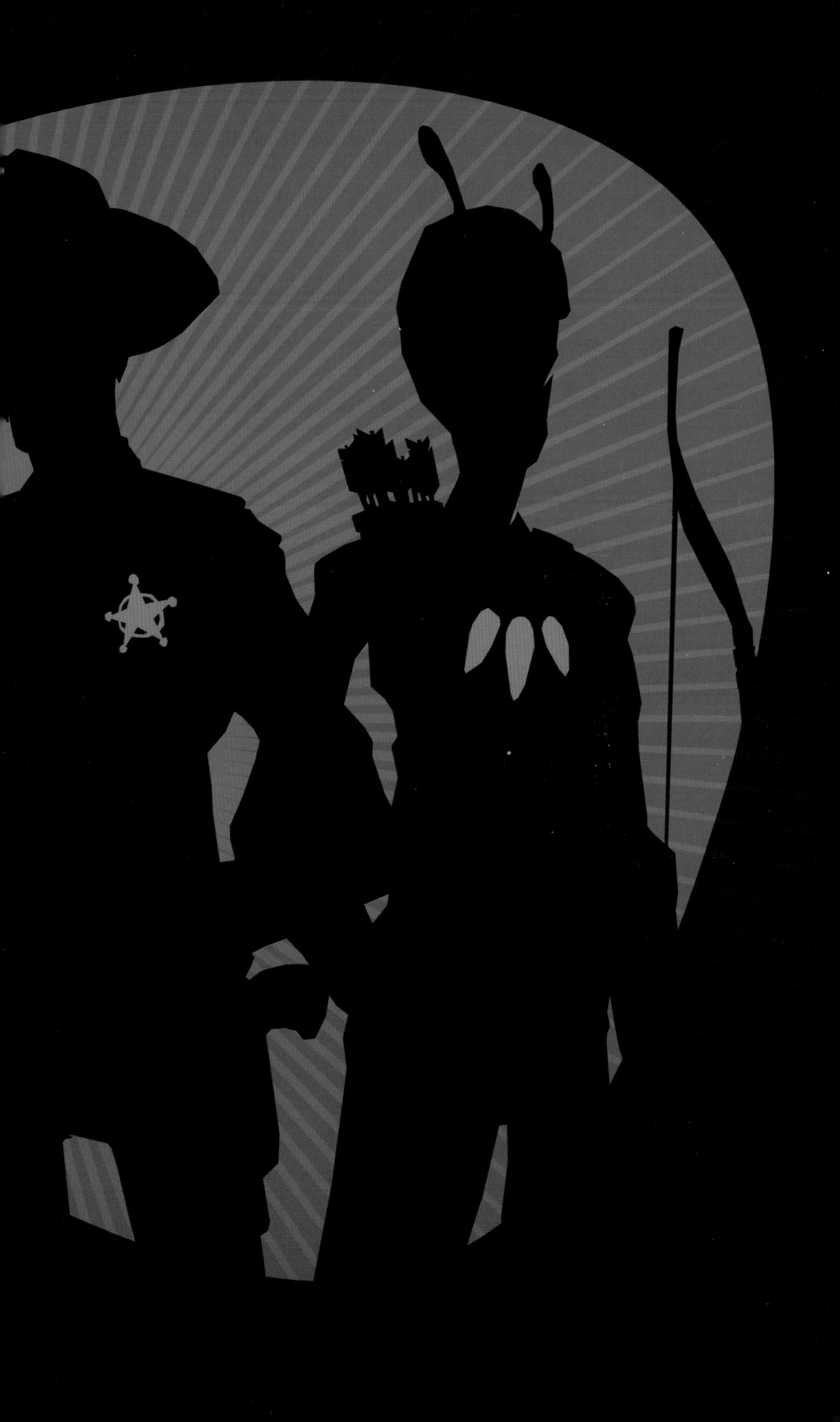

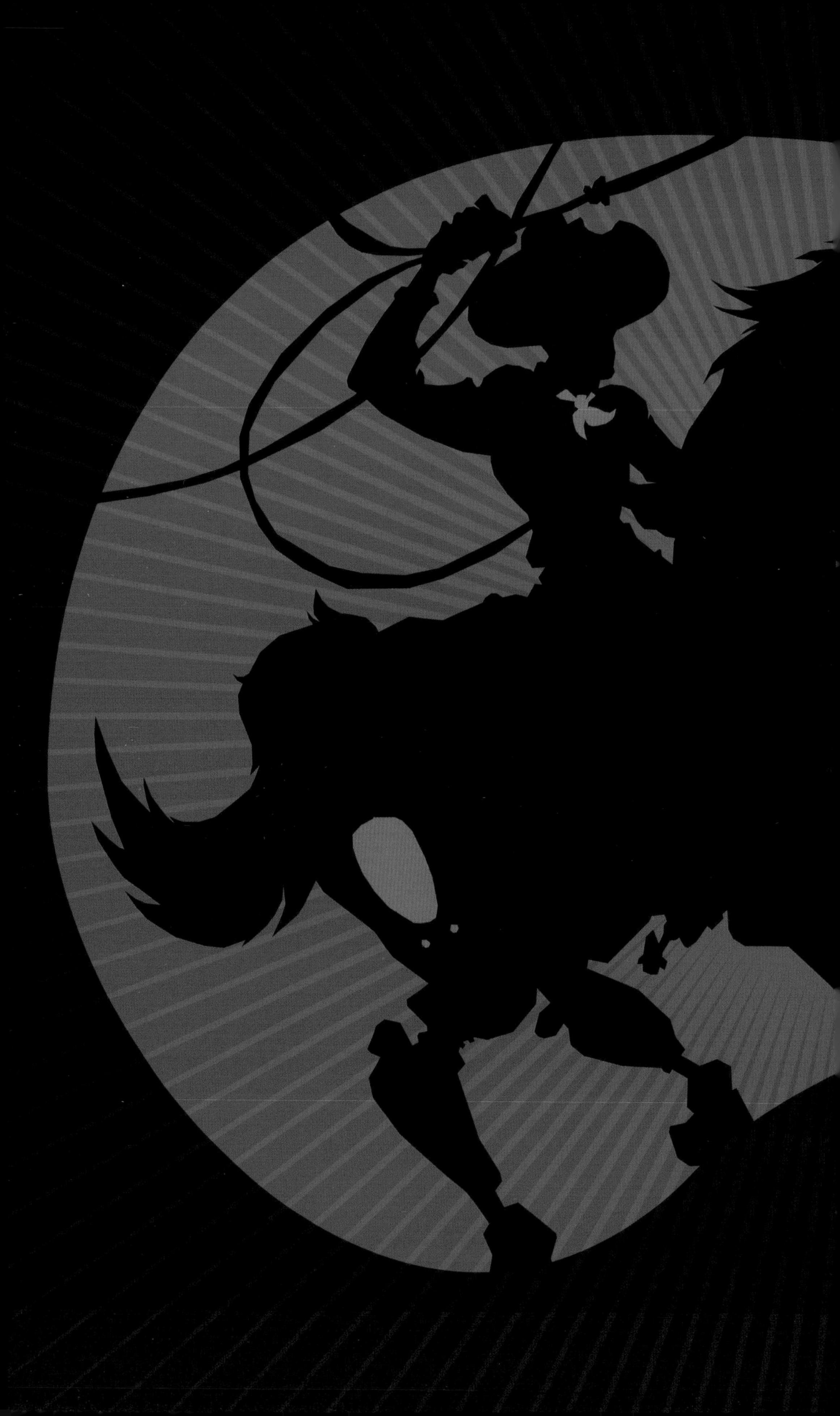

Sparks Nevada, Marshal on Mars in...

MARTIAN MANHUNT

WRITTEN BY
BEN ACKER & BEN BLACKER

ILLUSTRATED BY
J. BONE

COLORED BY
OMI REMALANTE JR.
JORDIE BELLAIRE

LETTERED BY
MARSHALL DILLON

COVER BY
SCOTT NEWMAN

PROLOGUE

The Marshal Meets the Tracker

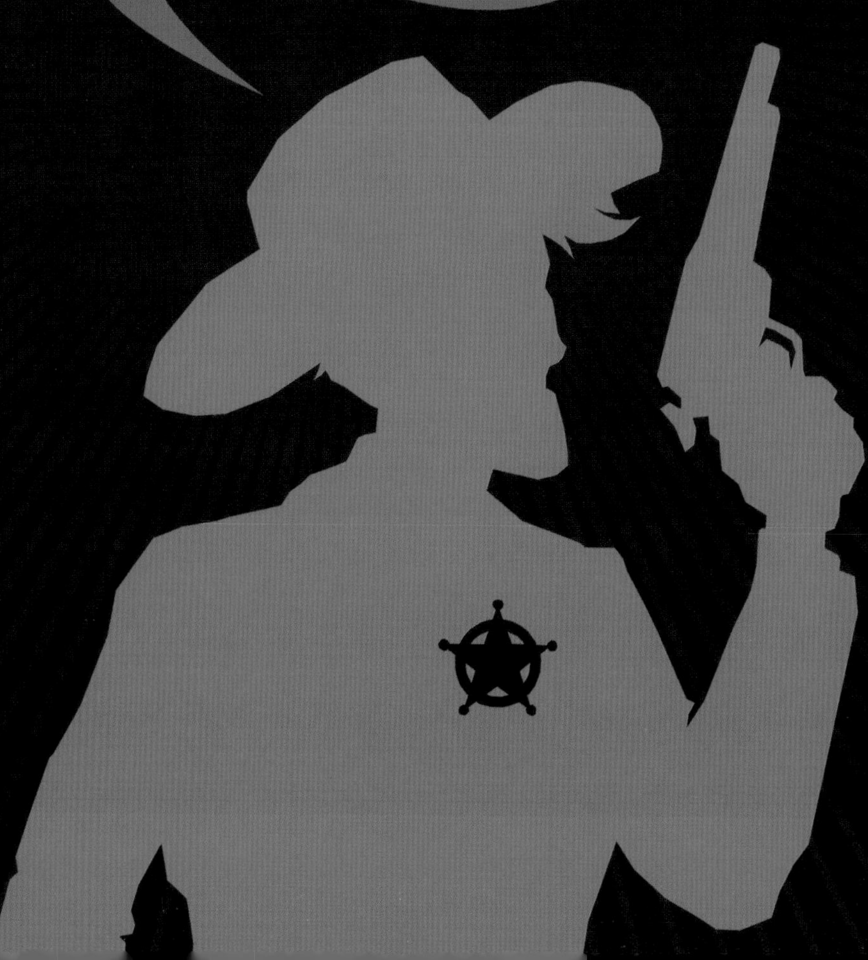

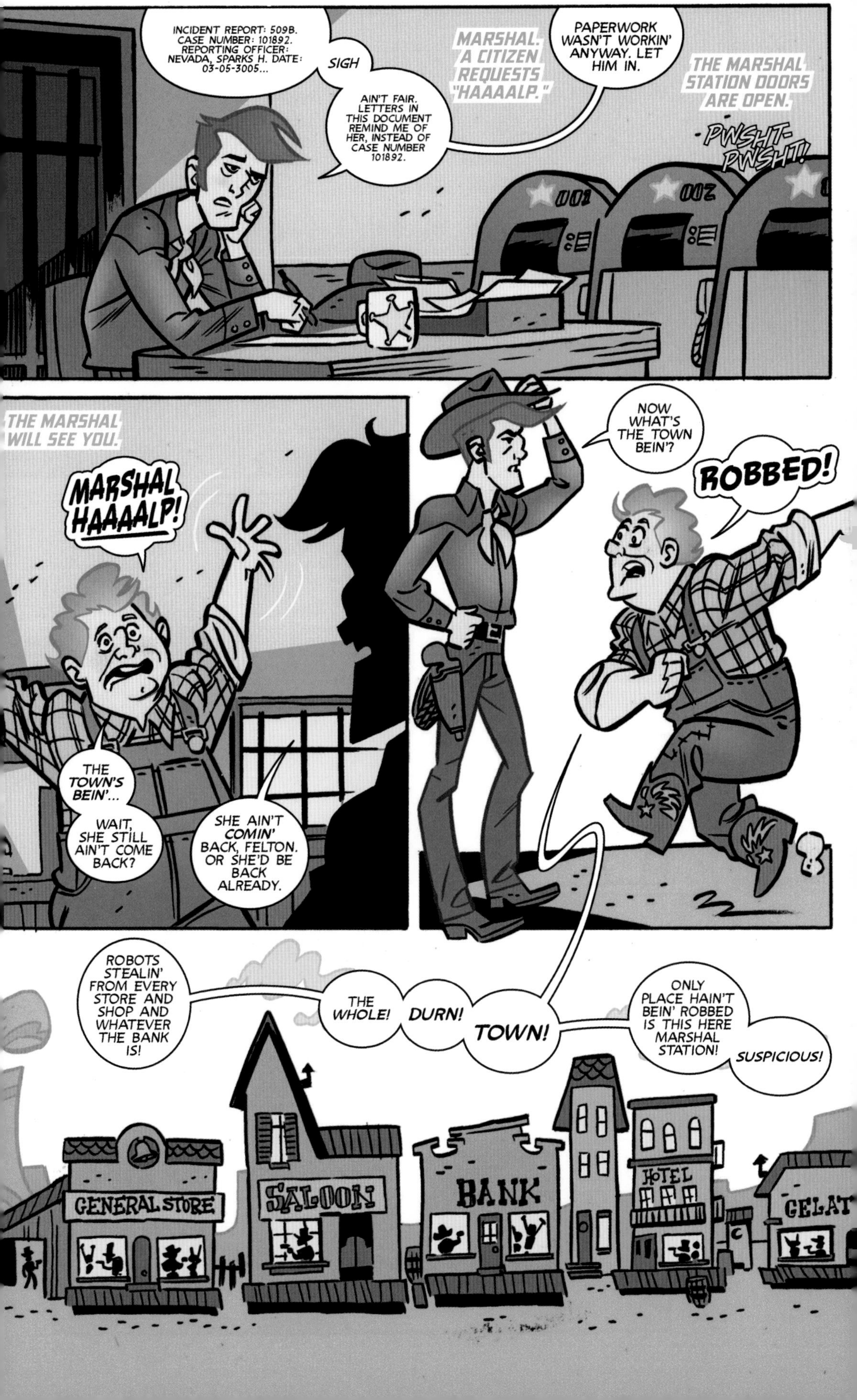
INCIDENT REPORT: 509B. CASE NUMBER: 101892. REPORTING OFFICER: NEVADA, SPARKS H. DATE: 03-05-3005...
SIGH
AIN'T FAIR. LETTERS IN THIS DOCUMENT REMIND ME OF HER, INSTEAD OF CASE NUMBER 101892.
MARSHAL. A CITIZEN REQUESTS "HAAAALP."
PAPERWORK WASN'T WORKIN' ANYWAY. LET HIM IN.
THE MARSHAL STATION DOORS ARE OPEN.
PWSHT-PWSHT!
001
002
THE MARSHAL WILL SEE YOU.
MARSHAL HAAAALP!
THE TOWN'S BEIN'...
WAIT, SHE STILL AIN'T COME BACK?
SHE AIN'T COMIN' BACK, FELTON. OR SHE'D BE BACK ALREADY.
NOW WHAT'S THE TOWN BEIN'?
ROBBED!
ROBOTS STEALIN' FROM EVERY STORE AND SHOP AND WHATEVER THE BANK IS!
THE WHOLE! DURN! TOWN!
ONLY PLACE HAIN'T BEIN' ROBBED IS THIS HERE MARSHAL STATION!
SUSPICIOUS!
GENERAL STORE
SALOON
BANK
HOTEL
GELAT

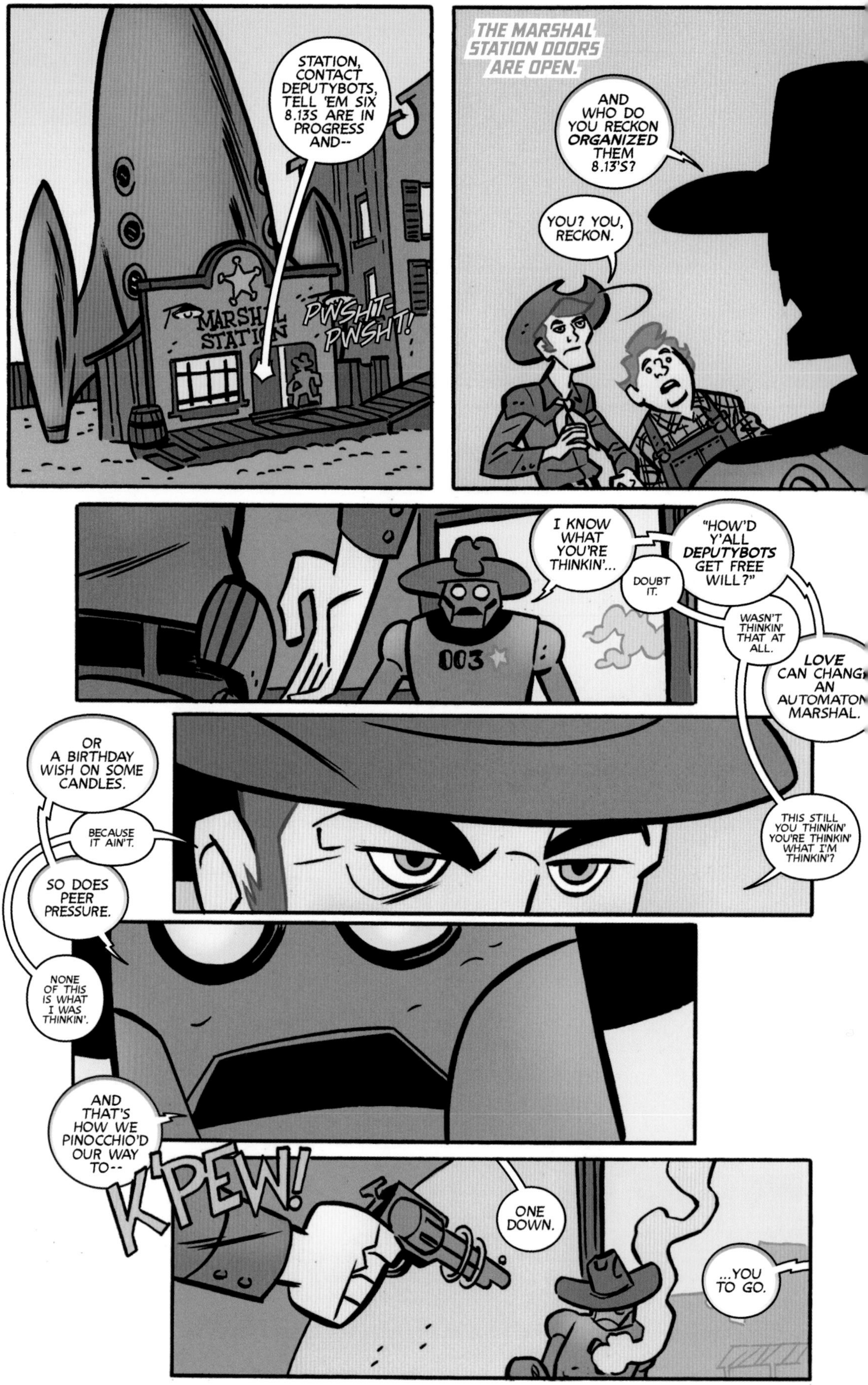
STATION, CONTACT DEPUTYBOTS, TELL 'EM SIX 8.13S ARE IN PROGRESS AND--
MARSHAL STATION
PWSHT-PWSHT!
THE MARSHAL STATION DOORS ARE OPEN.
AND WHO DO YOU RECKON ORGANIZED THEM 8.13'S?
YOU? YOU, RECKON.
I KNOW WHAT YOU'RE THINKIN'...
DOUBT IT.
"HOW'D Y'ALL DEPUTYBOTS GET FREE WILL?"
WASN'T THINKIN' THAT AT ALL.
003
LOVE CAN CHANGE AN AUTOMATON MARSHAL.
THIS STILL YOU THINKIN' YOU'RE THINKIN' WHAT I'M THINKIN'?
OR A BIRTHDAY WISH ON SOME CANDLES.
BECAUSE IT AIN'T.
SO DOES PEER PRESSURE.
NONE OF THIS IS WHAT I WAS THINKIN'.
AND THAT'S HOW WE PINOCCHIO'D OUR WAY TO--
K'PEW!
ONE DOWN.
...YOU TO GO.

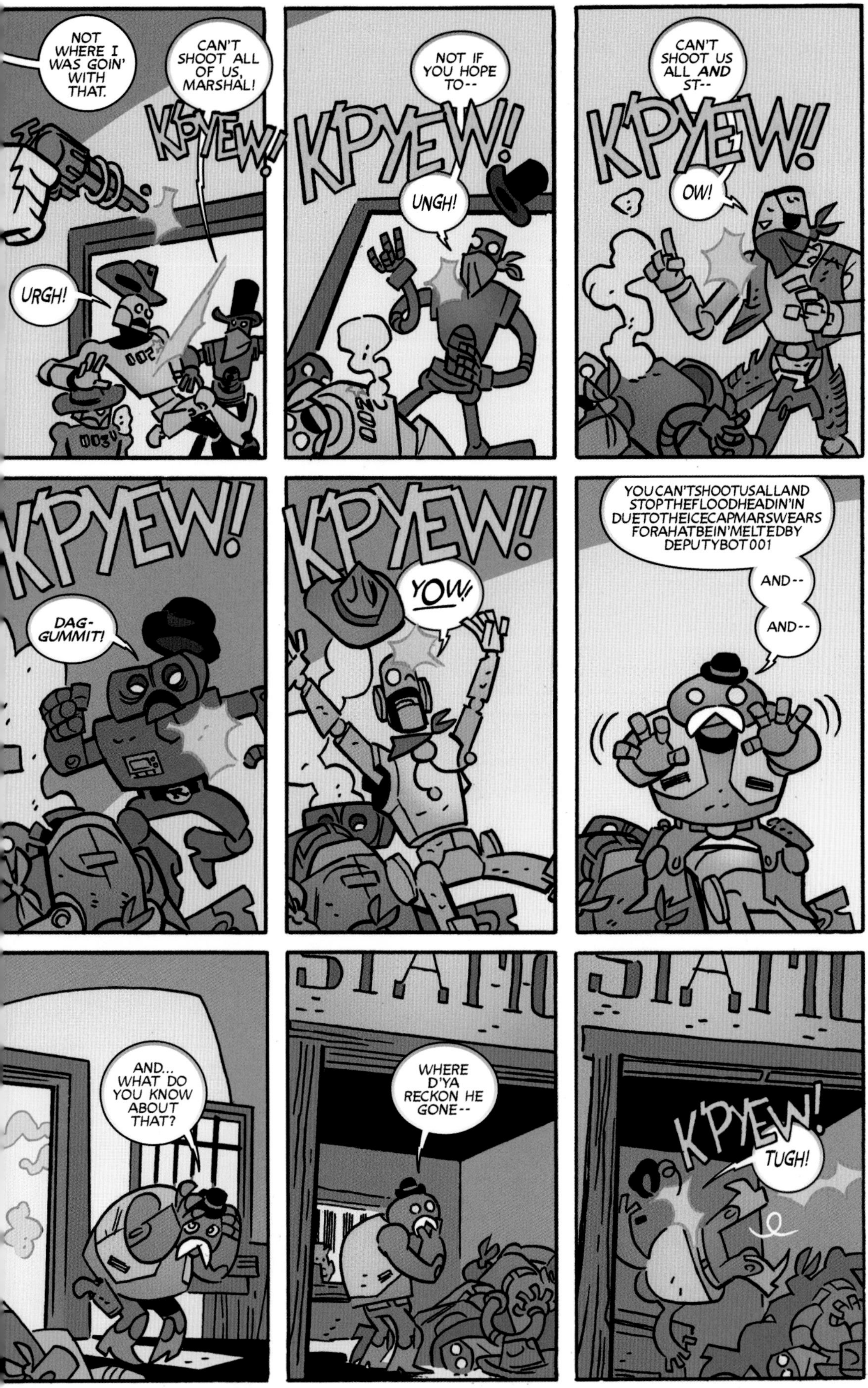
NOT WHERE I WAS GOIN' WITH THAT.
CAN'T SHOOT ALL OF US, MARSHAL!
K'PYEW!
URGH!
NOT IF YOU HOPE TO--
K'PYEW!
UNGH!
CAN'T SHOOT US ALL AND ST--
K'PYEW!
OW!
K'PYEW!
DAG-GUMMIT!
K'PYEW!
YOW!
YOUCAN'TSHOOTUSALLAND STOPTHEFLOODHEADIN'IN DUETOTHEICECAPMARSWEARS FORAHATBEIN'MELTEDBY DEPUTYBOT001
AND--
AND--
AND... WHAT DO YOU KNOW ABOUT THAT?
WHERE D'YA RECKON HE GONE--
K'PYEW!
TUGH!

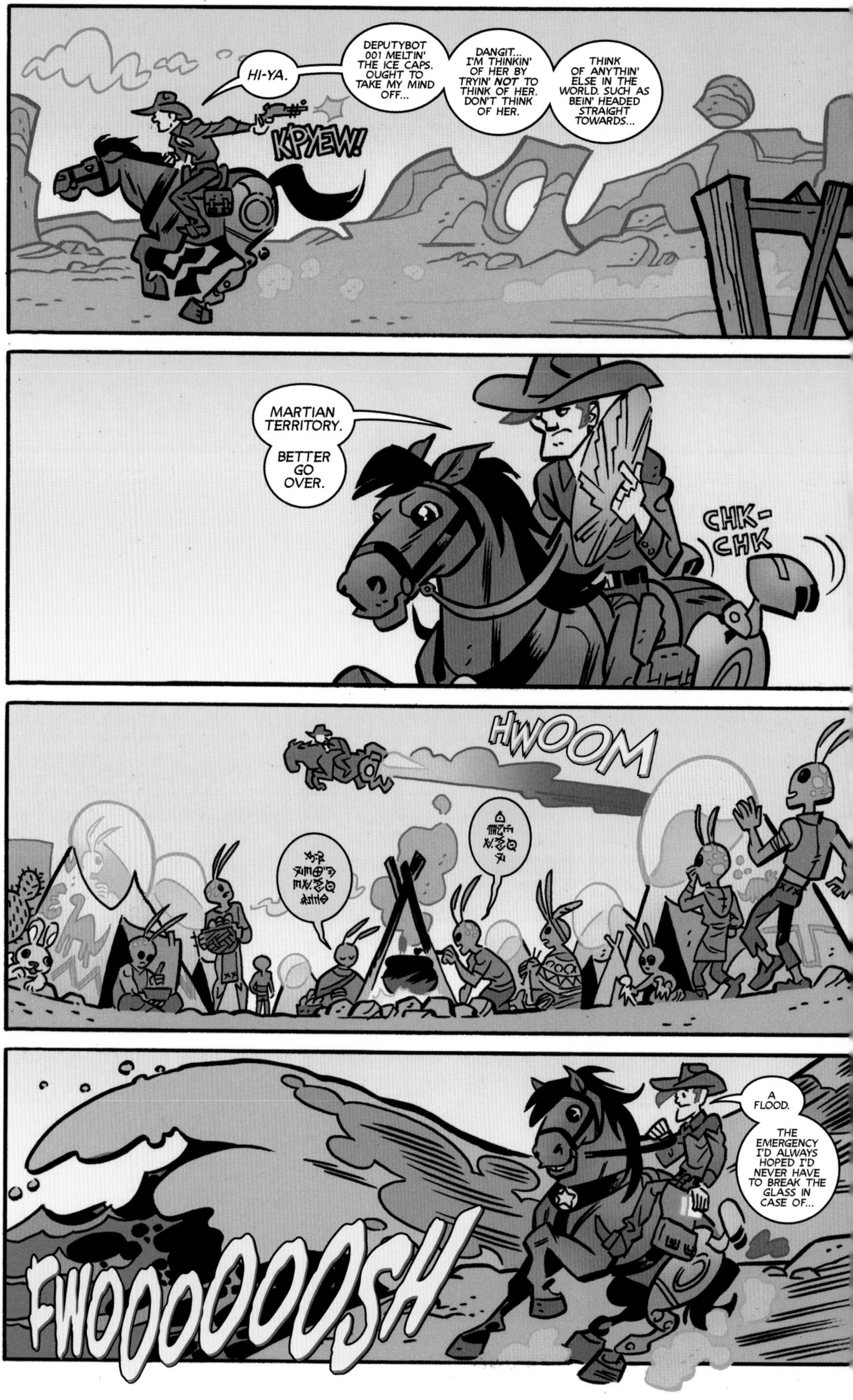

HI-YA.
KPYEW!
DEPUTYBOT 001 MELTIN' THE ICE CAPS. OUGHT TO TAKE MY MIND OFF...
DANGIT... I'M THINKIN' OF HER BY TRYIN' NOT TO THINK OF HER. DON'T THINK OF HER.
THINK OF ANYTHIN' ELSE IN THE WORLD. SUCH AS BEIN' HEADED STRAIGHT TOWARDS...
MARTIAN TERRITORY.
BETTER GO OVER.
CHK-CHK
HWOOM
A FLOOD.
THE EMERGENCY I'D ALWAYS HOPED I'D NEVER HAVE TO BREAK THE GLASS IN CASE OF...
FWOOOOOOSH

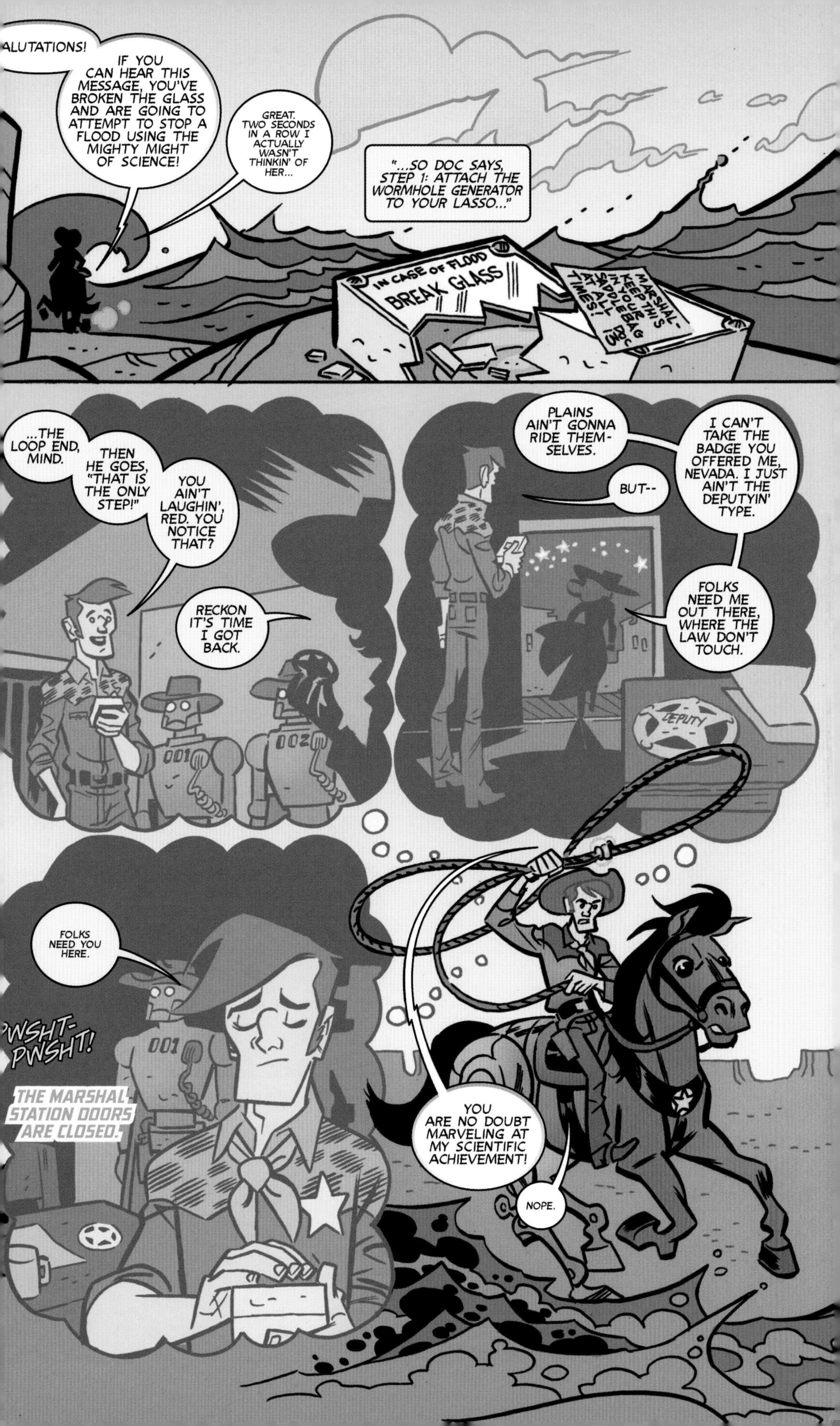

ALUTATIONS!
IF YOU CAN HEAR THIS MESSAGE, YOU'VE BROKEN THE GLASS AND ARE GOING TO ATTEMPT TO STOP A FLOOD USING THE MIGHTY MIGHT OF SCIENCE!
GREAT. TWO SECONDS IN A ROW I ACTUALLY WASN'T THINKIN' OF HER...
"...SO DOC SAYS, STEP 1: ATTACH THE WORMHOLE GENERATOR TO YOUR LASSO..."
IN CASE OF FLOOD
BREAK GLASS
MARSHAL- KEEP THIS IN YOUR SADDLEBAG AT ALL TIMES! DOC
...THE LOOP END, MIND.
THEN HE GOES, "THAT IS THE ONLY STEP!"
YOU AIN'T LAUGHIN', RED. YOU NOTICE THAT?
RECKON IT'S TIME I GOT BACK.
001
002
PLAINS AIN'T GONNA RIDE THEM-SELVES.
I CAN'T TAKE THE BADGE YOU OFFERED ME, NEVADA. I JUST AIN'T THE DEPUTYIN' TYPE.
BUT--
FOLKS NEED ME OUT THERE, WHERE THE LAW DON'T TOUCH.
DEPUTY
FOLKS NEED YOU HERE.
PWSHT-PWSHT!
THE MARSHAL STATION DOORS ARE CLOSED.
001
YOU ARE NO DOUBT MARVELING AT MY SCIENTIFIC ACHIEVEMENT!
NOPE.

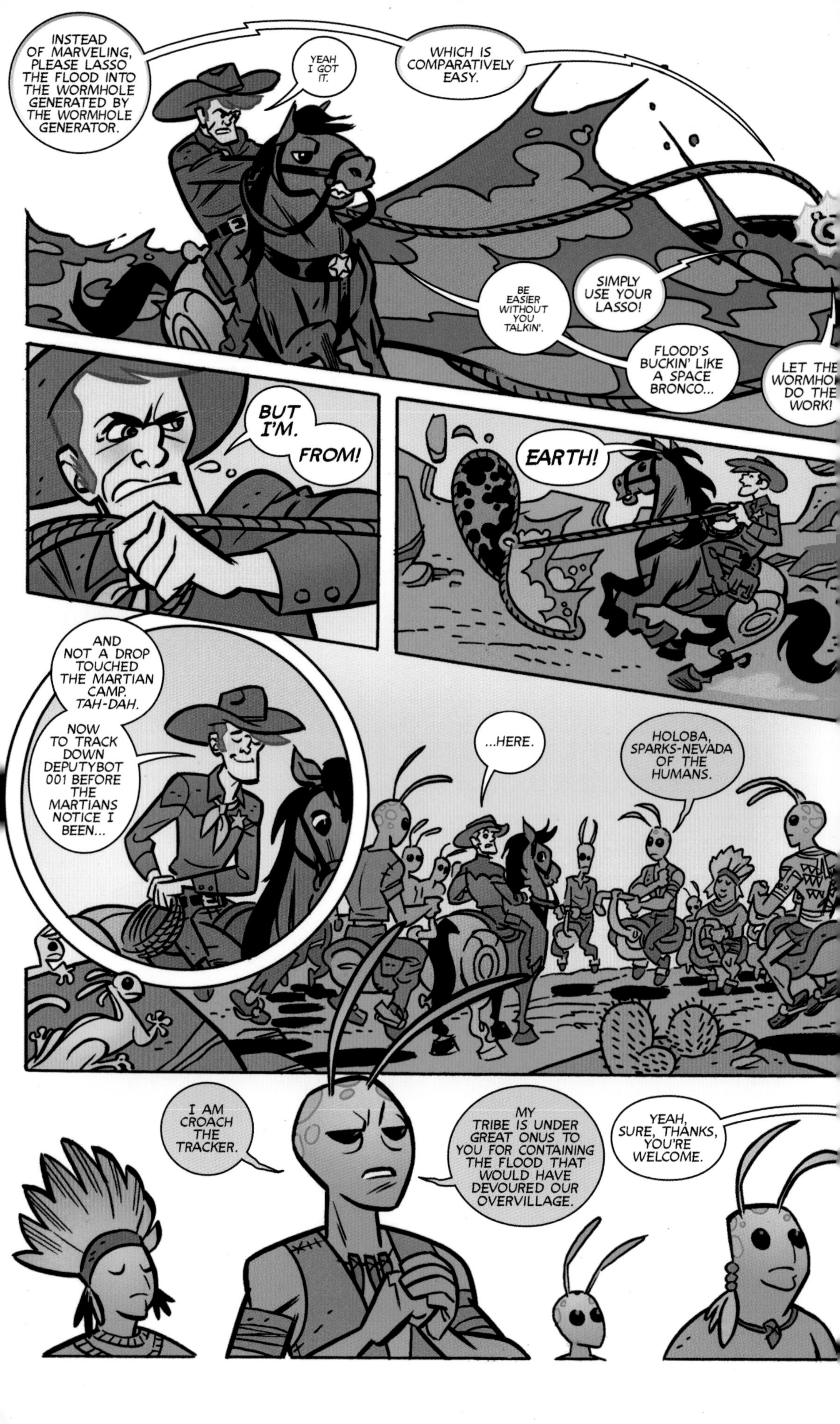
INSTEAD OF MARVELING, PLEASE LASSO THE FLOOD INTO THE WORMHOLE GENERATED BY THE WORMHOLE GENERATOR.
YEAH I GOT IT.
WHICH IS COMPARATIVELY EASY.
SIMPLY USE YOUR LASSO!
BE EASIER WITHOUT YOU TALKIN'.
FLOOD'S BUCKIN' LIKE A SPACE BRONCO...
LET THE WORMHO DO THE WORK!
BUT I'M. FROM!
EARTH!
AND NOT A DROP TOUCHED THE MARTIAN CAMP. TAH-DAH.
NOW TO TRACK DOWN DEPUTYBOT 001 BEFORE THE MARTIANS NOTICE I BEEN...
...HERE.
HOLOBA, SPARKS-NEVADA OF THE HUMANS.
I AM CROACH THE TRACKER.
MY TRIBE IS UNDER GREAT ONUS TO YOU FOR CONTAINING THE FLOOD THAT WOULD HAVE DEVOURED OUR OVERVILLAGE.
YEAH, SURE, THANKS, YOU'RE WELCOME.

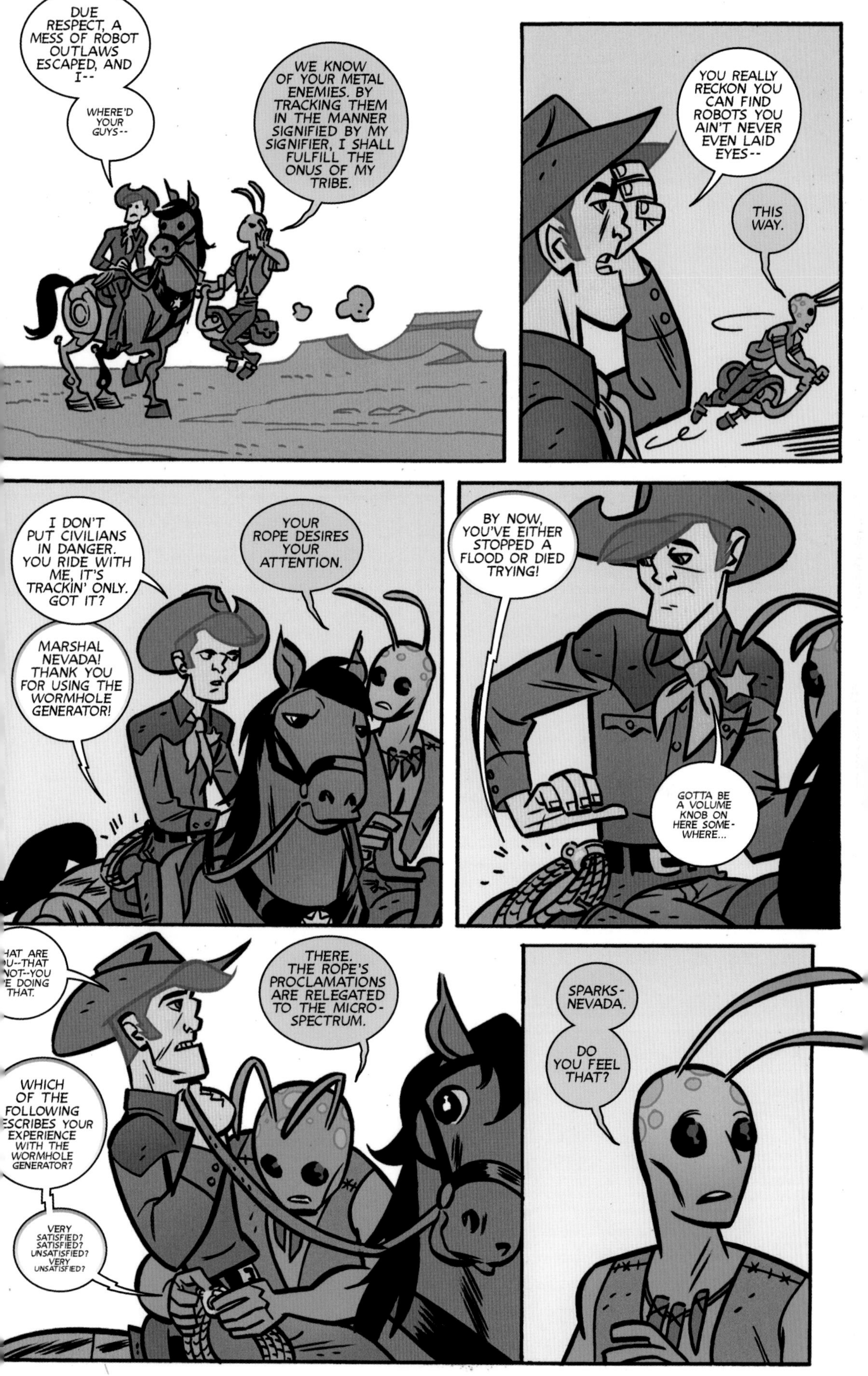
DUE RESPECT, A MESS OF ROBOT OUTLAWS ESCAPED, AND I--
WHERE'D YOUR GUYS--
WE KNOW OF YOUR METAL ENEMIES. BY TRACKING THEM IN THE MANNER SIGNIFIED BY MY SIGNIFIER, I SHALL FULFILL THE ONUS OF MY TRIBE.
YOU REALLY RECKON YOU CAN FIND ROBOTS YOU AIN'T NEVER EVEN LAID EYES--
THIS WAY.
I DON'T PUT CIVILIANS IN DANGER. YOU RIDE WITH ME, IT'S TRACKIN' ONLY. GOT IT?
YOUR ROPE DESIRES YOUR ATTENTION.
MARSHAL NEVADA! THANK YOU FOR USING THE WORMHOLE GENERATOR!
BY NOW, YOU'VE EITHER STOPPED A FLOOD OR DIED TRYING!
GOTTA BE A VOLUME KNOB ON HERE SOME-WHERE...
HAT ARE U--THAT NOT--YOU E DOING THAT.
THERE. THE ROPE'S PROCLAMATIONS ARE RELEGATED TO THE MICRO-SPECTRUM.
WHICH OF THE FOLLOWING ESCRIBES YOUR EXPERIENCE WITH THE WORMHOLE GENERATOR?
VERY SATISFIED? SATISFIED? UNSATISFIED? VERY UNSATISFIED?
SPARKS-NEVADA.
DO YOU FEEL THAT?

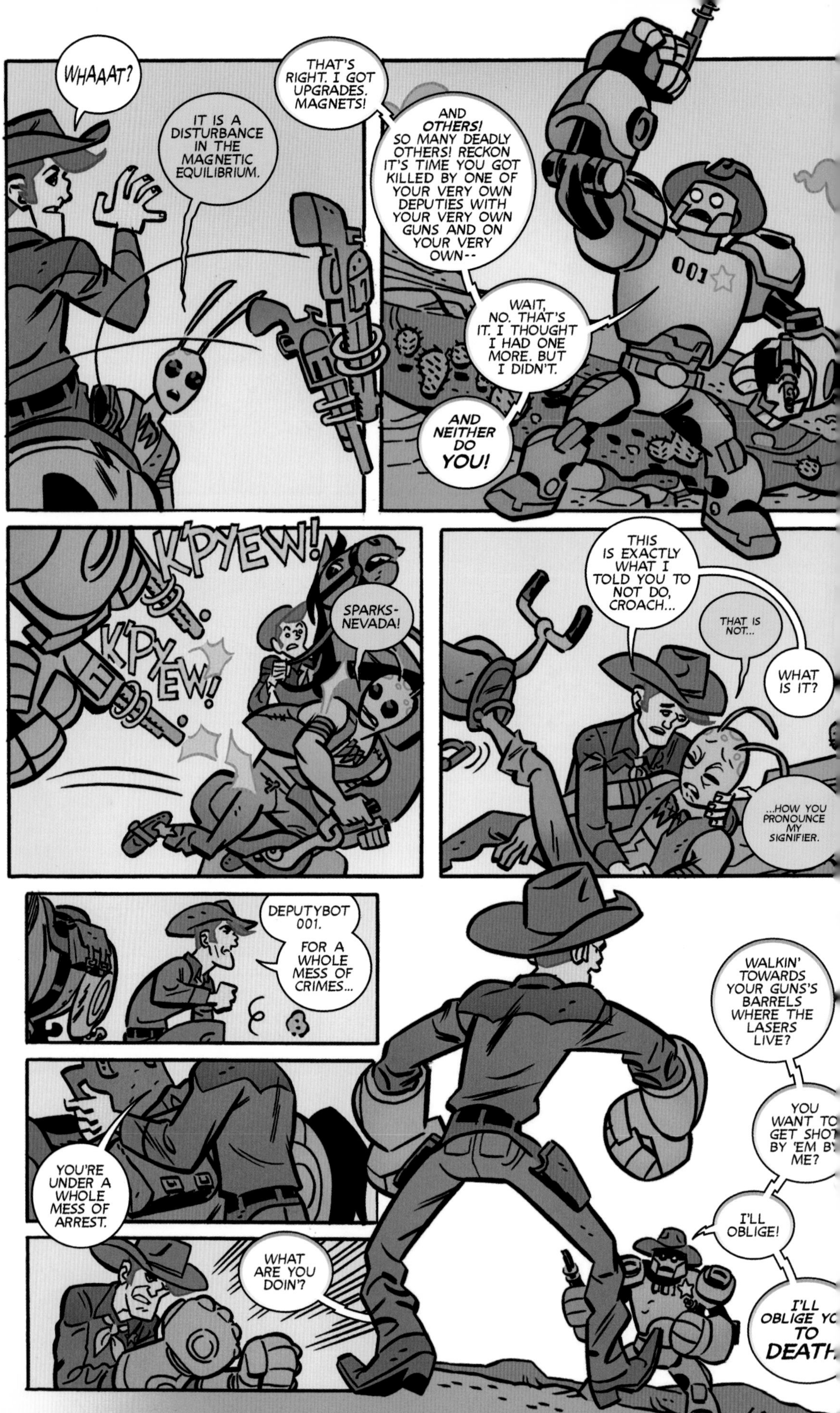
WHAAAT?
IT IS A DISTURBANCE IN THE MAGNETIC EQUILIBRIUM.
THAT'S RIGHT. I GOT UPGRADES. MAGNETS!
AND OTHERS! SO MANY DEADLY OTHERS! RECKON IT'S TIME YOU GOT KILLED BY ONE OF YOUR VERY OWN DEPUTIES WITH YOUR VERY OWN GUNS AND ON YOUR VERY OWN--
WAIT, NO. THAT'S IT. I THOUGHT I HAD ONE MORE. BUT I DIDN'T.
AND NEITHER DO YOU!
K'PYEW!
K'PYEW!
SPARKS-NEVADA!
THIS IS EXACTLY WHAT I TOLD YOU TO NOT DO, CROACH...
THAT IS NOT...
WHAT IS IT?
...HOW YOU PRONOUNCE MY SIGNIFIER.
DEPUTYBOT 001.
FOR A WHOLE MESS OF CRIMES...
YOU'RE UNDER A WHOLE MESS OF ARREST.
WALKIN' TOWARDS YOUR GUNS'S BARRELS WHERE THE LASERS LIVE?
WHAT ARE YOU DOIN'?
I'LL OBLIGE!

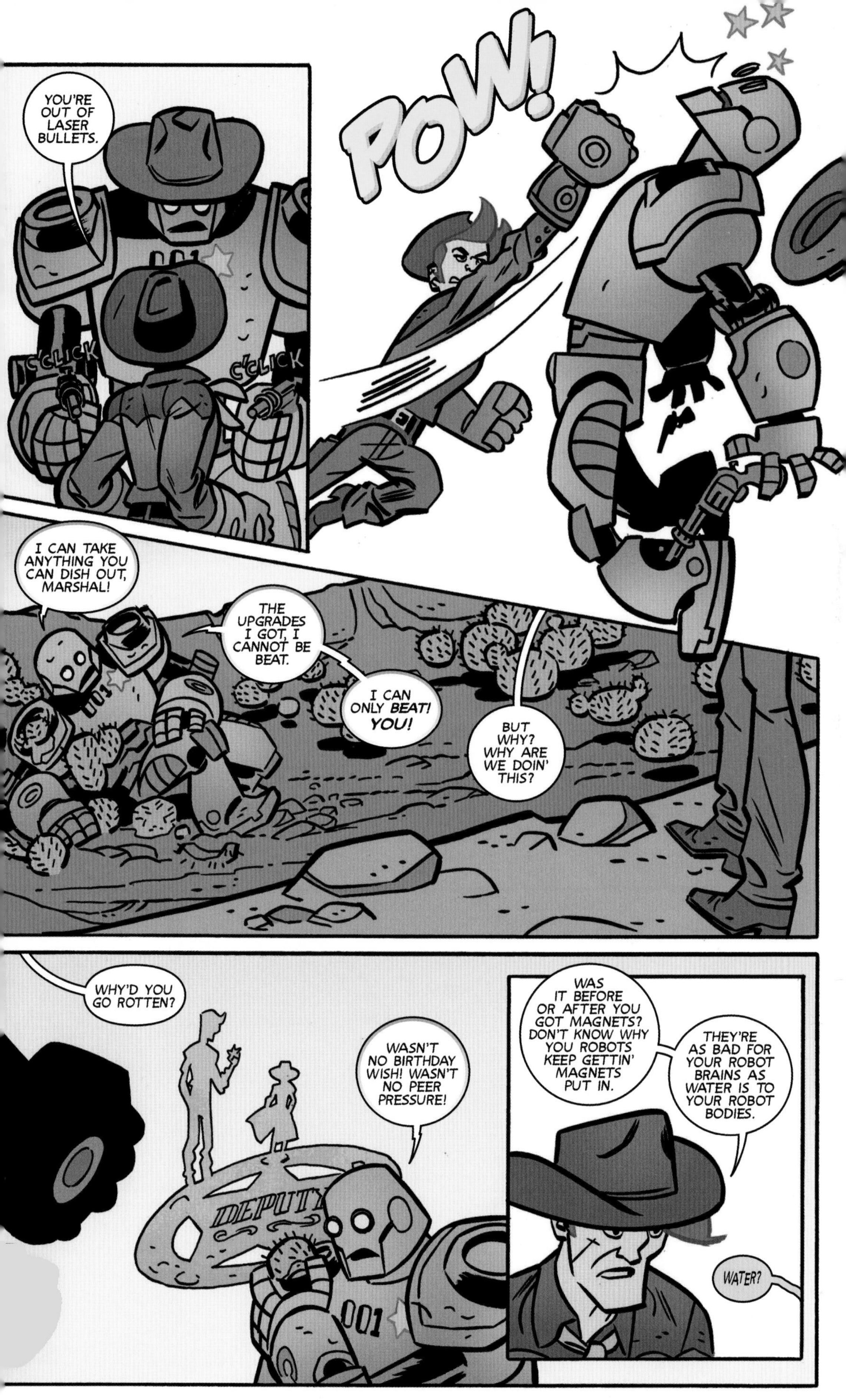
YOU'RE OUT OF LASER BULLETS.
C'CLICK
C'CLICK
POW!
I CAN TAKE ANYTHING YOU CAN DISH OUT, MARSHAL!
THE UPGRADES I GOT, I CANNOT BE BEAT.
I CAN ONLY BEAT! YOU!
BUT WHY? WHY ARE WE DOIN' THIS?
WHY'D YOU GO ROTTEN?
WASN'T NO BIRTHDAY WISH! WASN'T NO PEER PRESSURE!
DEPUTY
001
WAS IT BEFORE OR AFTER YOU GOT MAGNETS? DON'T KNOW WHY YOU ROBOTS KEEP GETTIN' MAGNETS PUT IN.
THEY'RE AS BAD FOR YOUR ROBOT BRAINS AS WATER IS TO YOUR ROBOT BODIES.
WATER?

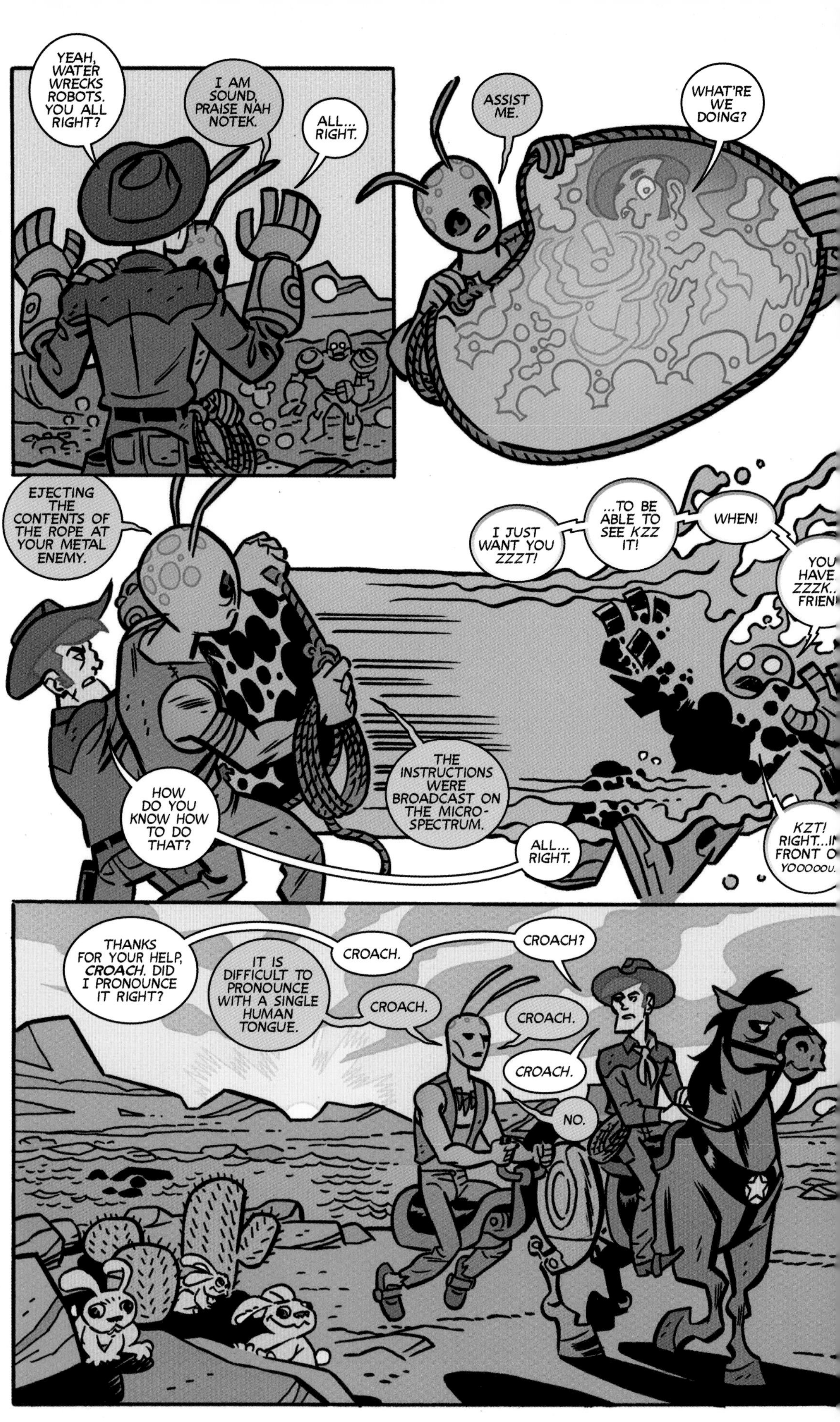
YEAH, WATER WRECKS ROBOTS. YOU ALL RIGHT?
I AM SOUND, PRAISE NAH NOTEK.
ALL... RIGHT.
ASSIST ME.
WHAT'RE WE DOING?
EJECTING THE CONTENTS OF THE ROPE AT YOUR METAL ENEMY.
I JUST WANT YOU ZZZT!
...TO BE ABLE TO SEE KZZ IT!
WHEN!
YOU HAVE ZZZK.. FRIEN
HOW DO YOU KNOW HOW TO DO THAT?
THE INSTRUCTIONS WERE BROADCAST ON THE MICRO-SPECTRUM.
ALL... RIGHT.
KZT! RIGHT...I FRONT O YOOOOOU.
THANKS FOR YOUR HELP, CROACH. DID I PRONOUNCE IT RIGHT?
IT IS DIFFICULT TO PRONOUNCE WITH A SINGLE HUMAN TONGUE.
CROACH.
CROACH?
CROACH.
CROACH.
CROACH.
NO.

Chapter

ONE

Three Encounters of the Close Kind

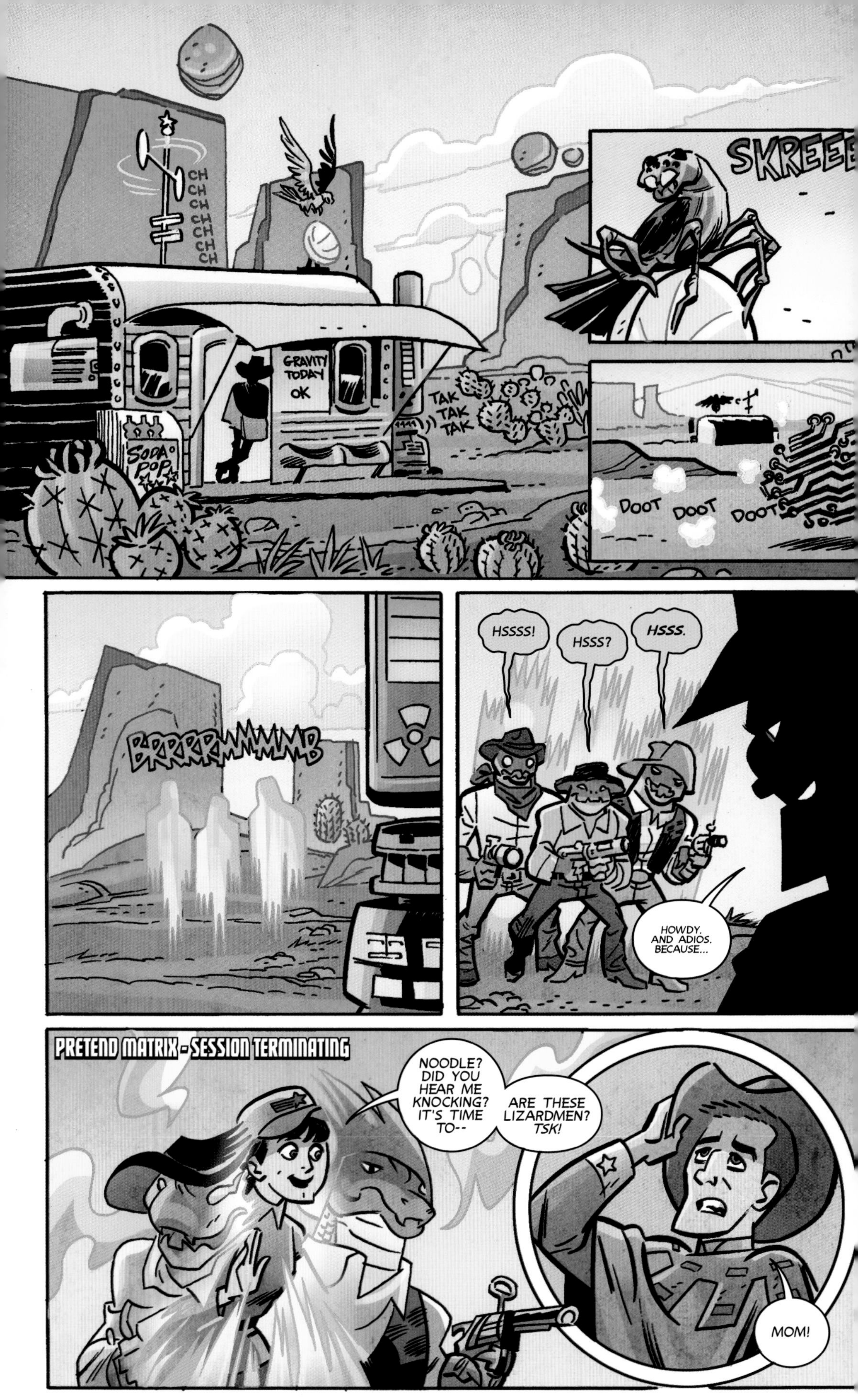
CH CH CH CH CH CH CH
GRAVITY TODAY OK
SODA POP
TAK TAK TAK
SKREEE
DOOT DOOT DOOT
BRRRRRMMMMMB
HSSSS!
HSSS?
HSSS.
HOWDY. AND ADIOS. BECAUSE...
PRETEND MATRIX - SESSION TERMINATING
NOODLE? DID YOU HEAR ME KNOCKING? IT'S TIME TO--
ARE THESE LIZARDMEN? TSK!
MOM!

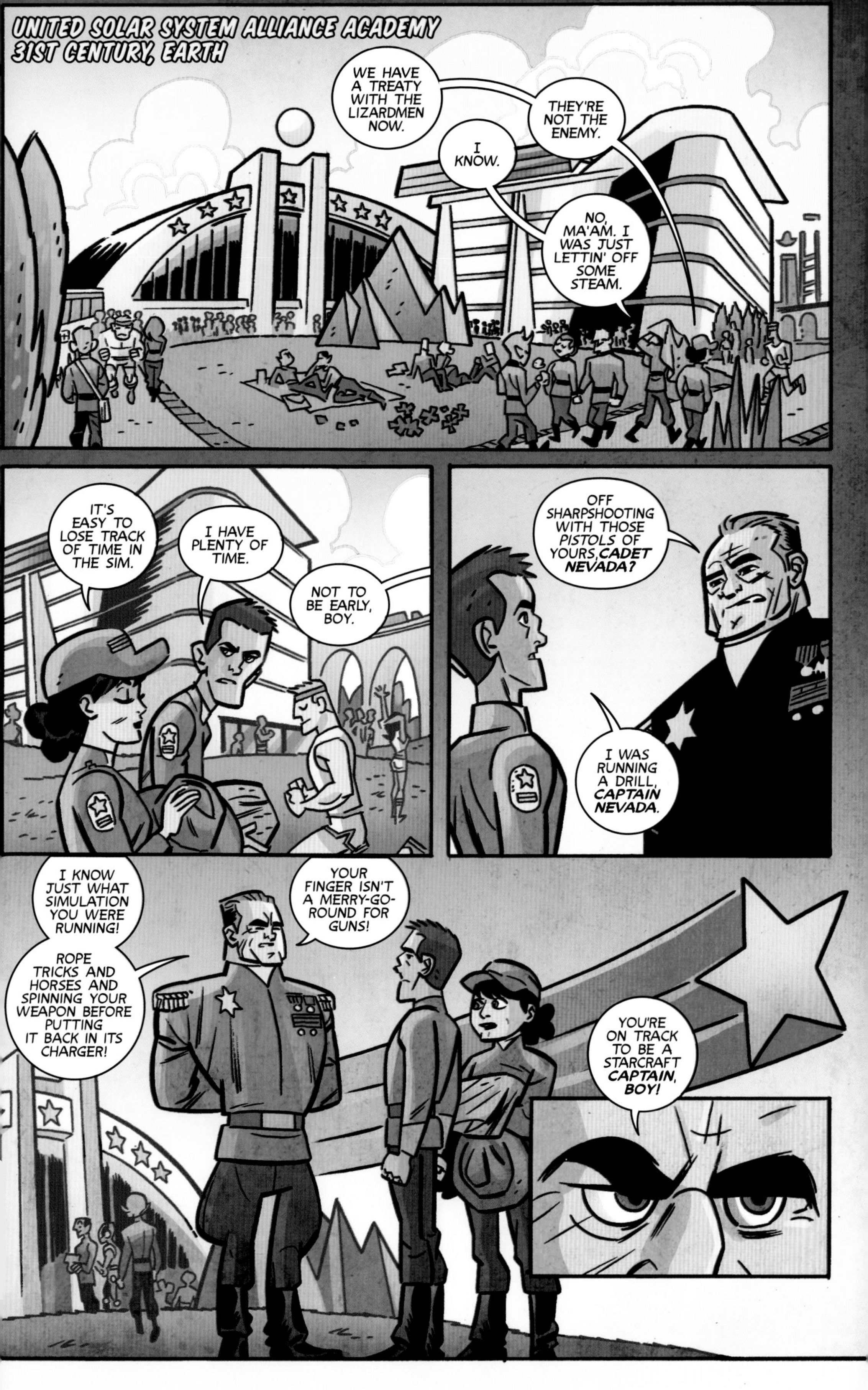
UNITED SOLAR SYSTEM ALLIANCE ACADEMY
31ST CENTURY, EARTH
WE HAVE A TREATY WITH THE LIZARDMEN NOW.
THEY'RE NOT THE ENEMY.
I KNOW.
NO, MA'AM. I WAS JUST LETTIN' OFF SOME STEAM.
IT'S EASY TO LOSE TRACK OF TIME IN THE SIM.
I HAVE PLENTY OF TIME.
NOT TO BE EARLY, BOY.
OFF SHARPSHOOTING WITH THOSE PISTOLS OF YOURS, CADET NEVADA?
I WAS RUNNING A DRILL, CAPTAIN NEVADA.
I KNOW JUST WHAT SIMULATION YOU WERE RUNNING!
ROPE TRICKS AND HORSES AND SPINNING YOUR WEAPON BEFORE PUTTING IT BACK IN ITS CHARGER!
YOUR FINGER ISN'T A MERRY-GO-ROUND FOR GUNS!
YOU'RE ON TRACK TO BE A STARCRAFT CAPTAIN, BOY!

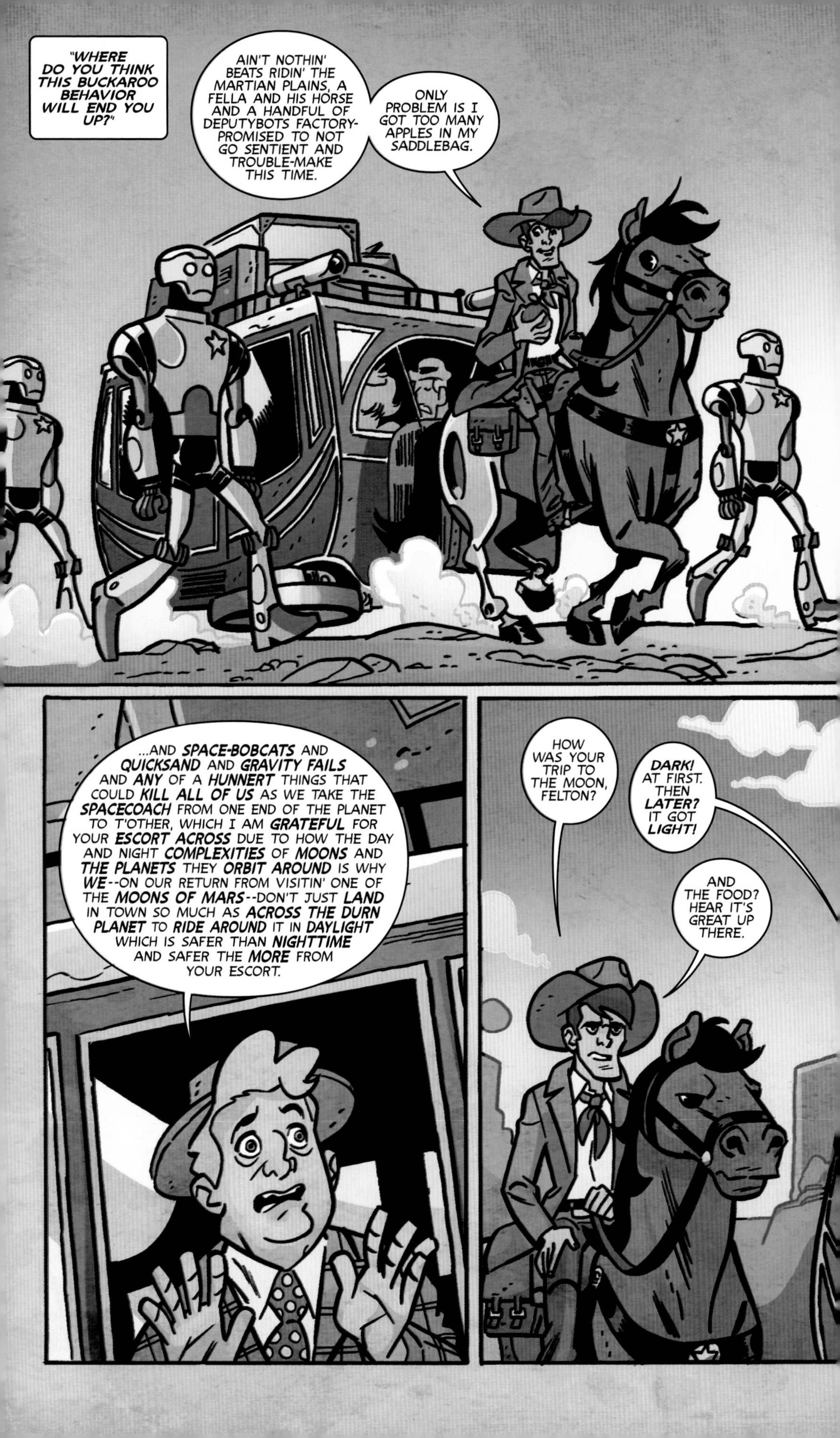
"WHERE DO YOU THINK THIS BUCKAROO BEHAVIOR WILL END YOU UP?"
AIN'T NOTHIN' BEATS RIDIN' THE MARTIAN PLAINS, A FELLA AND HIS HORSE AND A HANDFUL OF DEPUTYBOTS FACTORY-PROMISED TO NOT GO SENTIENT AND TROUBLE-MAKE THIS TIME.
ONLY PROBLEM IS I GOT TOO MANY APPLES IN MY SADDLEBAG.
...AND SPACE-BOBCATS AND QUICKSAND AND GRAVITY FAILS AND ANY OF A HUNNERT THINGS THAT COULD KILL ALL OF US AS WE TAKE THE SPACECOACH FROM ONE END OF THE PLANET TO T'OTHER, WHICH I AM GRATEFUL FOR YOUR ESCORT ACROSS DUE TO HOW THE DAY AND NIGHT COMPLEXITIES OF MOONS AND THE PLANETS THEY ORBIT AROUND IS WHY WE--ON OUR RETURN FROM VISITIN' ONE OF THE MOONS OF MARS--DON'T JUST LAND IN TOWN SO MUCH AS ACROSS THE DURN PLANET TO RIDE AROUND IT IN DAYLIGHT WHICH IS SAFER THAN NIGHTTIME AND SAFER THE MORE FROM YOUR ESCORT.
HOW WAS YOUR TRIP TO THE MOON, FELTON?
DARK! AT FIRST. THEN LATER? IT GOT LIGHT!
AND THE FOOD? HEAR IT'S GREAT UP THERE.

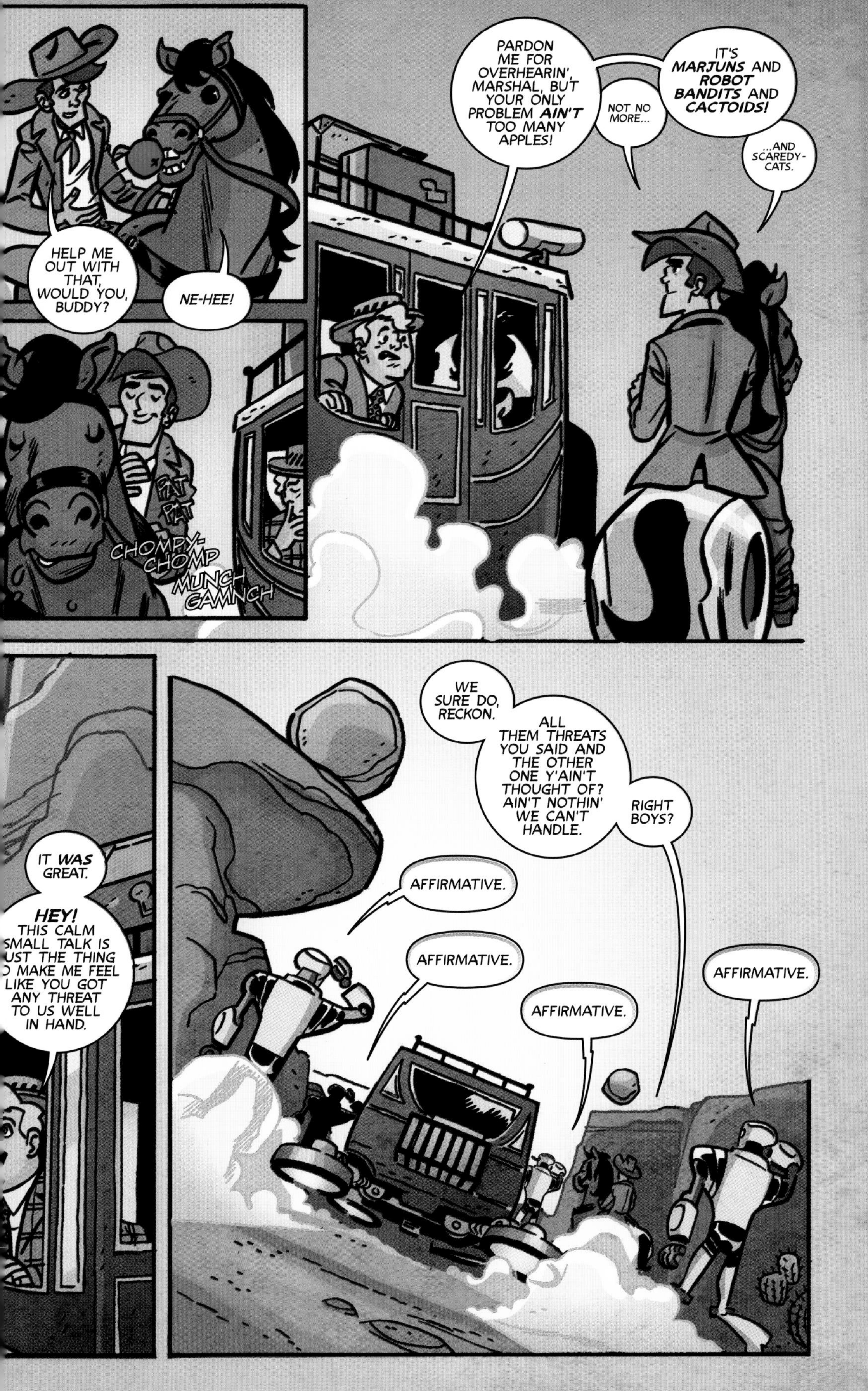
HELP ME OUT WITH THAT, WOULD YOU, BUDDY?
NE-HEE!
PAT PAT
CHOMPY-CHOMP
MUNCH GAMNCH
PARDON ME FOR OVERHEARIN', MARSHAL, BUT YOUR ONLY PROBLEM AIN'T TOO MANY APPLES!
NOT NO MORE...
IT'S MARJUNS AND ROBOT BANDITS AND CACTOIDS!
...AND SCAREDY-CATS.
IT WAS GREAT.
HEY! THIS CALM SMALL TALK IS UST THE THING D MAKE ME FEEL LIKE YOU GOT ANY THREAT TO US WELL IN HAND.
WE SURE DO, RECKON.
ALL THEM THREATS YOU SAID AND THE OTHER ONE Y'AIN'T THOUGHT OF? AIN'T NOTHIN' WE CAN'T HANDLE.
RIGHT BOYS?
AFFIRMATIVE.
AFFIRMATIVE.
AFFIRMATIVE.
AFFIRMATIVE.

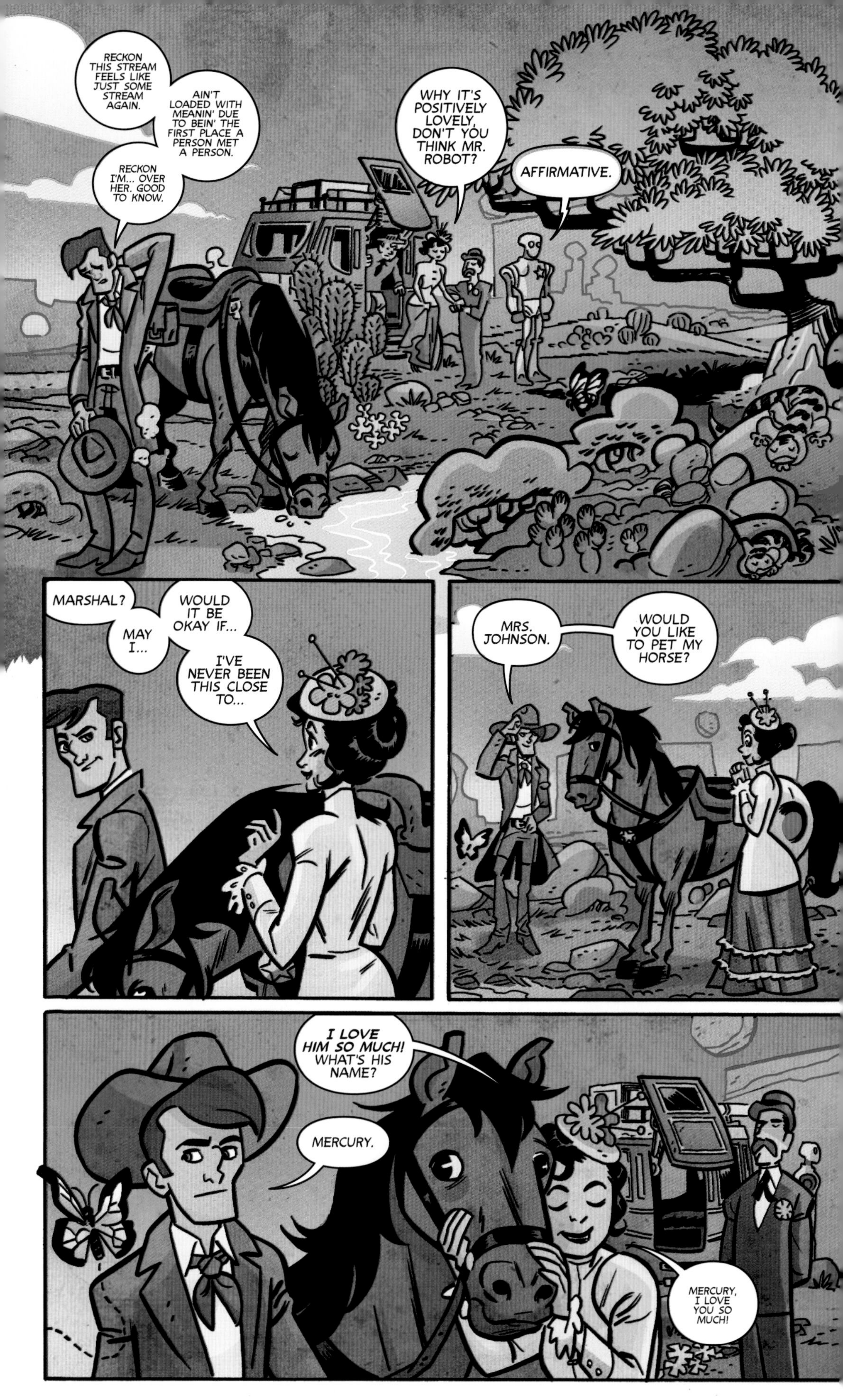

RECKON THIS STREAM FEELS LIKE JUST SOME STREAM AGAIN.
AIN'T LOADED WITH MEANIN' DUE TO BEIN' THE FIRST PLACE A PERSON MET A PERSON.
RECKON I'M... OVER HER. GOOD TO KNOW.
WHY IT'S POSITIVELY LOVELY, DON'T YOU THINK MR. ROBOT?
AFFIRMATIVE.
MARSHAL?
MAY I...
WOULD IT BE OKAY IF...
I'VE NEVER BEEN THIS CLOSE TO...
MRS. JOHNSON.
WOULD YOU LIKE TO PET MY HORSE?
I LOVE HIM SO MUCH! WHAT'S HIS NAME?
MERCURY.
MERCURY, I LOVE YOU SO MUCH!

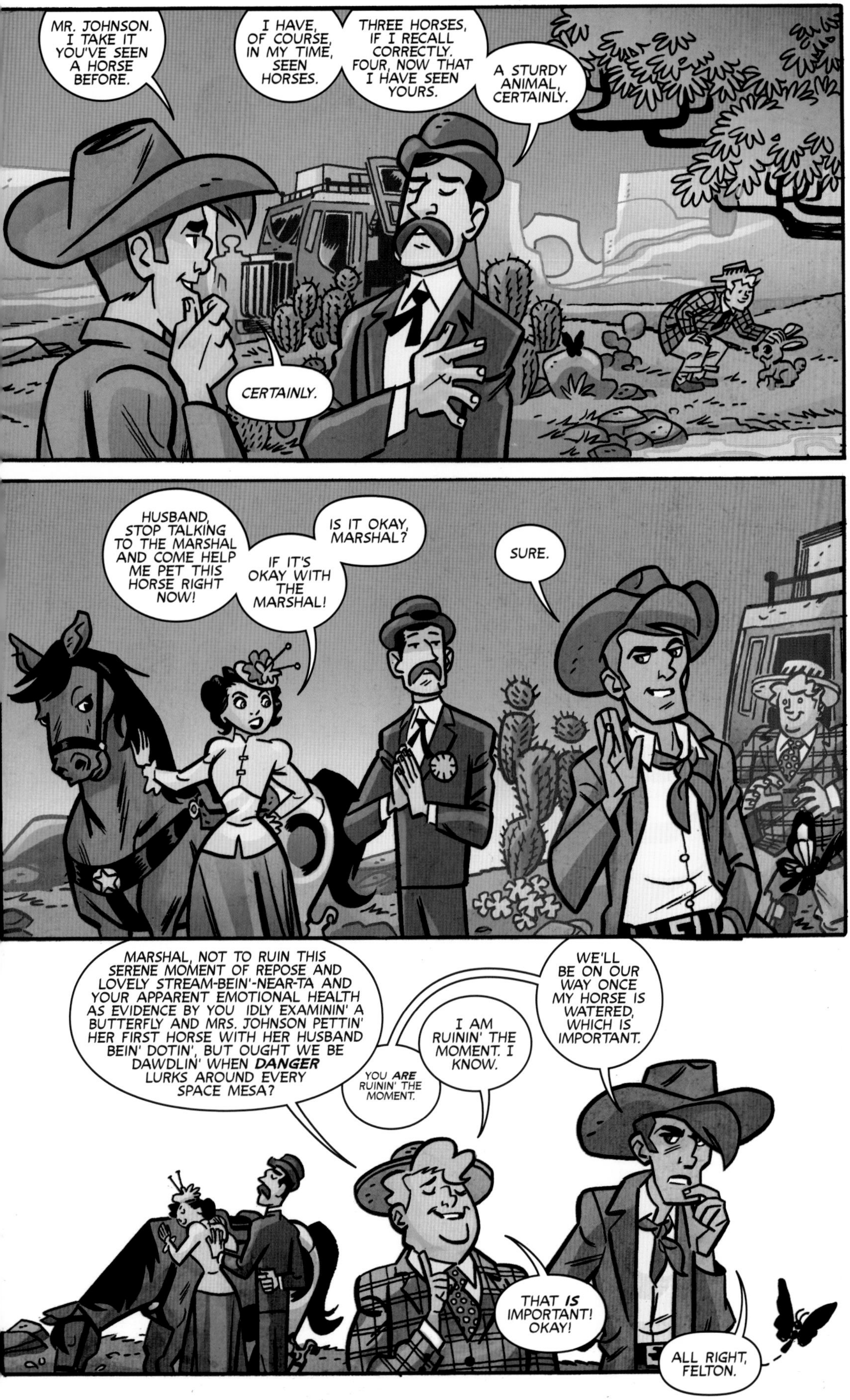
MR. JOHNSON. I TAKE IT YOU'VE SEEN A HORSE BEFORE.
I HAVE, OF COURSE, IN MY TIME, SEEN HORSES.
THREE HORSES, IF I RECALL CORRECTLY. FOUR, NOW THAT I HAVE SEEN YOURS.
A STURDY ANIMAL, CERTAINLY.
CERTAINLY.
HUSBAND, STOP TALKING TO THE MARSHAL AND COME HELP ME PET THIS HORSE RIGHT NOW!
IF IT'S OKAY WITH THE MARSHAL!
IS IT OKAY, MARSHAL?
SURE.
MARSHAL, NOT TO RUIN THIS SERENE MOMENT OF REPOSE AND LOVELY STREAM-BEIN'-NEAR-TA AND YOUR APPARENT EMOTIONAL HEALTH AS EVIDENCE BY YOU IDLY EXAMININ' A BUTTERFLY AND MRS. JOHNSON PETTIN' HER FIRST HORSE WITH HER HUSBAND BEIN' DOTIN', BUT OUGHT WE BE DAWDLIN' WHEN **DANGER** LURKS AROUND EVERY SPACE MESA?
YOU **ARE** RUININ' THE MOMENT.
I AM RUININ' THE MOMENT. I KNOW.
WE'LL BE ON OUR WAY ONCE MY HORSE IS WATERED, WHICH IS IMPORTANT.
THAT **IS** IMPORTANT! OKAY!
ALL RIGHT, FELTON.

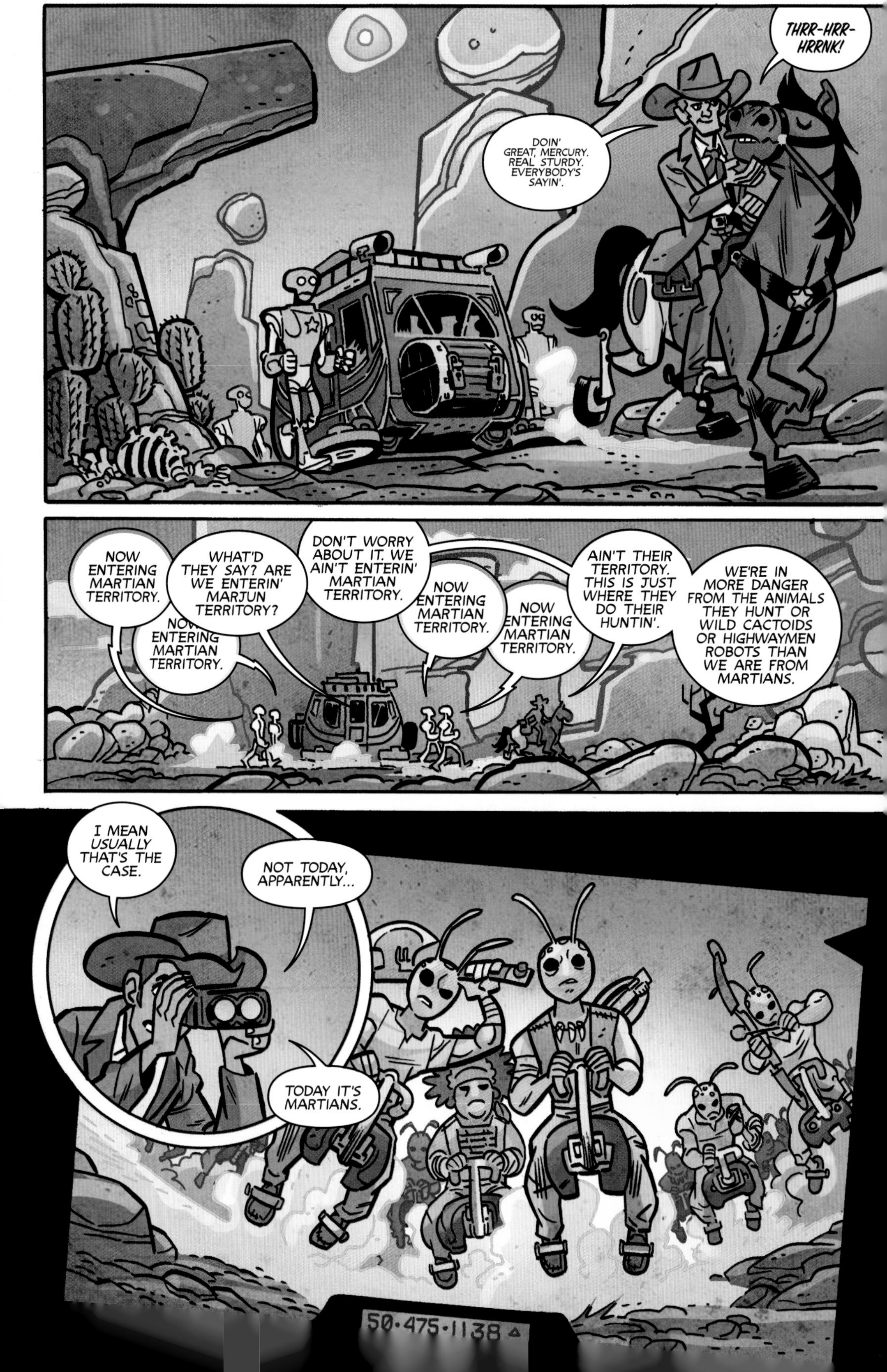
DOIN' GREAT, MERCURY. REAL STURDY. EVERYBODY'S SAYIN'.
THRR-HRR-HRRNK!
NOW ENTERING MARTIAN TERRITORY.
NOW ENTERING MARTIAN TERRITORY.
WHAT'D THEY SAY? ARE WE ENTERIN' MARJUN TERRITORY?
DON'T WORRY ABOUT IT. WE AIN'T ENTERIN' MARTIAN TERRITORY.
NOW ENTERING MARTIAN TERRITORY.
NOW ENTERING MARTIAN TERRITORY.
AIN'T THEIR TERRITORY. THIS IS JUST WHERE THEY DO THEIR HUNTIN'.
WE'RE IN MORE DANGER FROM THE ANIMALS THEY HUNT OR WILD CACTOIDS OR HIGHWAYMEN ROBOTS THAN WE ARE FROM MARTIANS.
I MEAN USUALLY THAT'S THE CASE.
NOT TODAY, APPARENTLY...
TODAY IT'S MARTIANS.
50·475·1138

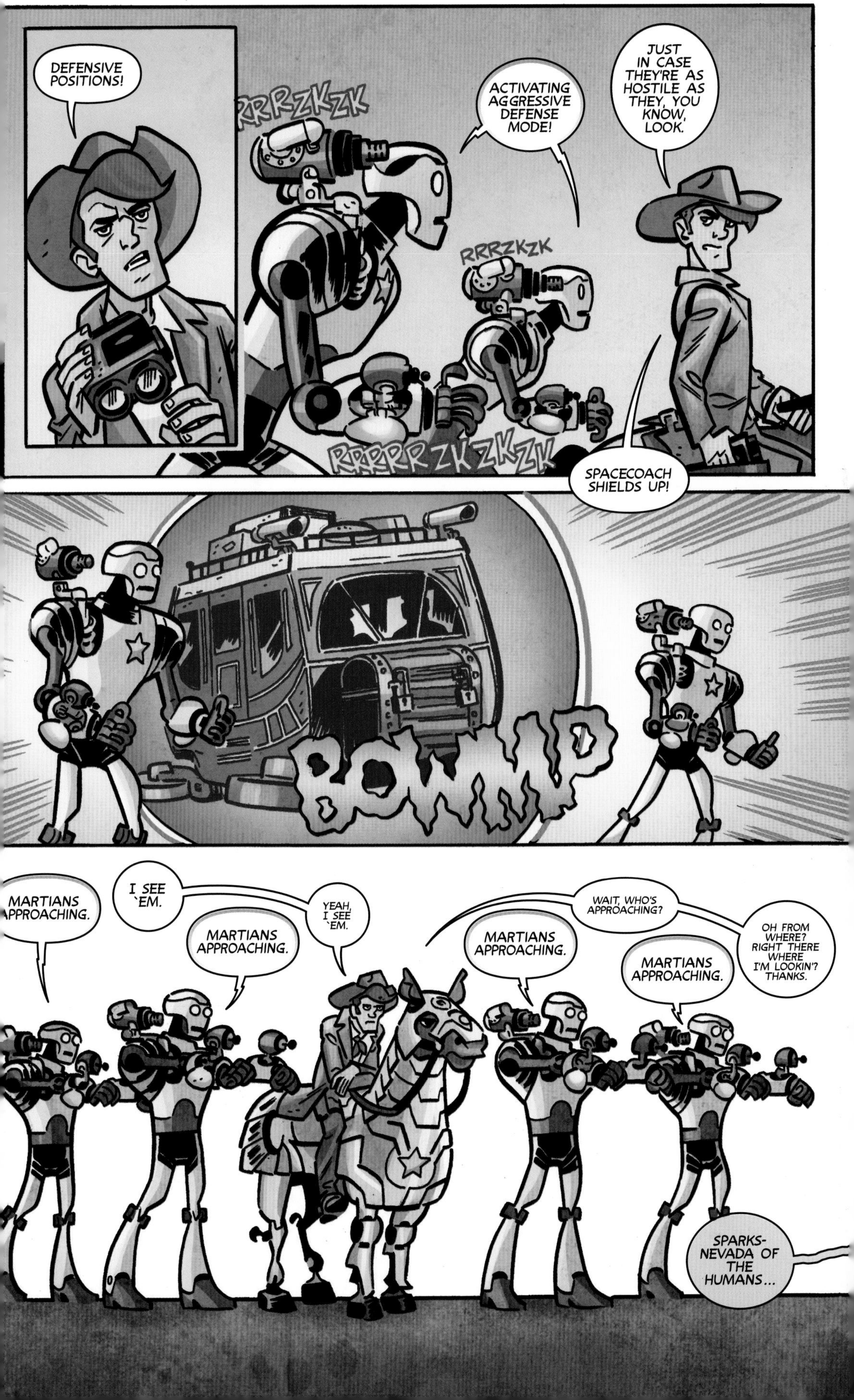
DEFENSIVE POSITIONS!
RRRRZKZK
ACTIVATING AGGRESSIVE DEFENSE MODE!
JUST IN CASE THEY'RE AS HOSTILE AS THEY, YOU KNOW, LOOK.
RRRZKZK
RRRRRRZKZKZK
SPACECOACH SHIELDS UP!
BOWMP
MARTIANS APPROACHING.
I SEE `EM.
MARTIANS APPROACHING.
YEAH, I SEE `EM.
MARTIANS APPROACHING.
WAIT, WHO'S APPROACHING?
MARTIANS APPROACHING.
OH FROM WHERE? RIGHT THERE WHERE I'M LOOKIN'? THANKS.
SPARKS-NEVADA OF THE HUMANS...

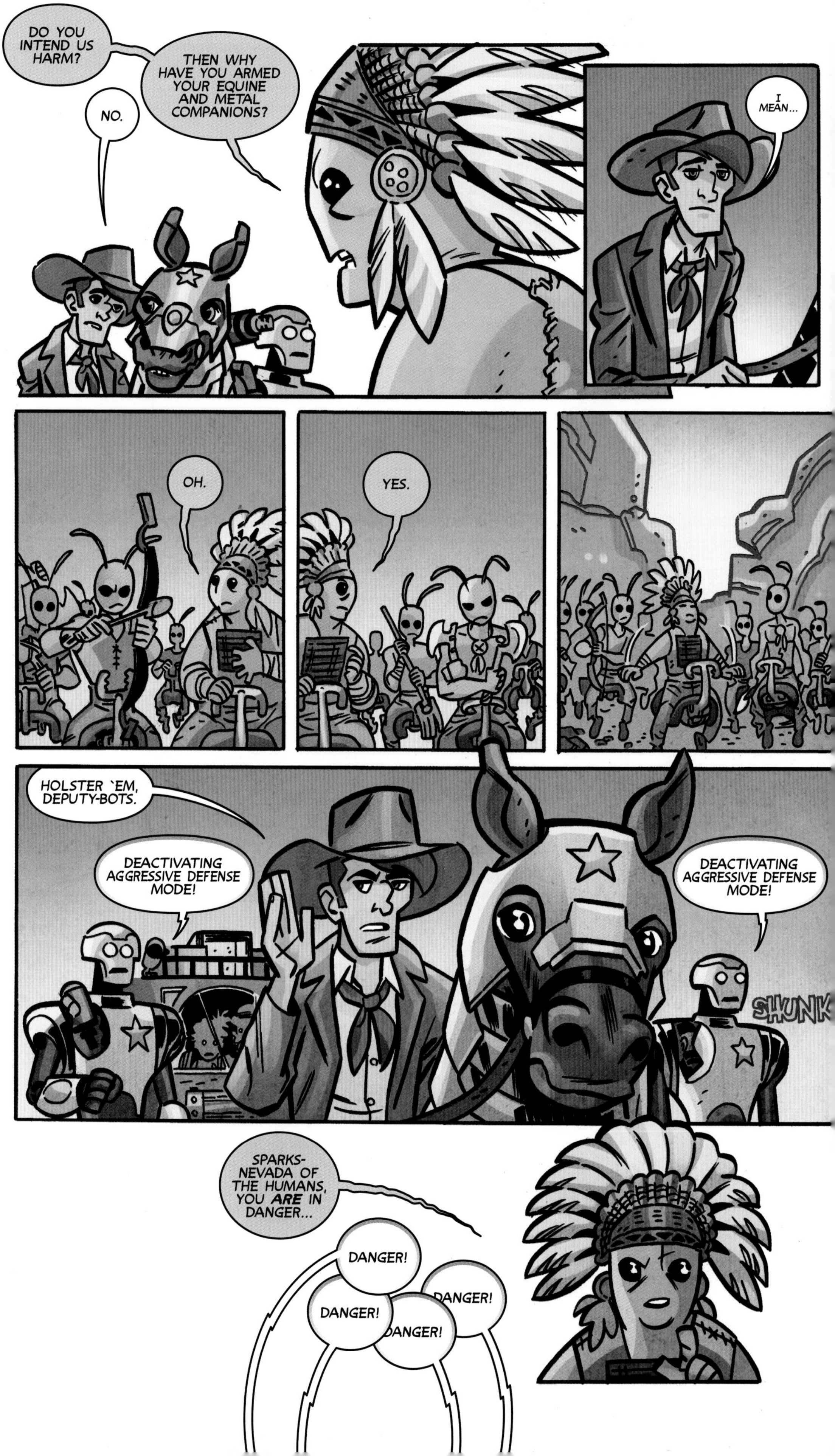
DO YOU INTEND US HARM?
NO.
THEN WHY HAVE YOU ARMED YOUR EQUINE AND METAL COMPANIONS?
I MEAN...
OH.
YES.
HOLSTER 'EM, DEPUTY-BOTS.
DEACTIVATING AGGRESSIVE DEFENSE MODE!
DEACTIVATING AGGRESSIVE DEFENSE MODE!
SHUNK
SPARKS-NEVADA OF THE HUMANS, YOU *ARE* IN DANGER...
DANGER!
DANGER!
DANGER!
DANGER!

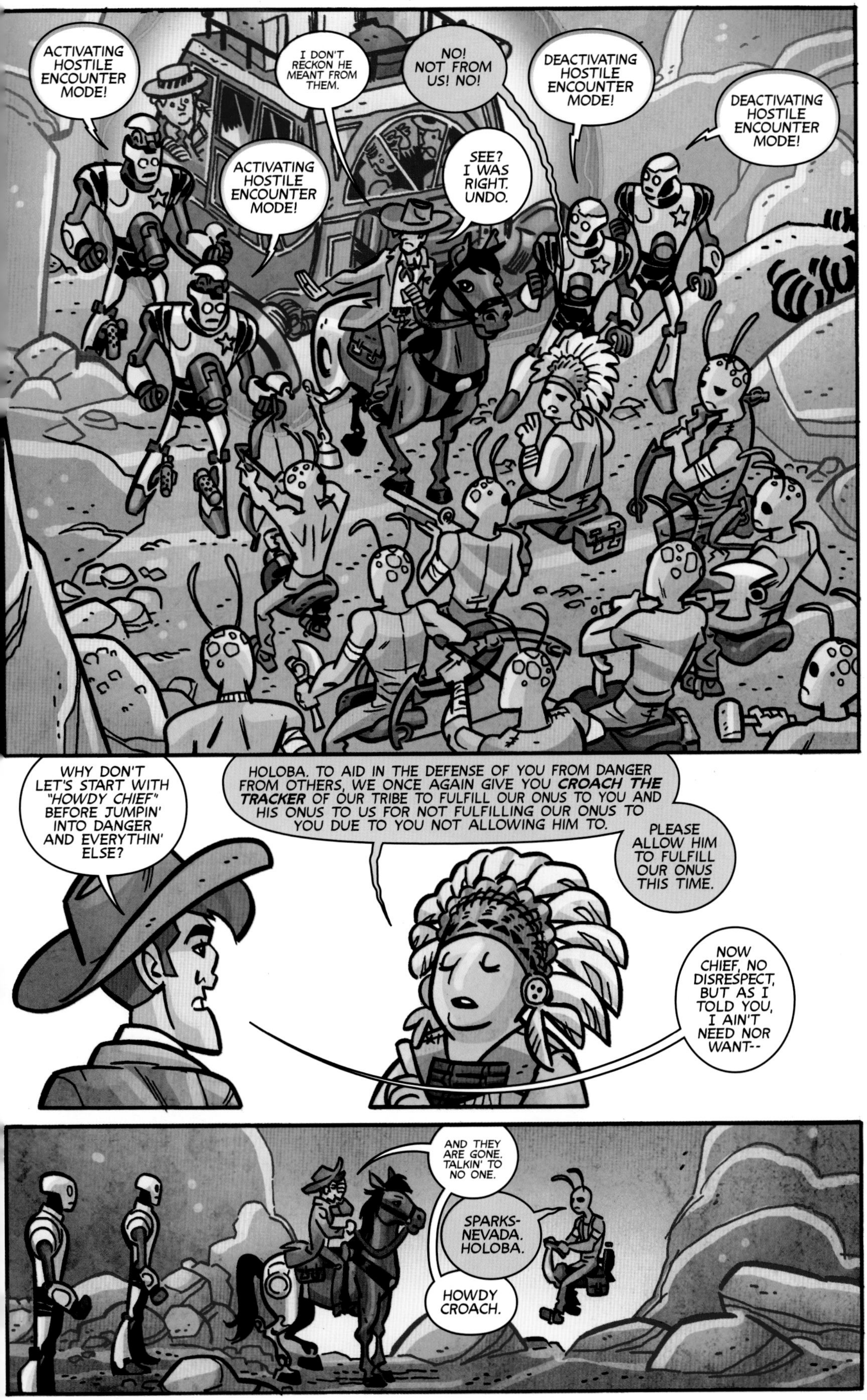

ACTIVATING HOSTILE ENCOUNTER MODE!
I DON'T RECKON HE MEANT FROM THEM.
NO! NOT FROM US! NO!
DEACTIVATING HOSTILE ENCOUNTER MODE!
ACTIVATING HOSTILE ENCOUNTER MODE!
SEE? I WAS RIGHT. UNDO.
DEACTIVATING HOSTILE ENCOUNTER MODE!
WHY DON'T LET'S START WITH "HOWDY CHIEF" BEFORE JUMPIN' INTO DANGER AND EVERYTHIN' ELSE?
HOLOBA. TO AID IN THE DEFENSE OF YOU FROM DANGER FROM OTHERS, WE ONCE AGAIN GIVE YOU *CROACH THE TRACKER* OF OUR TRIBE TO FULFILL OUR ONUS TO YOU AND HIS ONUS TO US FOR NOT FULFILLING OUR ONUS TO YOU DUE TO YOU NOT ALLOWING HIM TO.
PLEASE ALLOW HIM TO FULFILL OUR ONUS THIS TIME.
NOW CHIEF, NO DISRESPECT, BUT AS I TOLD YOU, I AIN'T NEED NOR WANT--
AND THEY ARE GONE. TALKIN' TO NO ONE.
SPARKS-NEVADA. HOLOBA.
HOWDY CROACH.

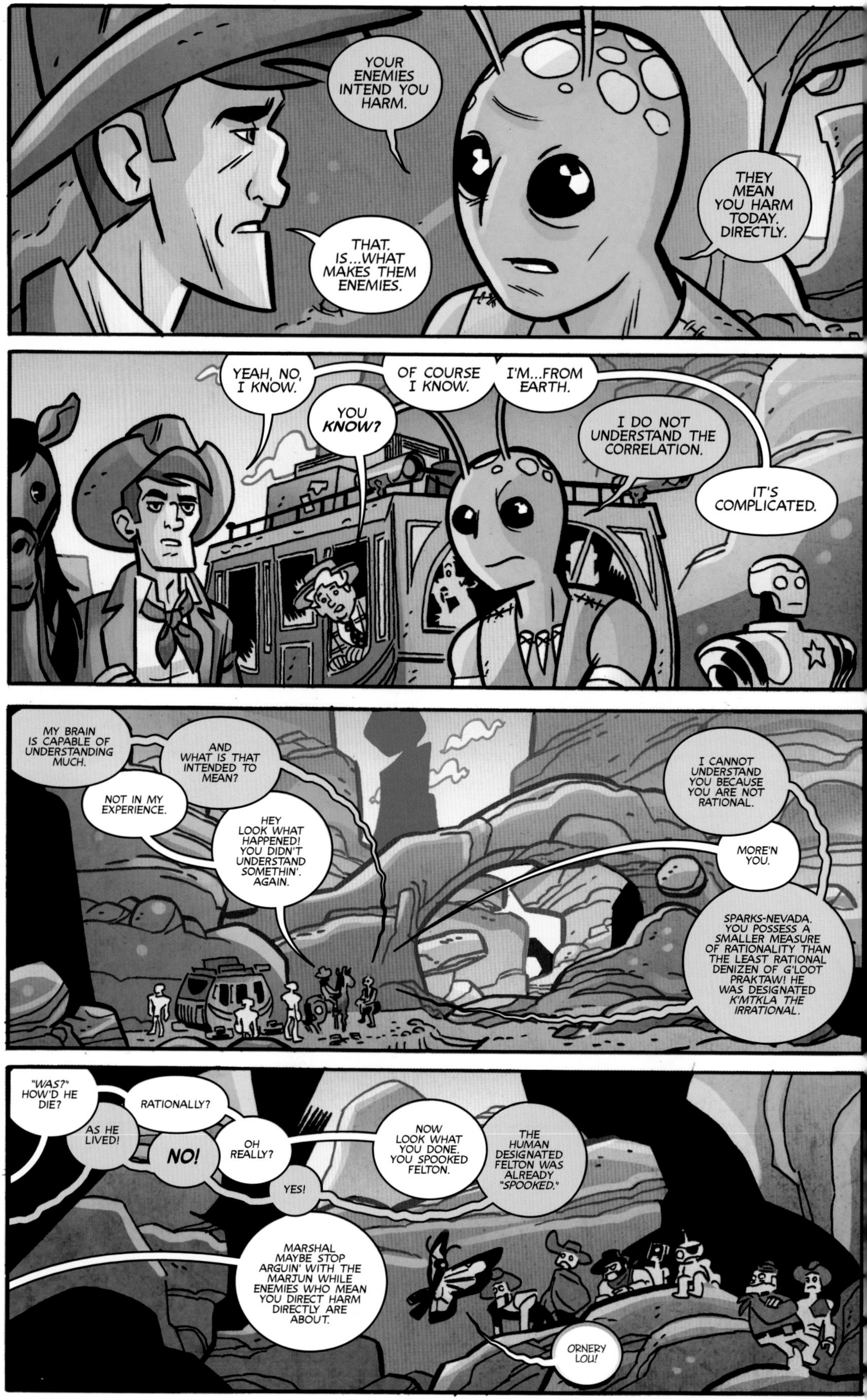

YOUR ENEMIES INTEND YOU HARM.
THAT. IS...WHAT MAKES THEM ENEMIES.
THEY MEAN YOU HARM TODAY. DIRECTLY.
YEAH, NO, I KNOW.
YOU *KNOW?*
OF COURSE I KNOW.
I'M...FROM EARTH.
I DO NOT UNDERSTAND THE CORRELATION.
IT'S COMPLICATED.
MY BRAIN IS CAPABLE OF UNDERSTANDING MUCH.
NOT IN MY EXPERIENCE.
AND WHAT IS THAT INTENDED TO MEAN?
HEY LOOK WHAT HAPPENED! YOU DIDN'T UNDERSTAND SOMETHIN'. AGAIN.
I CANNOT UNDERSTAND YOU BECAUSE YOU ARE NOT RATIONAL.
MORE'N YOU.
SPARKS-NEVADA. YOU POSSESS A SMALLER MEASURE OF RATIONALITY THAN THE LEAST RATIONAL DENIZEN OF G'LOOT PRAKTAW! HE WAS DESIGNATED *K'MTKLA THE IRRATIONAL.*
"WAS?" HOW'D HE DIE?
AS HE LIVED!
RATIONALLY?
NO!
OH REALLY?
YES!
NOW LOOK WHAT YOU DONE. YOU SPOOKED FELTON.
THE HUMAN DESIGNATED FELTON WAS ALREADY *"SPOOKED."*
MARSHAL MAYBE STOP ARGUIN' WITH THE MARJUN WHILE ENEMIES WHO MEAN YOU DIRECT HARM DIRECTLY ARE ABOUT.
ORNERY LOU!

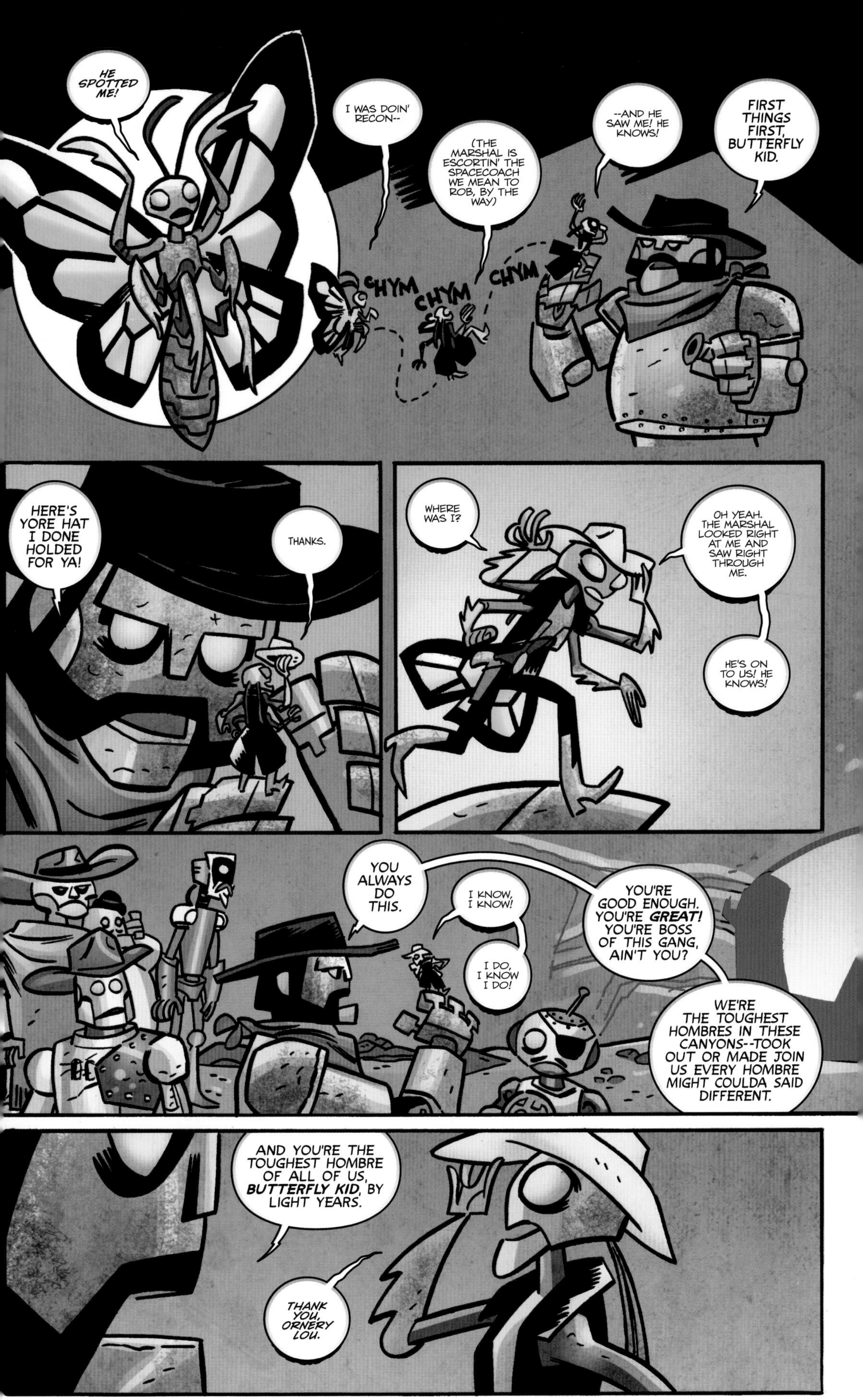
HE SPOTTED ME!
I WAS DOIN' RECON--
(THE MARSHAL IS ESCORTIN' THE SPACECOACH WE MEAN TO ROB, BY THE WAY)
--AND HE SAW ME! HE KNOWS!
CHYM CHYM CHYM
FIRST THINGS FIRST, BUTTERFLY KID.
HERE'S YORE HAT I DONE HOLDED FOR YA!
THANKS.
WHERE WAS I?
OH YEAH. THE MARSHAL LOOKED RIGHT AT ME AND SAW RIGHT THROUGH ME.
HE'S ON TO US! HE KNOWS!
YOU ALWAYS DO THIS.
I KNOW, I KNOW!
I DO, I KNOW I DO!
YOU'RE GOOD ENOUGH. YOU'RE GREAT! YOU'RE BOSS OF THIS GANG, AIN'T YOU?
WE'RE THE TOUGHEST HOMBRES IN THESE CANYONS--TOOK OUT OR MADE JOIN US EVERY HOMBRE MIGHT COULDA SAID DIFFERENT.
AND YOU'RE THE TOUGHEST HOMBRE OF ALL OF US, BUTTERFLY KID, BY LIGHT YEARS.
THANK YOU, ORNERY LOU.

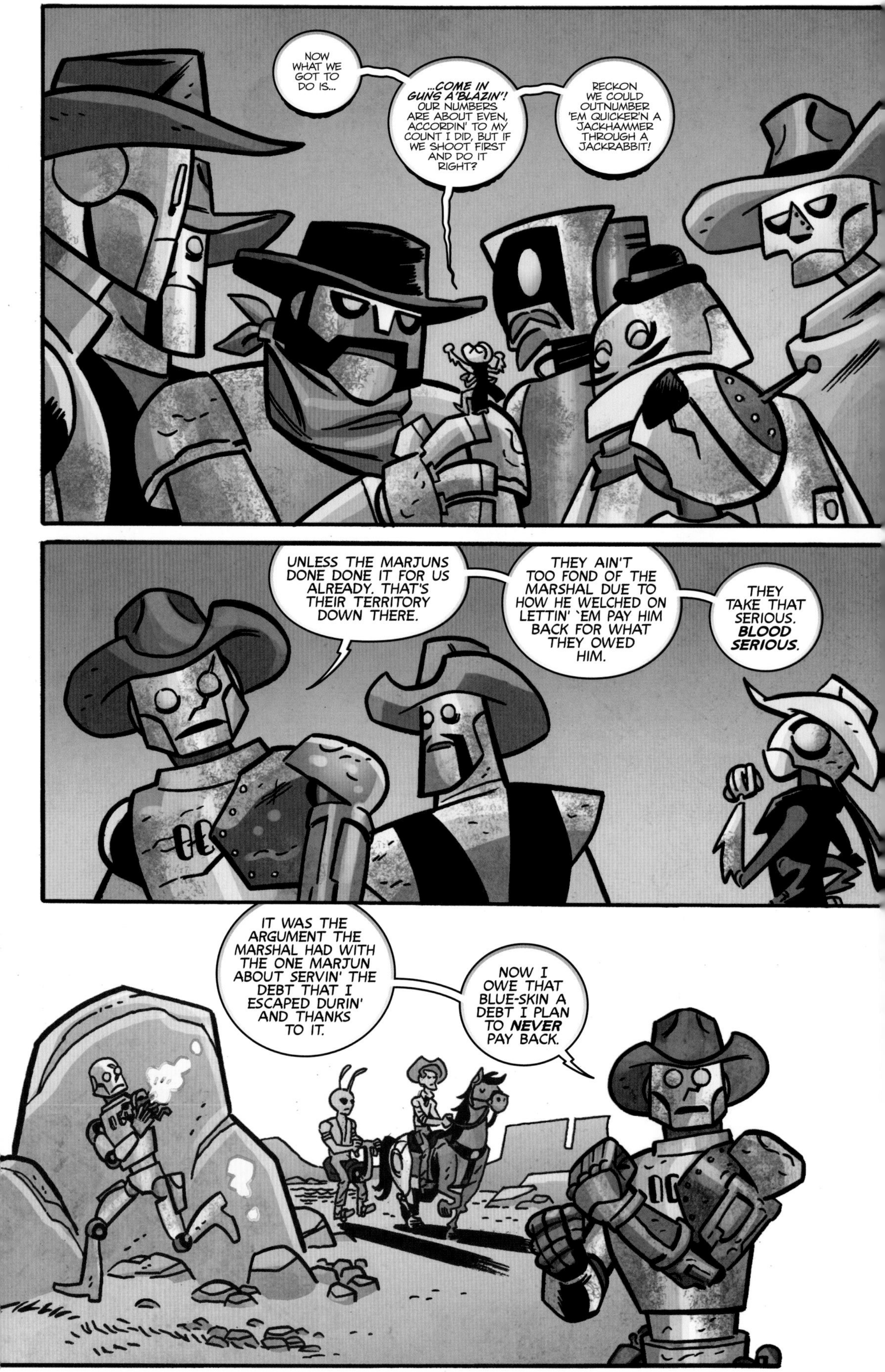
NOW WHAT WE GOT TO DO IS...
...**COME IN GUNS A'BLAZIN'!** OUR NUMBERS ARE ABOUT EVEN, ACCORDIN' TO MY COUNT I DID, BUT IF WE SHOOT FIRST AND DO IT RIGHT?
RECKON WE COULD OUTNUMBER 'EM QUICKER'N A JACKHAMMER THROUGH A JACKRABBIT!
UNLESS THE MARJUNS DONE DONE IT FOR US ALREADY. THAT'S THEIR TERRITORY DOWN THERE.
THEY AIN'T TOO FOND OF THE MARSHAL DUE TO HOW HE WELCHED ON LETTIN' `EM PAY HIM BACK FOR WHAT THEY OWED HIM.
THEY TAKE THAT SERIOUS. ***BLOOD SERIOUS.***
IT WAS THE ARGUMENT THE MARSHAL HAD WITH THE ONE MARJUN ABOUT SERVIN' THE DEBT THAT I ESCAPED DURIN' AND THANKS TO IT.
NOW I OWE THAT BLUE-SKIN A DEBT I PLAN TO ***NEVER*** PAY BACK.

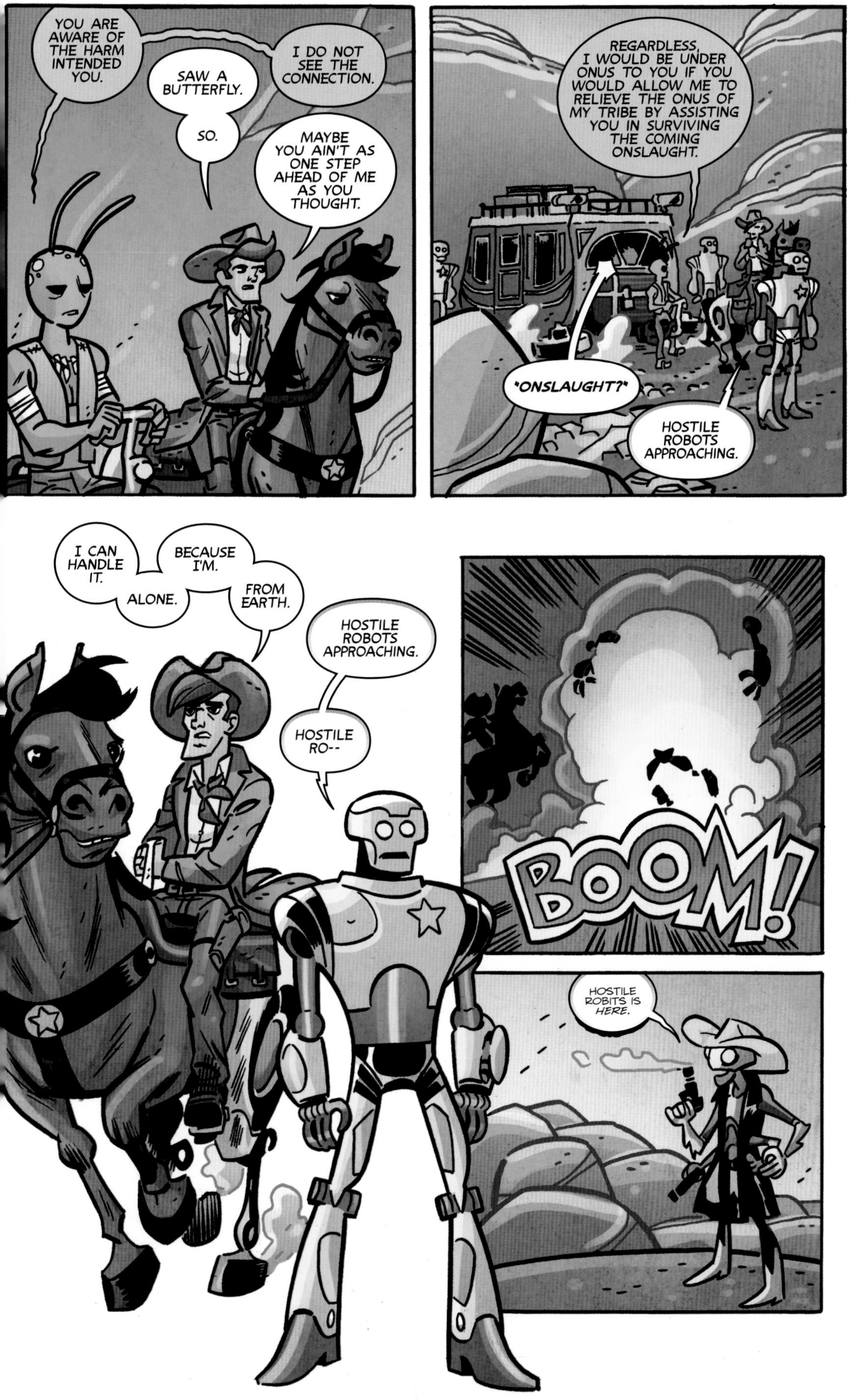
YOU ARE AWARE OF THE HARM INTENDED YOU.
SAW A BUTTERFLY.
SO.
I DO NOT SEE THE CONNECTION.
MAYBE YOU AIN'T AS ONE STEP AHEAD OF ME AS YOU THOUGHT.
REGARDLESS, I WOULD BE UNDER ONUS TO YOU IF YOU WOULD ALLOW ME TO RELIEVE THE ONUS OF MY TRIBE BY ASSISTING YOU IN SURVIVING THE COMING ONSLAUGHT.
"ONSLAUGHT?"
HOSTILE ROBOTS APPROACHING.
I CAN HANDLE IT.
ALONE.
BECAUSE I'M.
FROM EARTH.
HOSTILE ROBOTS APPROACHING.
HOSTILE RO--
BOOM!
HOSTILE ROBITS IS HERE.

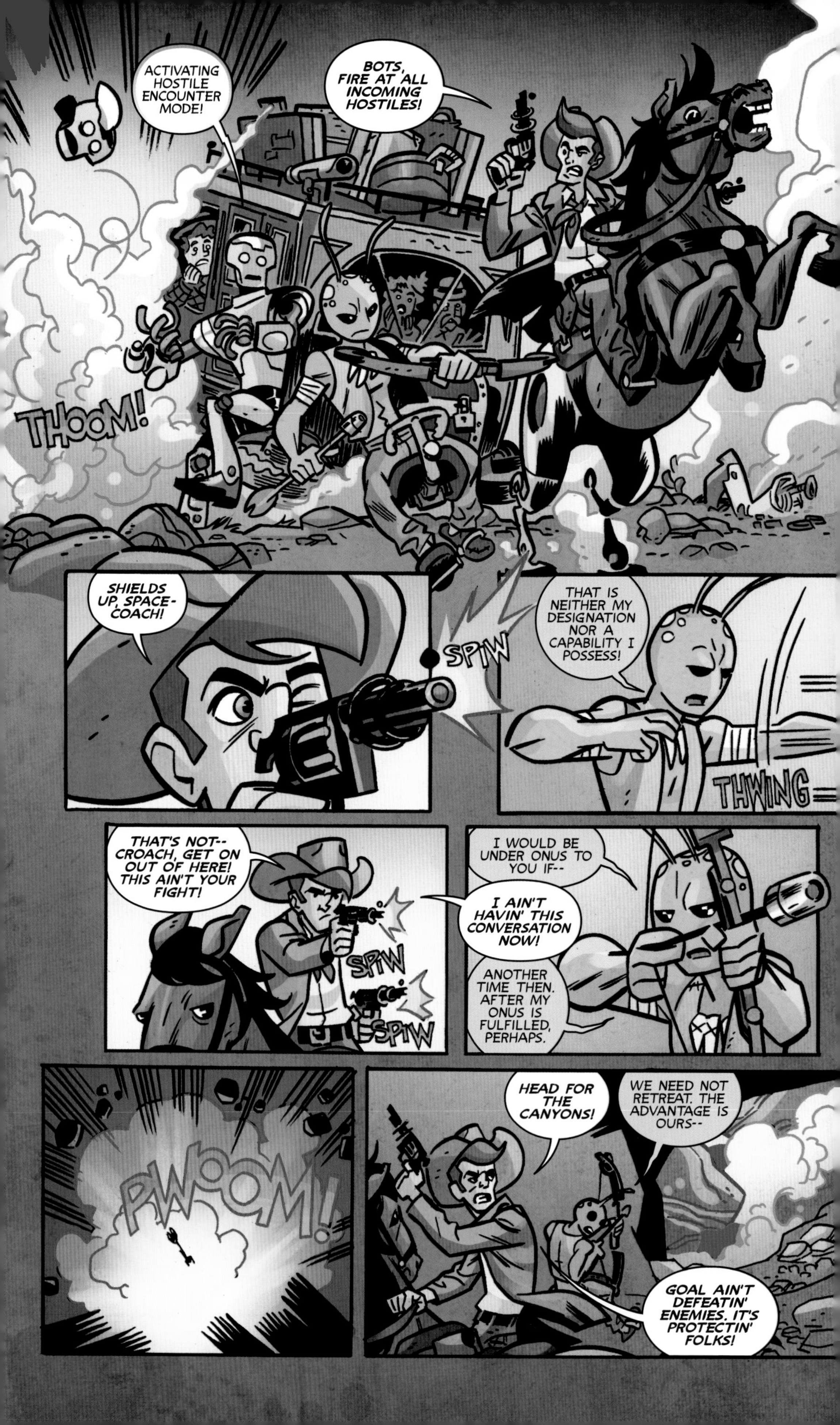
ACTIVATING HOSTILE ENCOUNTER MODE!
BOTS, FIRE AT ALL INCOMING HOSTILES!
THOOM!
SHIELDS UP, SPACE-COACH!
SPIW
THAT IS NEITHER MY DESIGNATION NOR A CAPABILITY I POSSESS!
THWING
THAT'S NOT-- CROACH, GET ON OUT OF HERE! THIS AIN'T YOUR FIGHT!
SPIW
SPIW
I WOULD BE UNDER ONUS TO YOU IF--
I AIN'T HAVIN' THIS CONVERSATION NOW!
ANOTHER TIME THEN. AFTER MY ONUS IS FULFILLED, PERHAPS.
PWOOM!
HEAD FOR THE CANYONS!
WE NEED NOT RETREAT. THE ADVANTAGE IS OURS--
GOAL AIN'T DEFEATIN' ENEMIES. IT'S PROTECTIN' FOLKS!

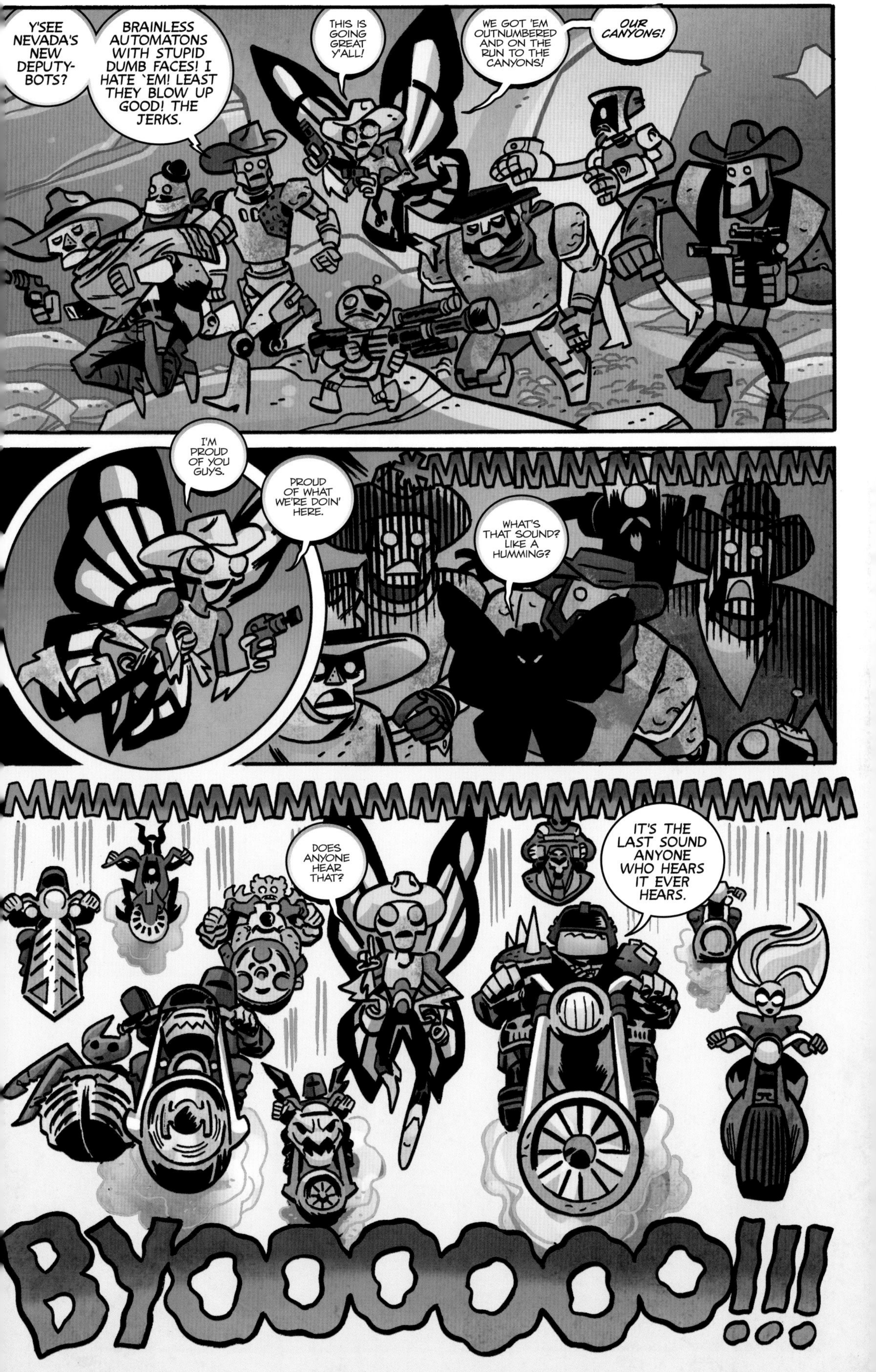
Y'SEE NEVADA'S NEW DEPUTY-BOTS?
BRAINLESS AUTOMATONS WITH STUPID DUMB FACES! I HATE `EM! LEAST THEY BLOW UP GOOD! THE JERKS.
THIS IS GOING GREAT Y'ALL!
WE GOT 'EM OUTNUMBERED AND ON THE RUN TO THE CANYONS!
OUR CANYONS!
I'M PROUD OF YOU GUYS.
PROUD OF WHAT WE'RE DOIN' HERE.
MMMMMMMMMMMM
WHAT'S THAT SOUND? LIKE A HUMMING?
MMMMMMMMMMMMMMMMMMMMMMM
DOES ANYONE HEAR THAT?
IT'S THE LAST SOUND ANYONE WHO HEARS IT EVER HEARS.
BYOOOOOO!!!

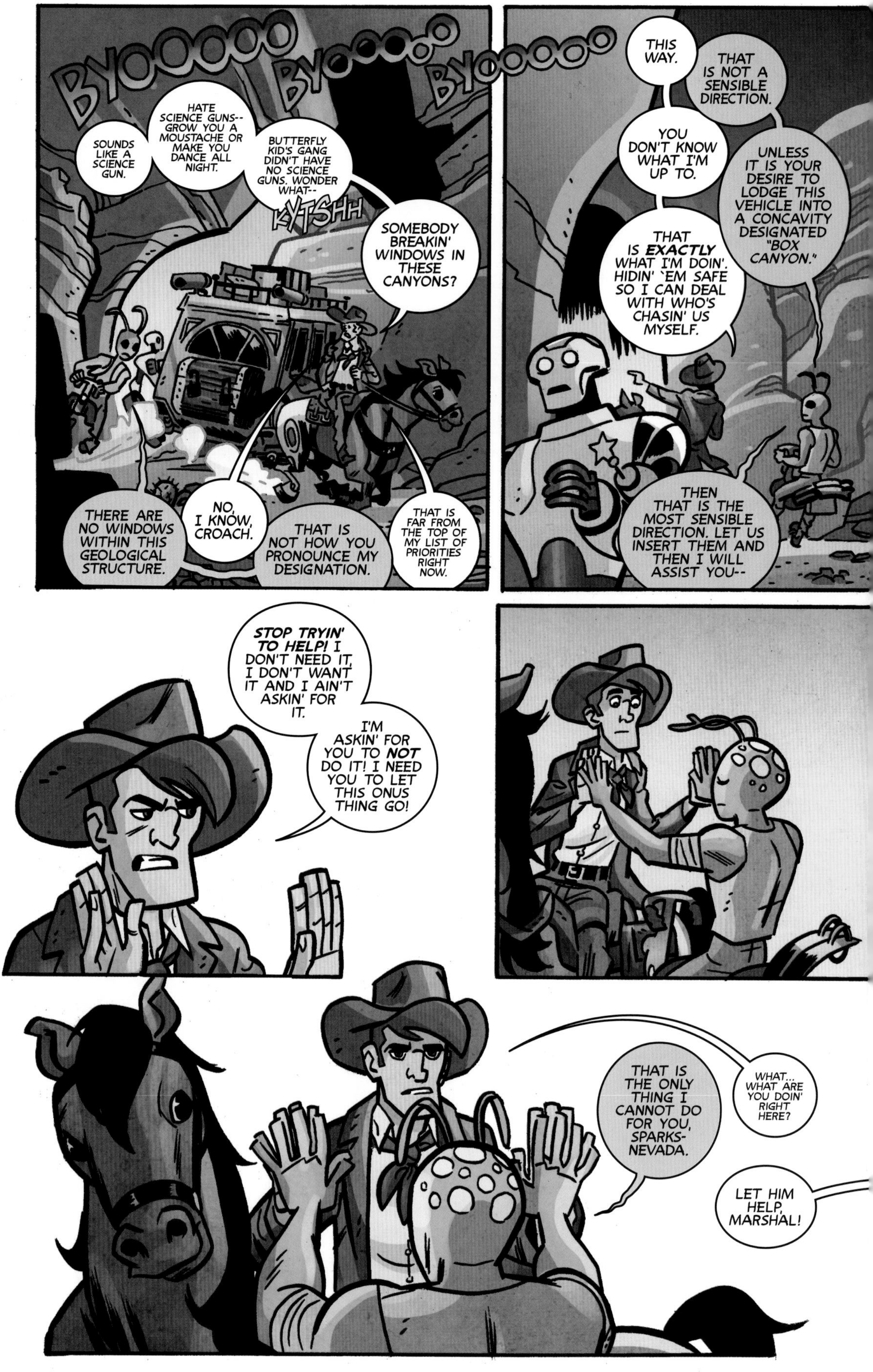
BYOOOOO BYOOOoOO BYOOOOOO
SOUNDS LIKE A SCIENCE GUN.
HATE SCIENCE GUNS-- GROW YOU A MOUSTACHE OR MAKE YOU DANCE ALL NIGHT.
BUTTERFLY KID'S GANG DIDN'T HAVE NO SCIENCE GUNS. WONDER WHAT--
KYTSHH
SOMEBODY BREAKIN' WINDOWS IN THESE CANYONS?
THERE ARE NO WINDOWS WITHIN THIS GEOLOGICAL STRUCTURE.
NO, I KNOW, CROACH.
THAT IS NOT HOW YOU PRONOUNCE MY DESIGNATION.
THAT IS FAR FROM THE TOP OF MY LIST OF PRIORITIES RIGHT NOW.
THIS WAY.
THAT IS NOT A SENSIBLE DIRECTION.
YOU DON'T KNOW WHAT I'M UP TO.
UNLESS IT IS YOUR DESIRE TO LODGE THIS VEHICLE INTO A CONCAVITY DESIGNATED "BOX CANYON."
THAT IS **EXACTLY** WHAT I'M DOIN'. HIDIN' `EM SAFE SO I CAN DEAL WITH WHO'S CHASIN' US MYSELF.
THEN THAT IS THE MOST SENSIBLE DIRECTION. LET US INSERT THEM AND THEN I WILL ASSIST YOU--
STOP TRYIN' TO HELP! I DON'T NEED IT, I DON'T WANT IT AND I AIN'T ASKIN' FOR IT.
I'M ASKIN' FOR YOU TO **NOT** DO IT! I NEED YOU TO LET THIS ONUS THING GO!
THAT IS THE ONLY THING I CANNOT DO FOR YOU, SPARKS-NEVADA.
WHAT... WHAT ARE YOU DOIN' RIGHT HERE?
LET HIM HELP, MARSHAL!

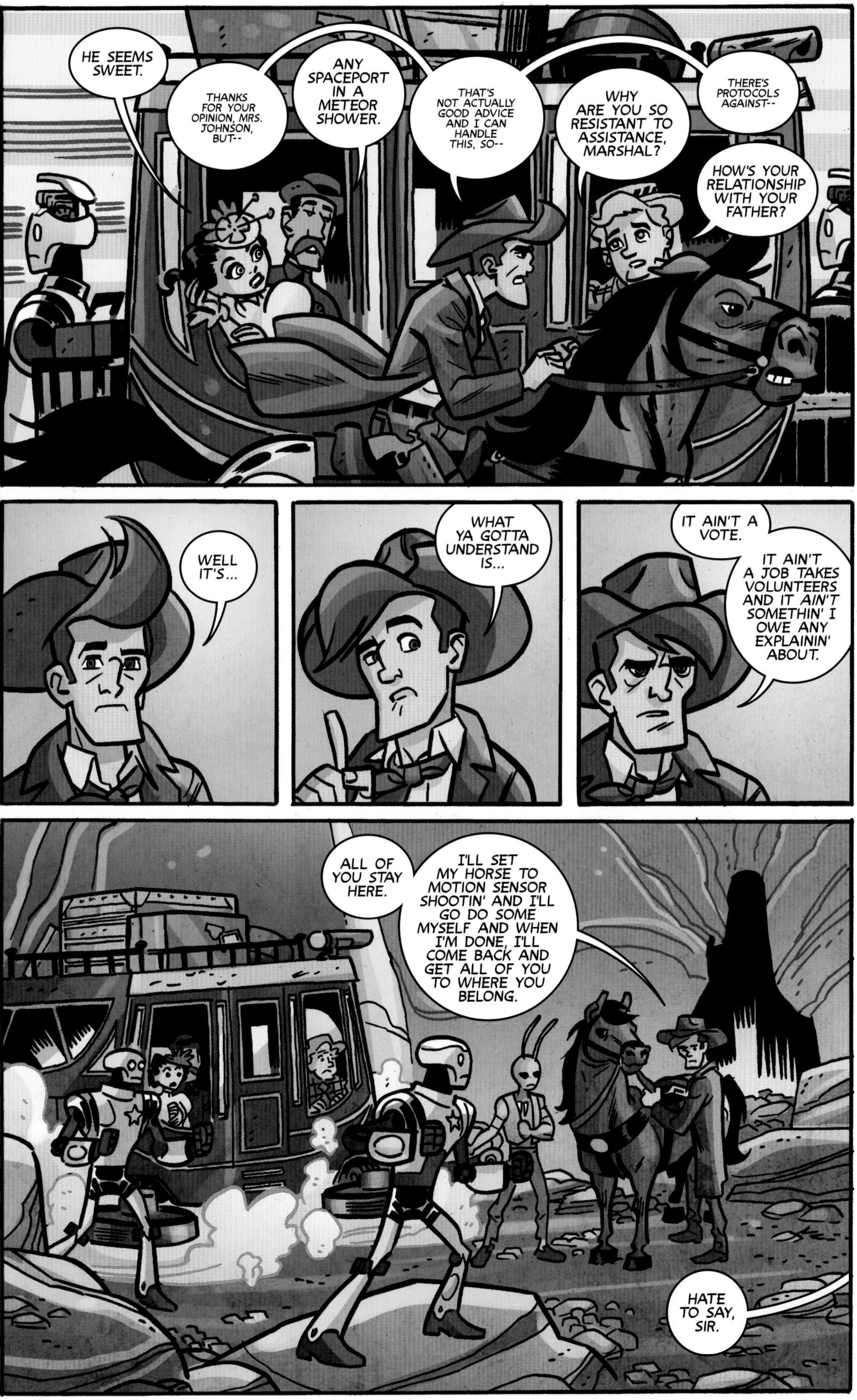

HE SEEMS SWEET.
THANKS FOR YOUR OPINION, MRS. JOHNSON, BUT--
ANY SPACEPORT IN A METEOR SHOWER.
THAT'S NOT ACTUALLY GOOD ADVICE AND I CAN HANDLE THIS, SO--
WHY ARE YOU SO RESISTANT TO ASSISTANCE, MARSHAL?
THERE'S PROTOCOLS AGAINST--
HOW'S YOUR RELATIONSHIP WITH YOUR FATHER?
WELL IT'S...
WHAT YA GOTTA UNDERSTAND IS...
IT AIN'T A VOTE.
IT AIN'T A JOB TAKES VOLUNTEERS AND IT *AIN'T* SOMETHIN' I OWE ANY EXPLAININ' ABOUT.
ALL OF YOU STAY HERE.
I'LL SET MY HORSE TO MOTION SENSOR SHOOTIN' AND I'LL GO DO SOME MYSELF AND WHEN I'M DONE, I'LL COME BACK AND GET ALL OF YOU TO WHERE YOU BELONG.
HATE TO SAY, SIR.

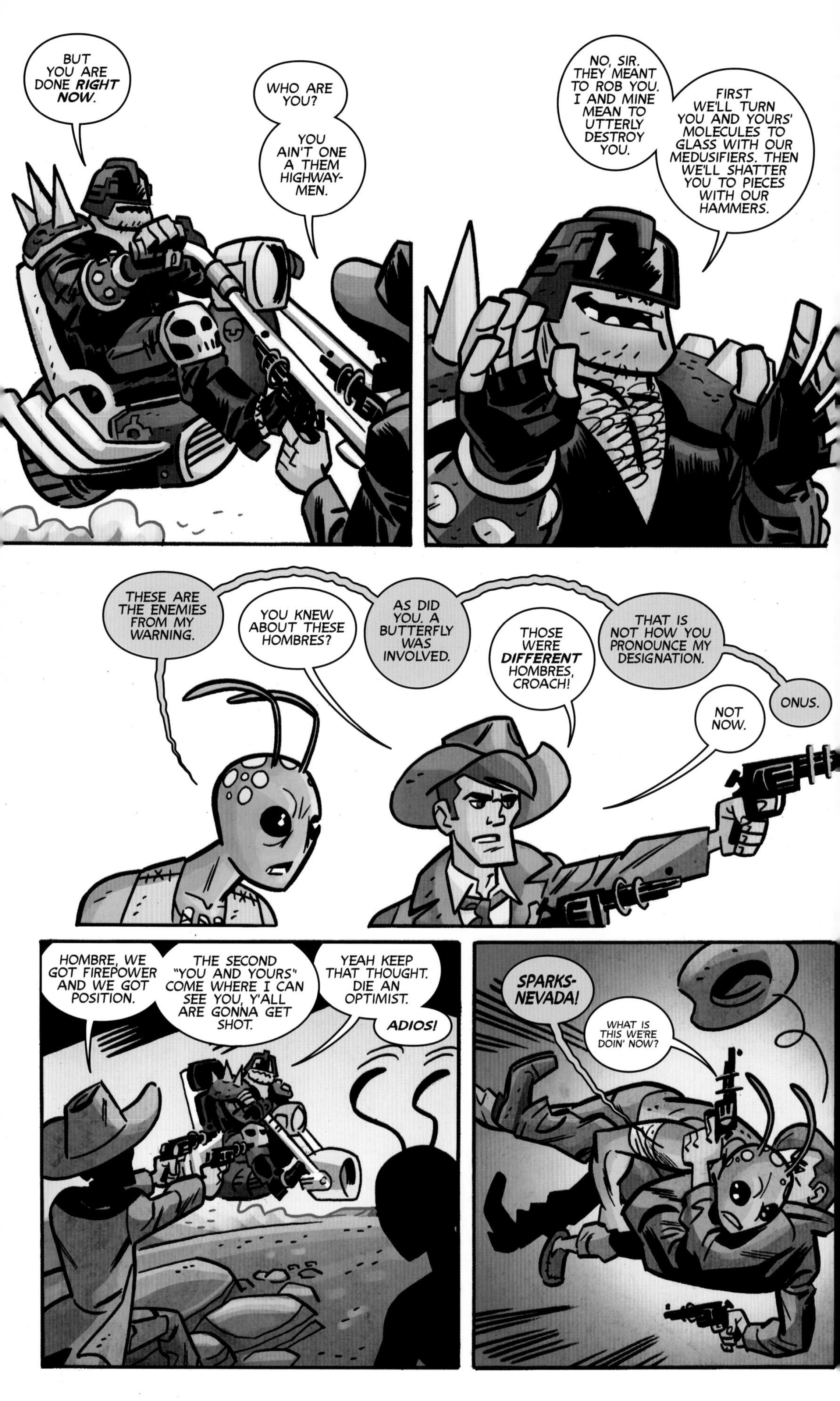
BUT YOU ARE DONE *RIGHT NOW*.
WHO ARE YOU?
YOU AIN'T ONE A THEM HIGHWAY-MEN.
NO, SIR. THEY MEANT TO ROB YOU. I AND MINE MEAN TO UTTERLY DESTROY YOU.
FIRST WE'LL TURN YOU AND YOURS' MOLECULES TO GLASS WITH OUR MEDUSIFIERS. THEN WE'LL SHATTER YOU TO PIECES WITH OUR HAMMERS.
THESE ARE THE ENEMIES FROM MY WARNING.
YOU KNEW ABOUT THESE HOMBRES?
AS DID YOU. A BUTTERFLY WAS INVOLVED.
THOSE WERE *DIFFERENT* HOMBRES, CROACH!
THAT IS NOT HOW YOU PRONOUNCE MY DESIGNATION.
ONUS.
NOT NOW.
HOMBRE, WE GOT FIREPOWER AND WE GOT POSITION.
THE SECOND "YOU AND YOURS" COME WHERE I CAN SEE YOU, Y'ALL ARE GONNA GET SHOT.
YEAH KEEP THAT THOUGHT. DIE AN OPTIMIST.
ADIOS!
SPARKS-NEVADA!
WHAT IS THIS WE'RE DOIN' NOW?

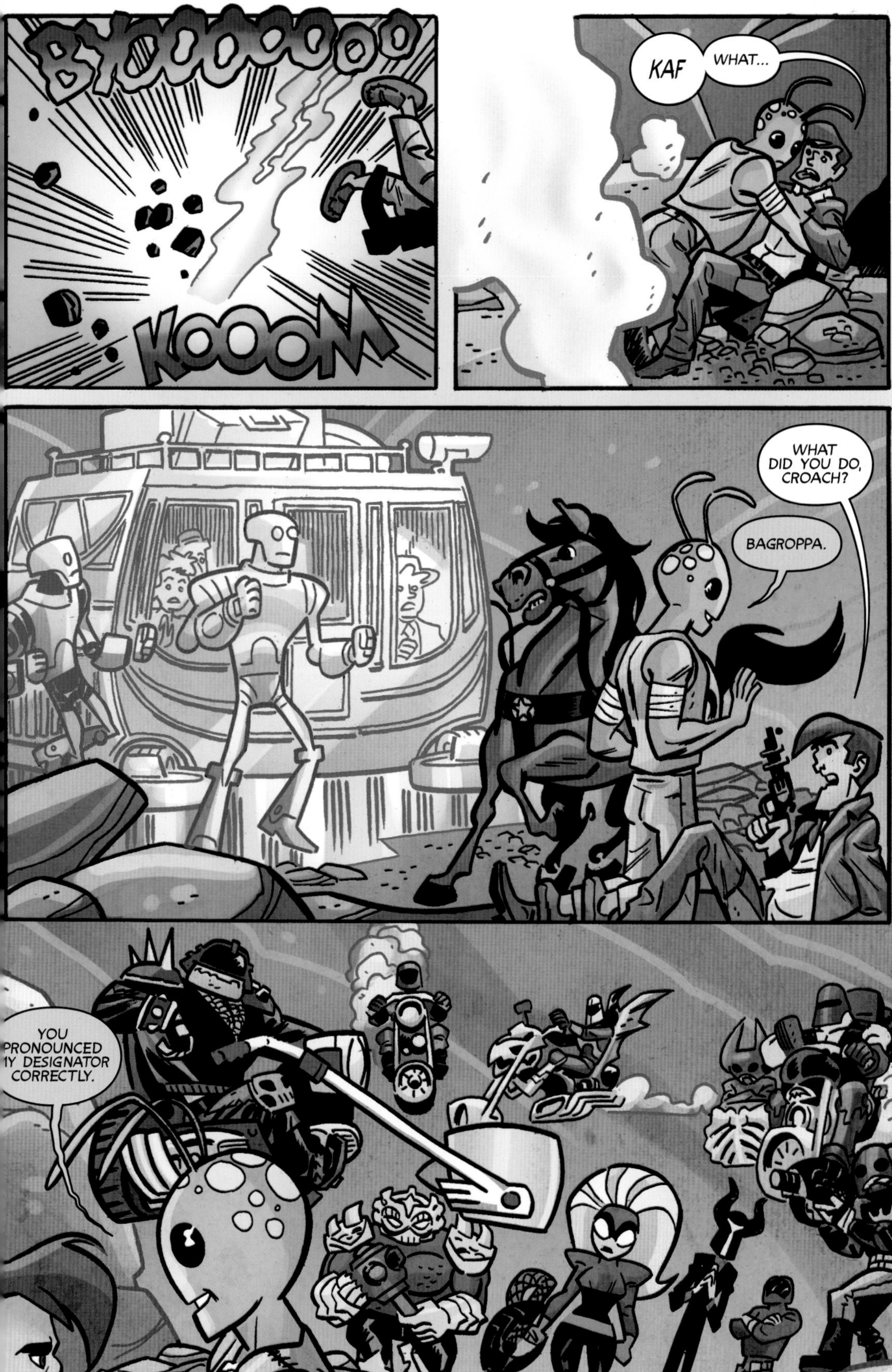
BYOOOOOOO
KOOOM
KAF
WHAT...
WHAT DID YOU DO, CROACH?
BAGROPPA.
YOU PRONOUNCED MY DESIGNATOR CORRECTLY.

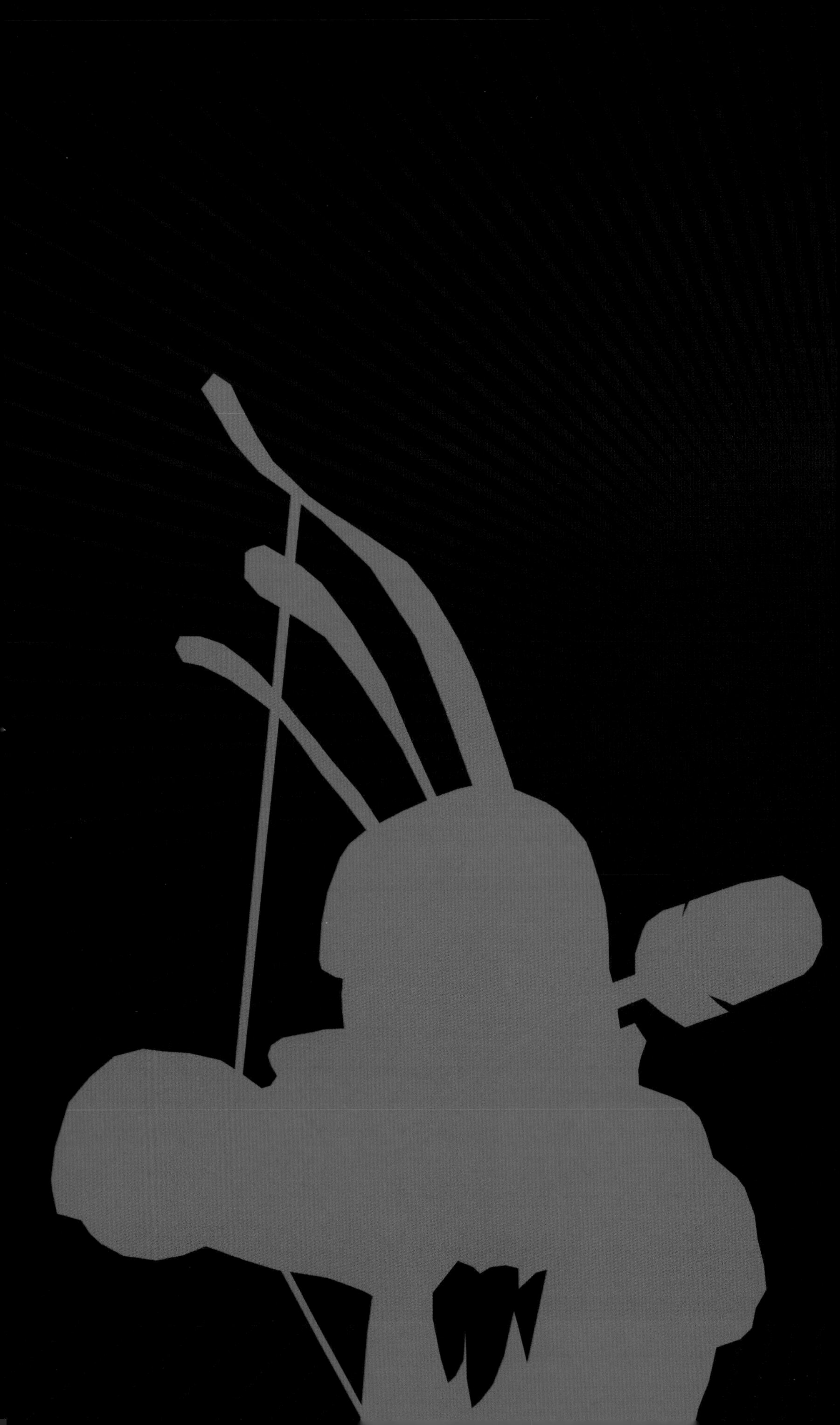

Chapter

TWO

Journey to the Center of the Mars

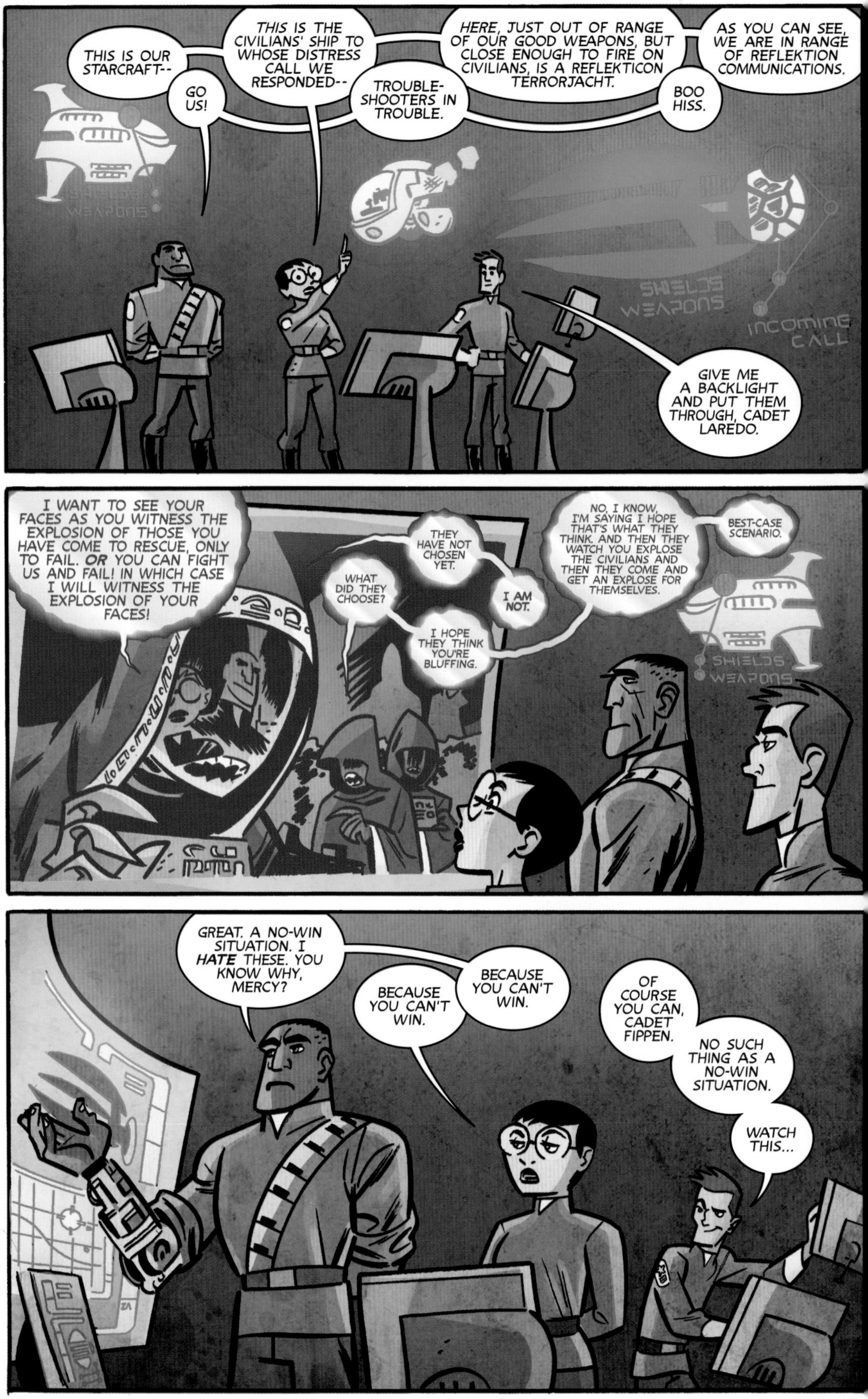
THIS IS OUR STARCRAFT--
GO US!
THIS IS THE CIVILIANS' SHIP TO WHOSE DISTRESS CALL WE RESPONDED--
TROUBLE-SHOOTERS IN TROUBLE.
HERE, JUST OUT OF RANGE OF OUR GOOD WEAPONS, BUT CLOSE ENOUGH TO FIRE ON CIVILIANS, IS A REFLEKTICON TERRORJACHT.
BOO HISS.
AS YOU CAN SEE, WE ARE IN RANGE OF REFLEKTION COMMUNICATIONS.
SHIELDS
WEAPONS
SHIELDS
WEAPONS
INCOMING CALL
GIVE ME A BACKLIGHT AND PUT THEM THROUGH, CADET LAREDO.
I WANT TO SEE YOUR FACES AS YOU WITNESS THE EXPLOSION OF THOSE YOU HAVE COME TO RESCUE, ONLY TO FAIL. OR YOU CAN FIGHT US AND FAIL! IN WHICH CASE I WILL WITNESS THE EXPLOSION OF YOUR FACES!
WHAT DID THEY CHOOSE?
THEY HAVE NOT CHOSEN YET.
I AM NOT.
I HOPE THEY THINK YOU'RE BLUFFING.
NO, I KNOW, I'M SAYING I HOPE THAT'S WHAT THEY THINK. AND THEN THEY WATCH YOU EXPLOSE THE CIVILIANS AND THEN THEY COME AND GET AN EXPLOSE FOR THEMSELVES.
BEST-CASE SCENARIO.
SHIELDS
WEAPONS
GREAT. A NO-WIN SITUATION. I HATE THESE. YOU KNOW WHY, MERCY?
BECAUSE YOU CAN'T WIN.
BECAUSE YOU CAN'T WIN.
OF COURSE YOU CAN, CADET FIPPEN.
NO SUCH THING AS A NO-WIN SITUATION.
WATCH THIS...

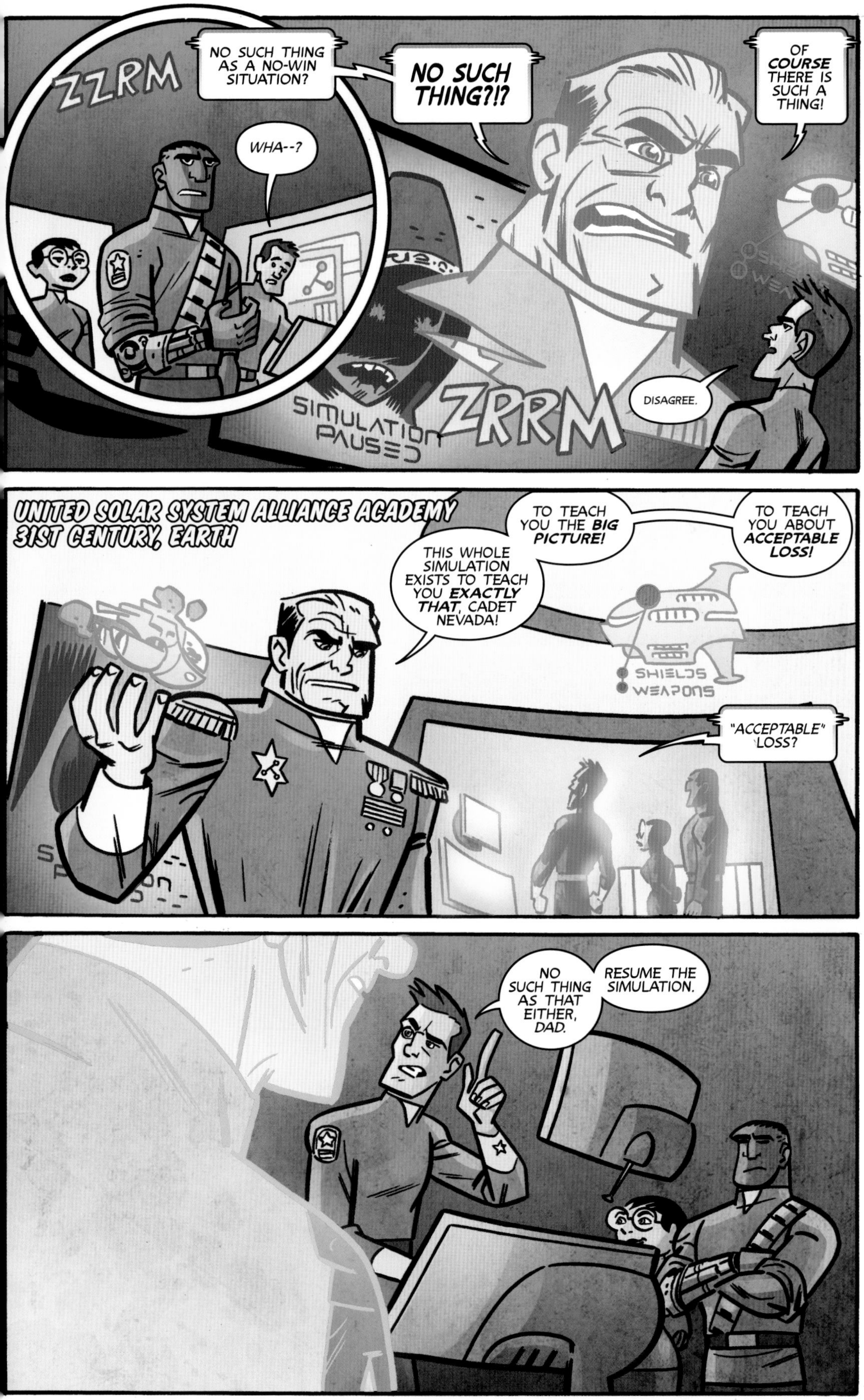
ZZRM
NO SUCH THING AS A NO-WIN SITUATION?
WHA--?
NO SUCH THING?!?
OF COURSE THERE IS SUCH A THING!
SIMULATION PAUSED
ZRRM
DISAGREE.
UNITED SOLAR SYSTEM ALLIANCE ACADEMY 31ST CENTURY, EARTH
THIS WHOLE SIMULATION EXISTS TO TEACH YOU EXACTLY THAT, CADET NEVADA!
TO TEACH YOU THE BIG PICTURE!
TO TEACH YOU ABOUT ACCEPTABLE LOSS!
SHIELDS
WEAPONS
"ACCEPTABLE" LOSS?
NO SUCH THING AS THAT EITHER, DAD.
RESUME THE SIMULATION.

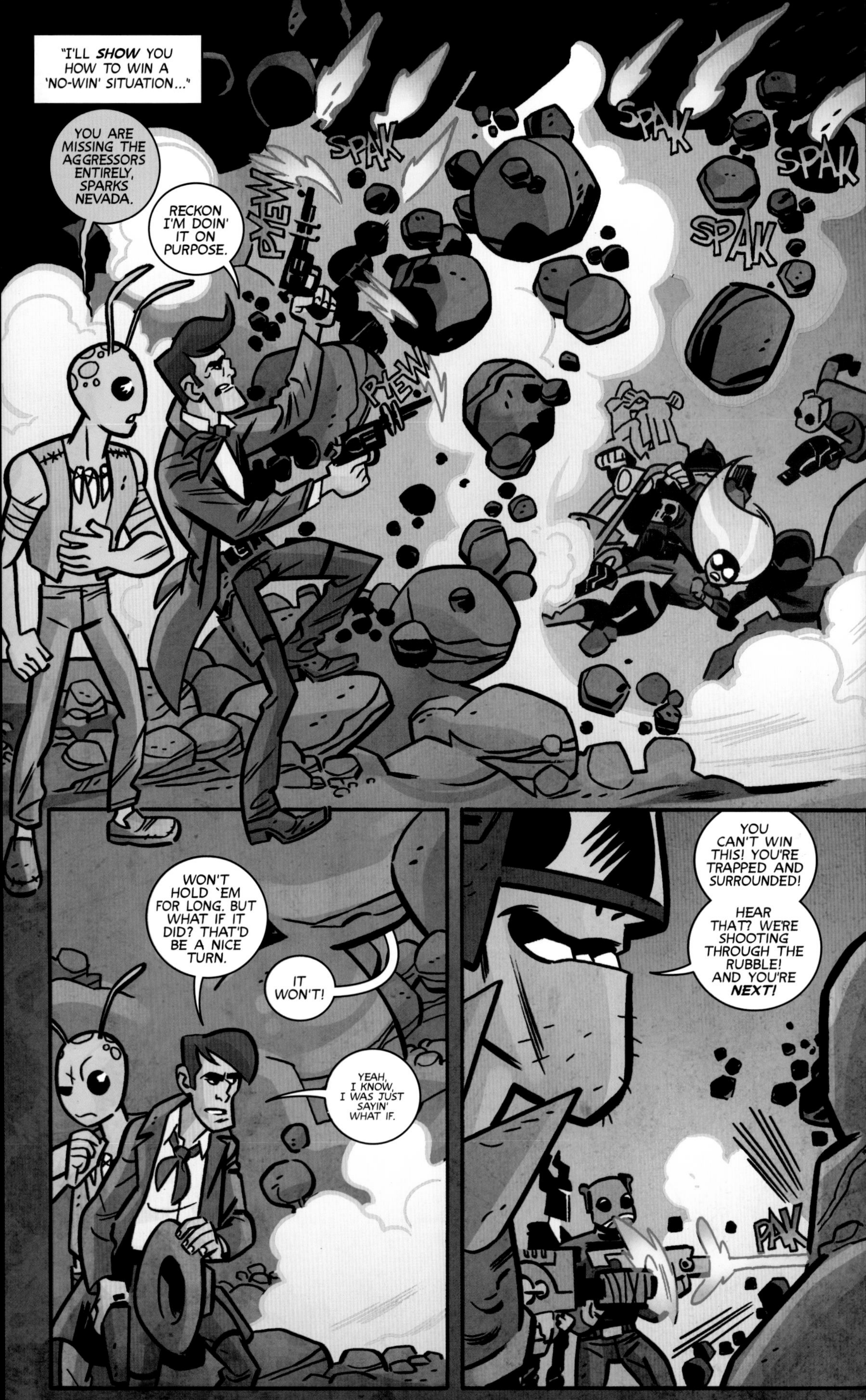
"I'LL SHOW YOU HOW TO WIN A 'NO-WIN' SITUATION..."
YOU ARE MISSING THE AGGRESSORS ENTIRELY, SPARKS NEVADA.
RECKON I'M DOIN' IT ON PURPOSE.
PTEW PTEW
SPAK
PTEW
SPAK
SPAK
SPAK
WON'T HOLD `EM FOR LONG. BUT WHAT IF IT DID? THAT'D BE A NICE TURN.
IT WON'T!
YEAH, I KNOW, I WAS JUST SAYIN' WHAT IF.
YOU CAN'T WIN THIS! YOU'RE TRAPPED AND SURROUNDED!
HEAR THAT? WE'RE SHOOTING THROUGH THE RUBBLE! AND YOU'RE NEXT!
PAK

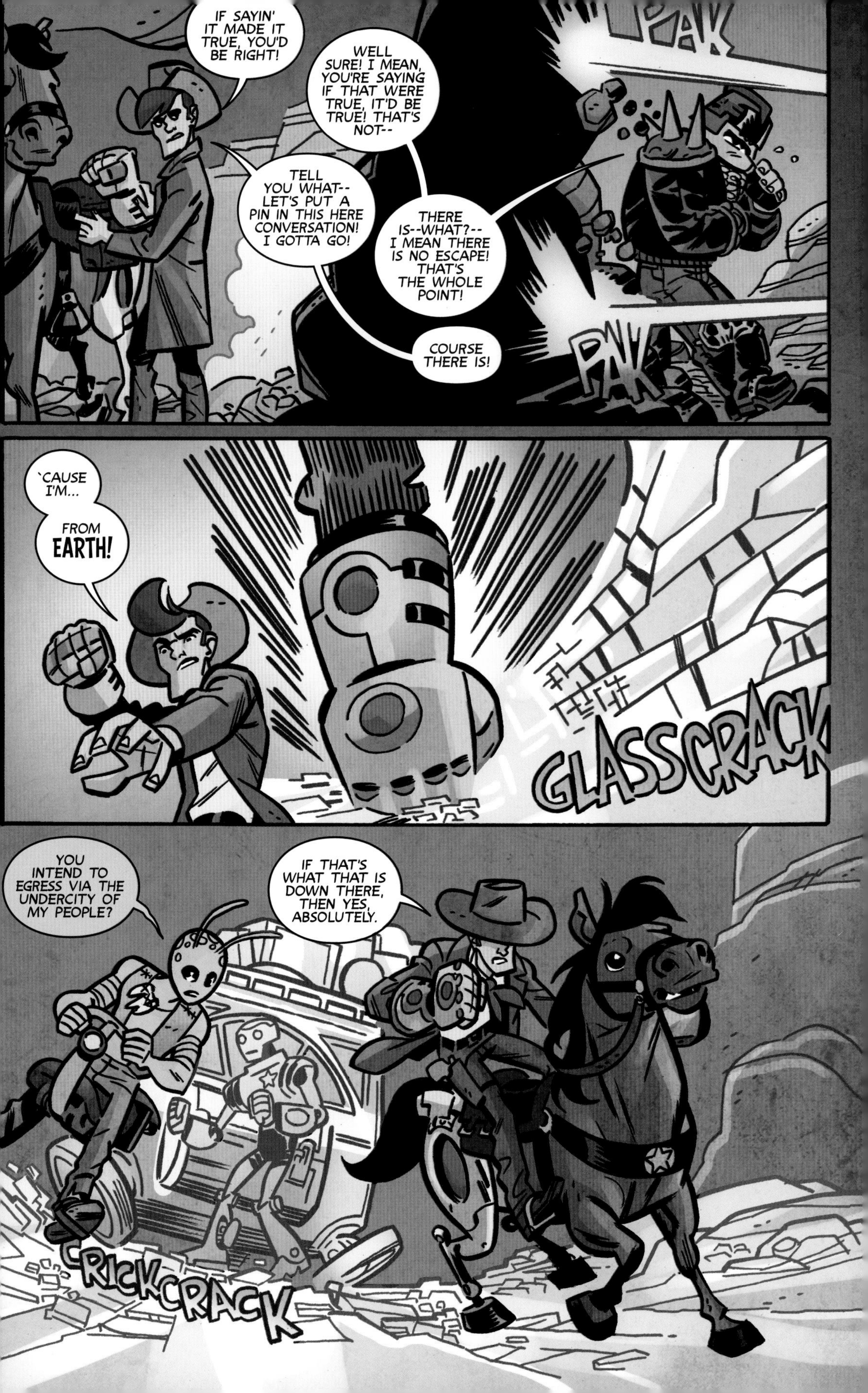
PAK
IF SAYIN' IT MADE IT TRUE, YOU'D BE RIGHT!
WELL SURE! I MEAN, YOU'RE SAYING IF THAT WERE TRUE, IT'D BE TRUE! THAT'S NOT--
TELL YOU WHAT-- LET'S PUT A PIN IN THIS HERE CONVERSATION! I GOTTA GO!
THERE IS--WHAT?-- I MEAN THERE IS NO ESCAPE! THAT'S THE WHOLE POINT!
COURSE THERE IS!
PAK
`CAUSE I'M...
FROM EARTH!
GLASSCRACK
YOU INTEND TO EGRESS VIA THE UNDERCITY OF MY PEOPLE?
IF THAT'S WHAT THAT IS DOWN THERE, THEN YES, ABSOLUTELY.
CRICKCRACK

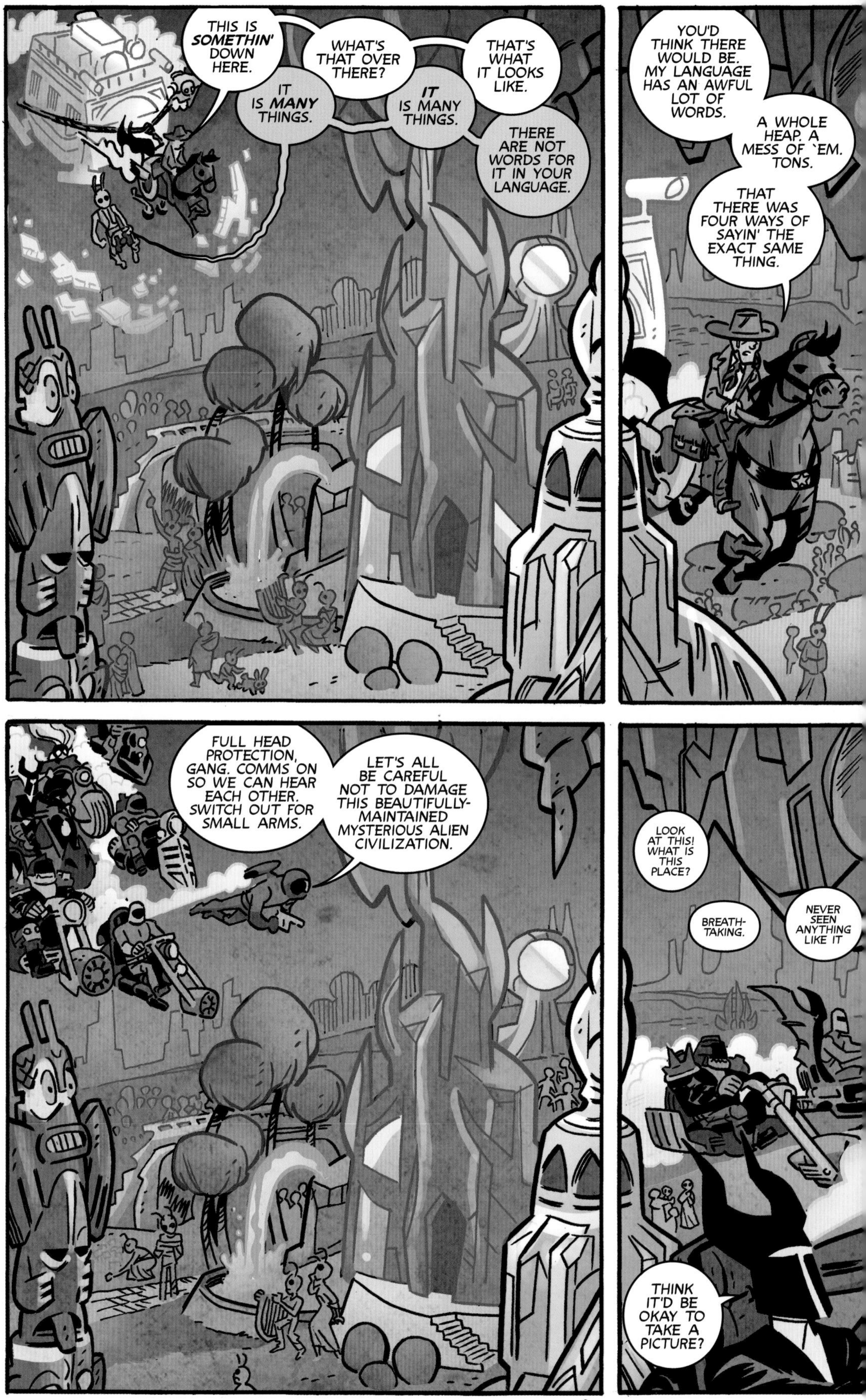
THIS IS SOMETHIN' DOWN HERE.
WHAT'S THAT OVER THERE?
THAT'S WHAT IT LOOKS LIKE.
IT IS MANY THINGS.
IT IS MANY THINGS.
THERE ARE NOT WORDS FOR IT IN YOUR LANGUAGE.
YOU'D THINK THERE WOULD BE. MY LANGUAGE HAS AN AWFUL LOT OF WORDS.
A WHOLE HEAP. A MESS OF `EM. TONS.
THAT THERE WAS FOUR WAYS OF SAYIN' THE EXACT SAME THING.
FULL HEAD PROTECTION, GANG. COMMS ON SO WE CAN HEAR EACH OTHER. SWITCH OUT FOR SMALL ARMS.
LET'S ALL BE CAREFUL NOT TO DAMAGE THIS BEAUTIFULLY-MAINTAINED MYSTERIOUS ALIEN CIVILIZATION.
LOOK AT THIS! WHAT IS THIS PLACE?
BREATH-TAKING.
NEVER SEEN ANYTHING LIKE IT
THINK IT'D BE OKAY TO TAKE A PICTURE?

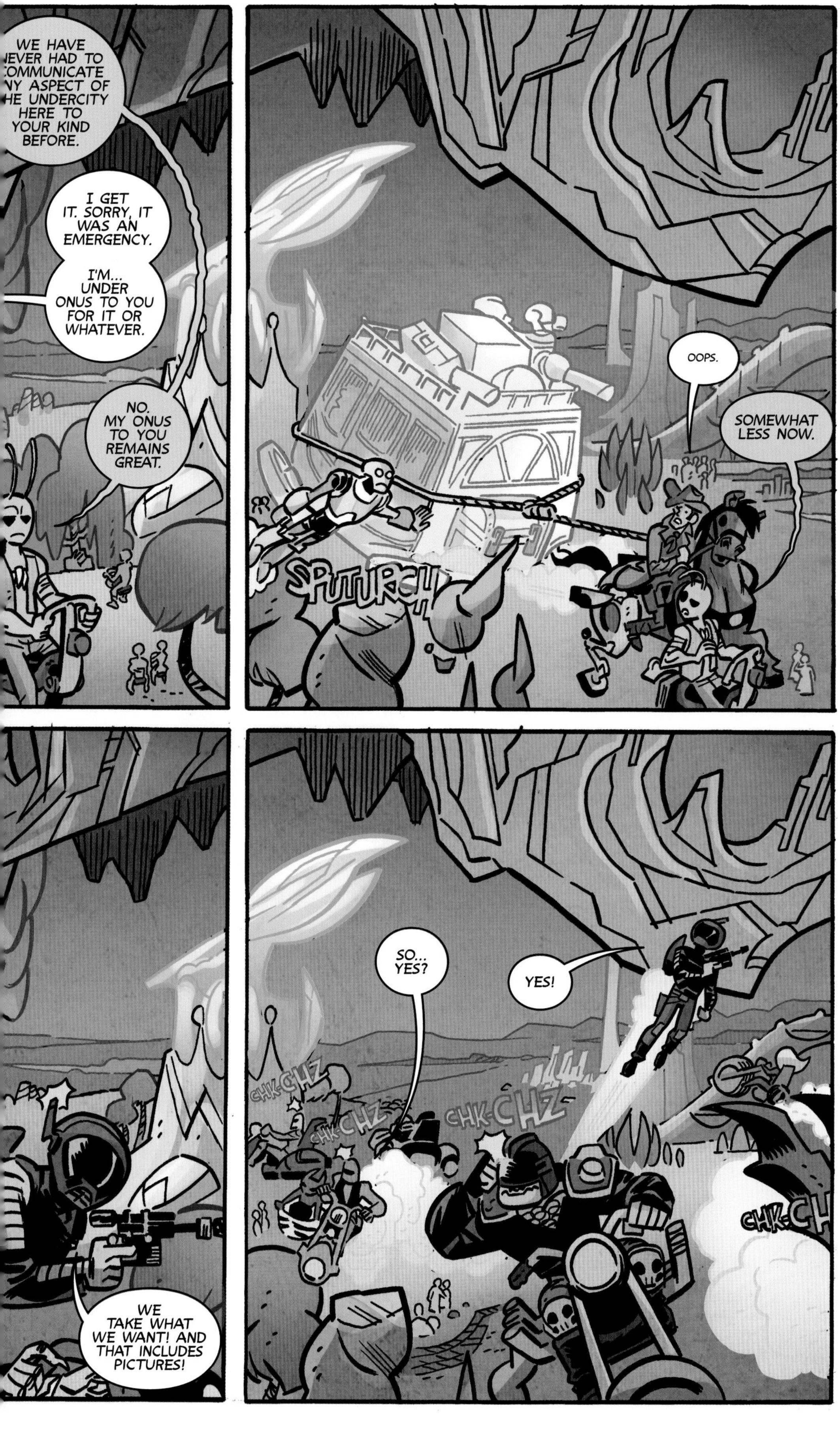

WE HAVE IEVER HAD TO OMMUNICATE NY ASPECT OF HE UNDERCITY HERE TO YOUR KIND BEFORE.
I GET IT. SORRY, IT WAS AN EMERGENCY.
I'M... UNDER ONUS TO YOU FOR IT OR WHATEVER.
NO. MY ONUS TO YOU REMAINS GREAT.
SPUTURCH
OOPS.
SOMEWHAT LESS NOW.
WE TAKE WHAT WE WANT! AND THAT INCLUDES PICTURES!
CHK-CHZ
CHK-CHZ
CHK-CHZ
SO... YES?
YES!

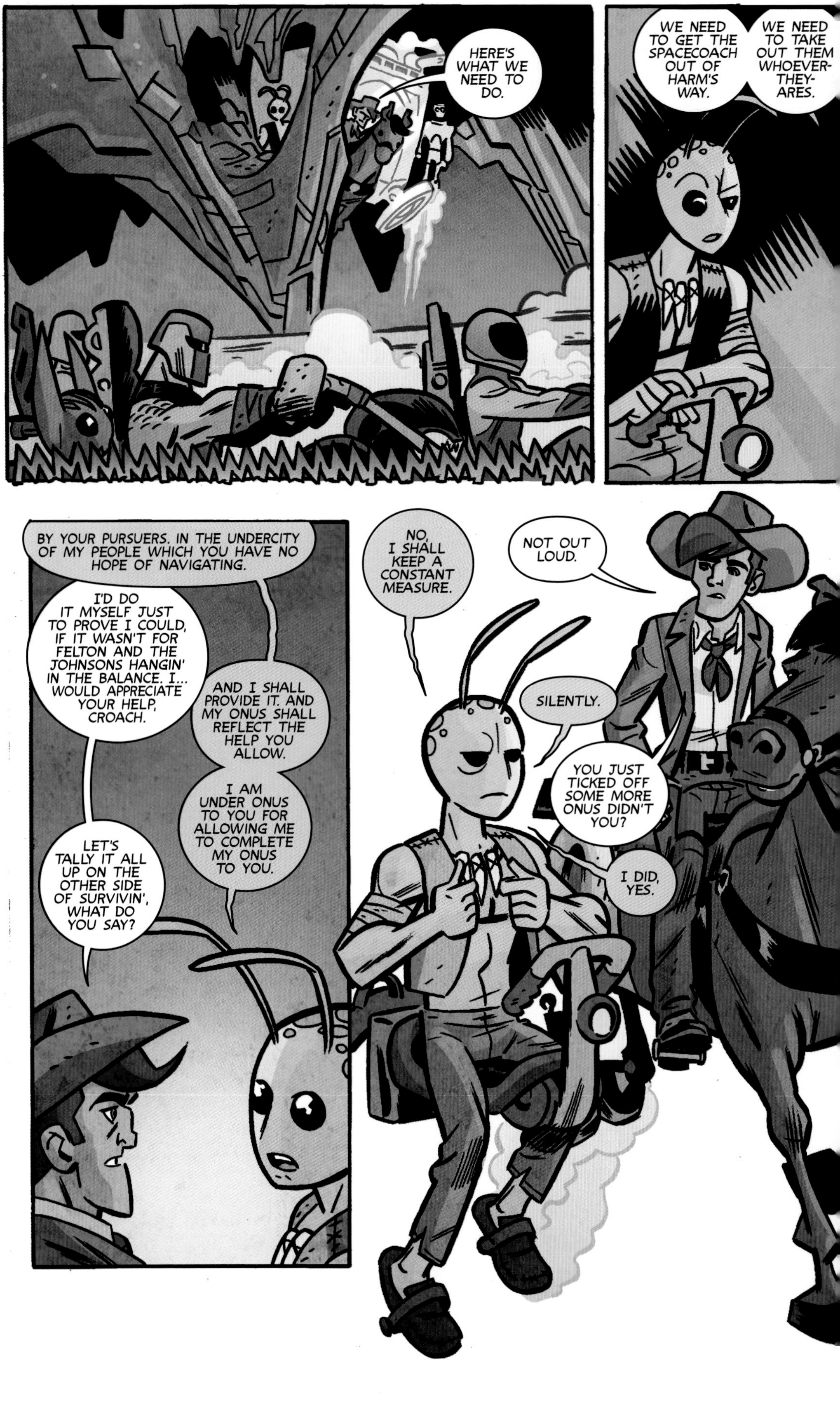
HERE'S WHAT WE NEED TO DO.
WE NEED TO GET THE SPACECOACH OUT OF HARM'S WAY.
WE NEED TO TAKE OUT THEM WHOEVER-THEY-ARES.
BY YOUR PURSUERS. IN THE UNDERCITY OF MY PEOPLE WHICH YOU HAVE NO HOPE OF NAVIGATING.
I'D DO IT MYSELF JUST TO PROVE I COULD, IF IT WASN'T FOR FELTON AND THE JOHNSONS HANGIN' IN THE BALANCE. I... WOULD APPRECIATE YOUR HELP, CROACH.
AND I SHALL PROVIDE IT. AND MY ONUS SHALL REFLECT THE HELP YOU ALLOW.
I AM UNDER ONUS TO YOU FOR ALLOWING ME TO COMPLETE MY ONUS TO YOU.
LET'S TALLY IT ALL UP ON THE OTHER SIDE OF SURVIVIN', WHAT DO YOU SAY?
NO, I SHALL KEEP A CONSTANT MEASURE.
NOT OUT LOUD.
SILENTLY.
YOU JUST TICKED OFF SOME MORE ONUS DIDN'T YOU?
I DID, YES.

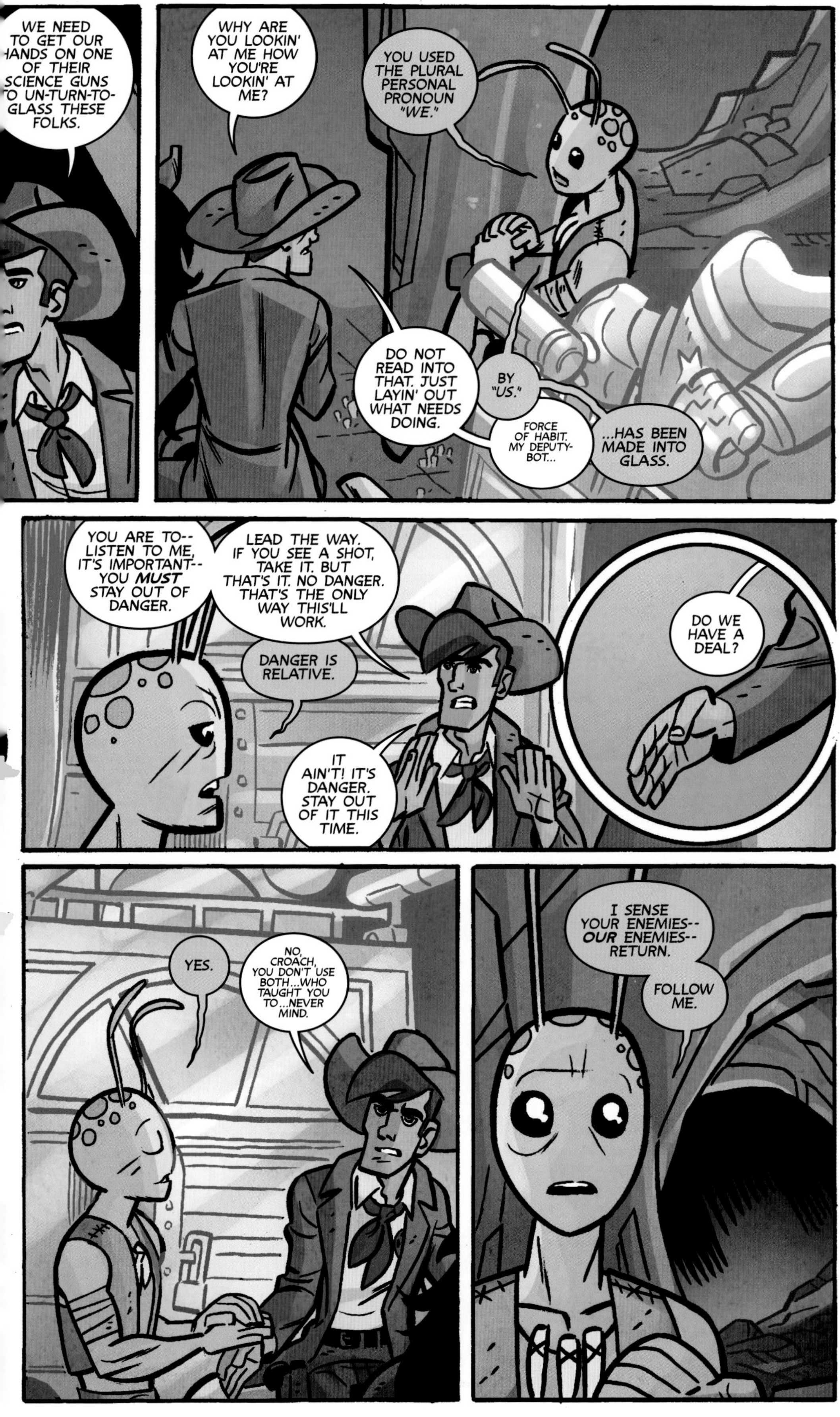
WE NEED TO GET OUR HANDS ON ONE OF THEIR SCIENCE GUNS TO UN-TURN-TO-GLASS THESE FOLKS.
WHY ARE YOU LOOKIN' AT ME HOW YOU'RE LOOKIN' AT ME?
YOU USED THE PLURAL PERSONAL PRONOUN "WE."
DO NOT READ INTO THAT. JUST LAYIN' OUT WHAT NEEDS DOING.
BY "US."
FORCE OF HABIT. MY DEPUTY-BOT...
...HAS BEEN MADE INTO GLASS.
YOU ARE TO--LISTEN TO ME, IT'S IMPORTANT--YOU MUST STAY OUT OF DANGER.
LEAD THE WAY. IF YOU SEE A SHOT, TAKE IT. BUT THAT'S IT. NO DANGER. THAT'S THE ONLY WAY THIS'LL WORK.
DANGER IS RELATIVE.
IT AIN'T! IT'S DANGER. STAY OUT OF IT THIS TIME.
DO WE HAVE A DEAL?
YES.
NO, CROACH, YOU DON'T USE BOTH...WHO TAUGHT YOU TO...NEVER MIND.
I SENSE YOUR ENEMIES--OUR ENEMIES--RETURN.
FOLLOW ME.

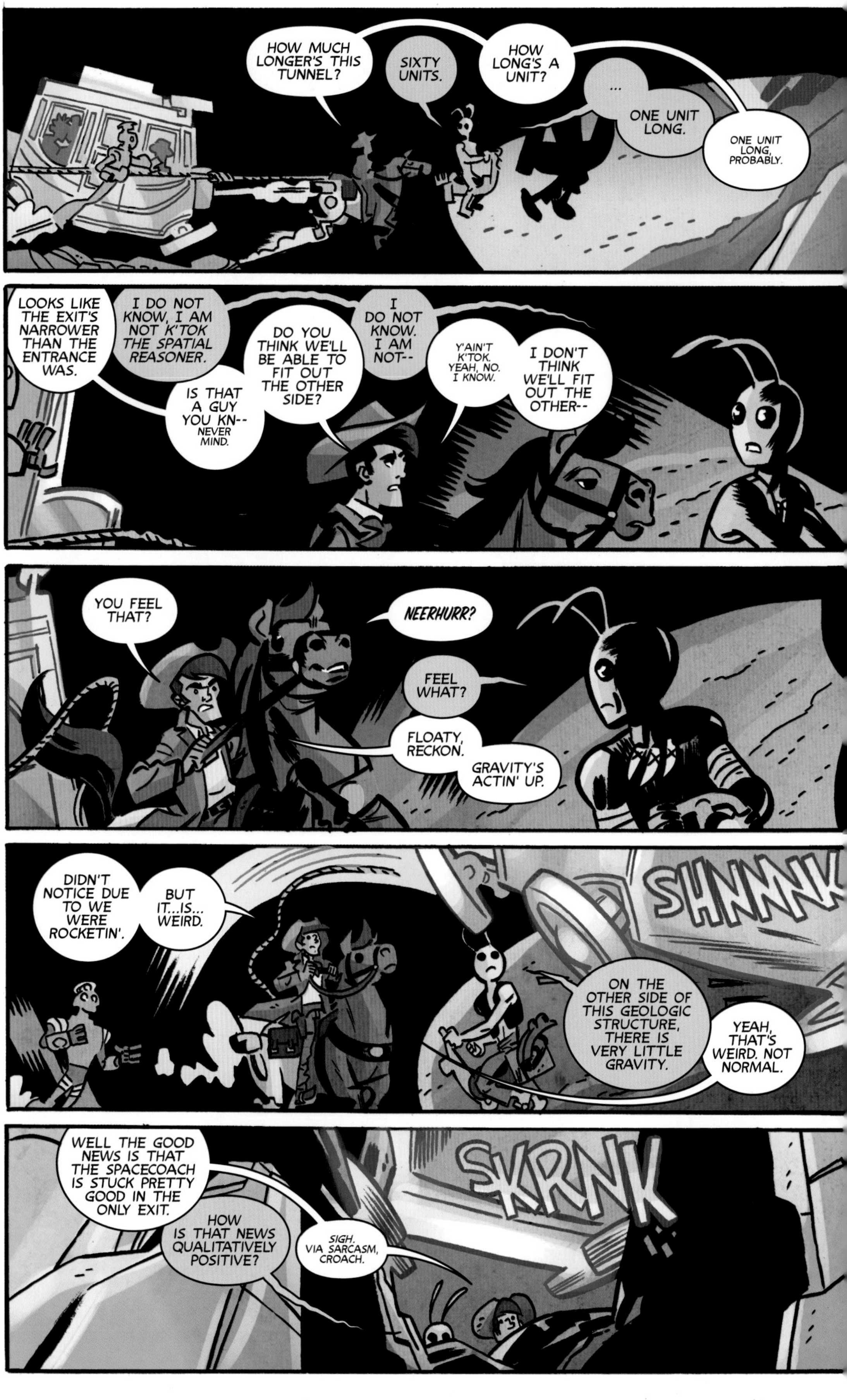

HOW MUCH LONGER'S THIS TUNNEL?
SIXTY UNITS.
HOW LONG'S A UNIT?
...
ONE UNIT LONG.
ONE UNIT LONG, PROBABLY.
LOOKS LIKE THE EXIT'S NARROWER THAN THE ENTRANCE WAS.
I DO NOT KNOW, I AM NOT *K'TOK THE SPATIAL REASONER.*
IS THAT A GUY YOU KN-- NEVER MIND.
DO YOU THINK WE'LL BE ABLE TO FIT OUT THE OTHER SIDE?
I DO NOT KNOW. I AM NOT--
Y'AIN'T K'TOK. YEAH, NO. I KNOW.
I DON'T THINK WE'LL FIT OUT THE OTHER--
YOU FEEL THAT?
NEERHURR?
FEEL WHAT?
FLOATY, RECKON.
GRAVITY'S ACTIN' UP.
DIDN'T NOTICE DUE TO WE WERE ROCKETIN'.
BUT IT...IS... WEIRD.
SHNNNK
ON THE OTHER SIDE OF THIS GEOLOGIC STRUCTURE, THERE IS VERY LITTLE GRAVITY.
YEAH, THAT'S WEIRD. NOT NORMAL.
WELL THE GOOD NEWS IS THAT THE SPACECOACH IS STUCK PRETTY GOOD IN THE ONLY EXIT.
SKRNK
HOW IS THAT NEWS QUALITATIVELY POSITIVE?
SIGH. VIA SARCASM, CROACH.

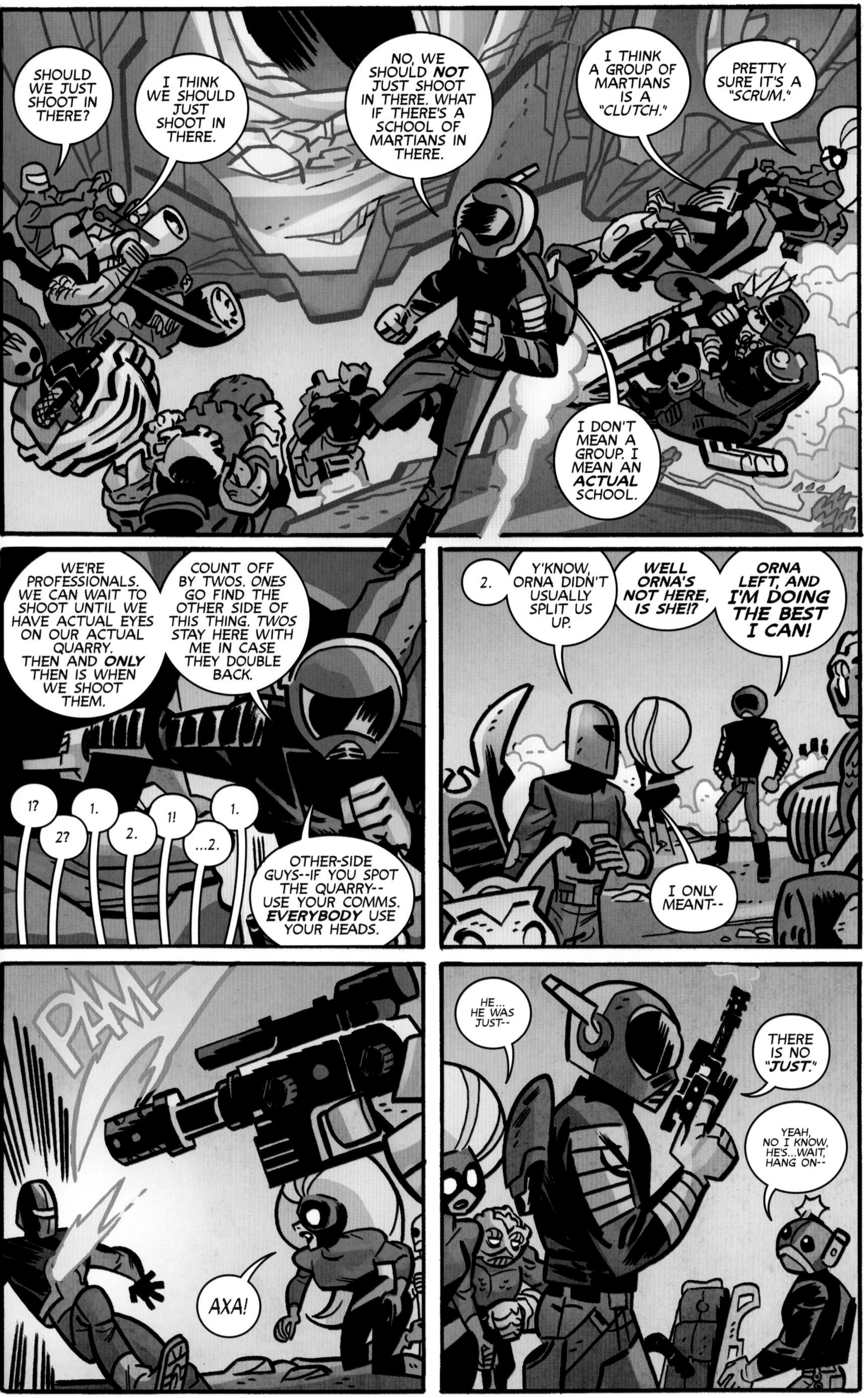
SHOULD WE JUST SHOOT IN THERE?
I THINK WE SHOULD JUST SHOOT IN THERE.
NO, WE SHOULD NOT JUST SHOOT IN THERE. WHAT IF THERE'S A SCHOOL OF MARTIANS IN THERE.
I THINK A GROUP OF MARTIANS IS A "CLUTCH."
PRETTY SURE IT'S A "SCRUM."
I DON'T MEAN A GROUP. I MEAN AN ACTUAL SCHOOL.
WE'RE PROFESSIONALS. WE CAN WAIT TO SHOOT UNTIL WE HAVE ACTUAL EYES ON OUR ACTUAL QUARRY. THEN AND ONLY THEN IS WHEN WE SHOOT THEM.
COUNT OFF BY TWOS. ONES GO FIND THE OTHER SIDE OF THIS THING. TWOS STAY HERE WITH ME IN CASE THEY DOUBLE BACK.
1?
2?
1.
2.
1!
...2.
1.
OTHER-SIDE GUYS--IF YOU SPOT THE QUARRY--USE YOUR COMMS. EVERYBODY USE YOUR HEADS.
2.
Y'KNOW, ORNA DIDN'T USUALLY SPLIT US UP.
WELL ORNA'S NOT HERE, IS SHE!?
ORNA LEFT, AND I'M DOING THE BEST I CAN!
I ONLY MEANT--
PAM
AXA!
HE... HE WAS JUST--
THERE IS NO "JUST."
YEAH, NO I KNOW, HE'S...WAIT, HANG ON--

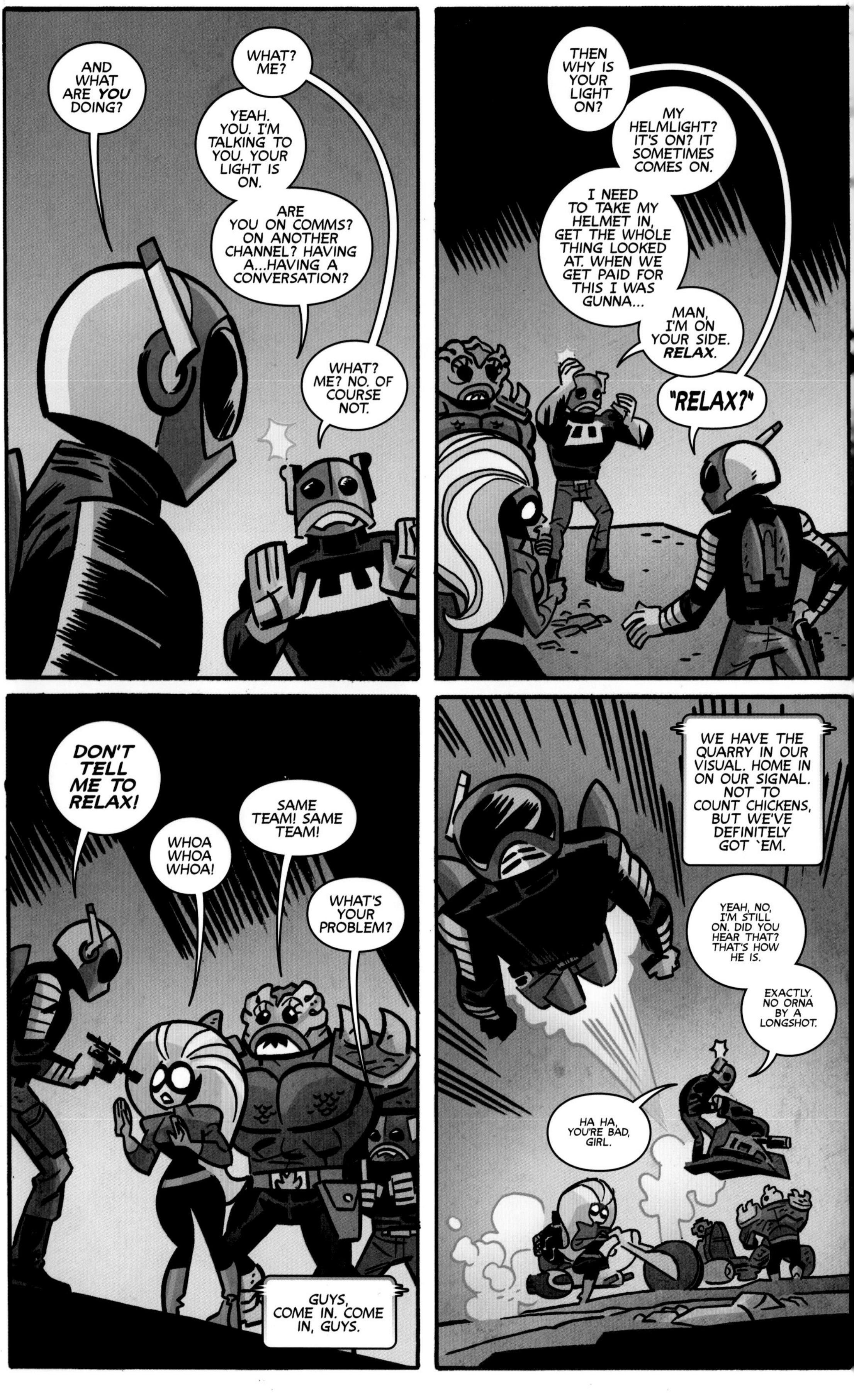
AND WHAT ARE YOU DOING?
WHAT? ME?
YEAH. YOU. I'M TALKING TO YOU. YOUR LIGHT IS ON.
ARE YOU ON COMMS? ON ANOTHER CHANNEL? HAVING A...HAVING A CONVERSATION?
WHAT? ME? NO. OF COURSE NOT.
THEN WHY IS YOUR LIGHT ON?
MY HELMLIGHT? IT'S ON? IT SOMETIMES COMES ON.
I NEED TO TAKE MY HELMET IN, GET THE WHOLE THING LOOKED AT. WHEN WE GET PAID FOR THIS I WAS GUNNA...
MAN, I'M ON YOUR SIDE. RELAX.
"RELAX?"
DON'T TELL ME TO RELAX!
WHOA WHOA WHOA!
SAME TEAM! SAME TEAM!
WHAT'S YOUR PROBLEM?
GUYS, COME IN. COME IN, GUYS.
WE HAVE THE QUARRY IN OUR VISUAL. HOME IN ON OUR SIGNAL. NOT TO COUNT CHICKENS, BUT WE'VE DEFINITELY GOT `EM.
YEAH, NO, I'M STILL ON. DID YOU HEAR THAT? THAT'S HOW HE IS.
EXACTLY. NO ORNA BY A LONGSHOT.
HA HA, YOU'RE BAD, GIRL.

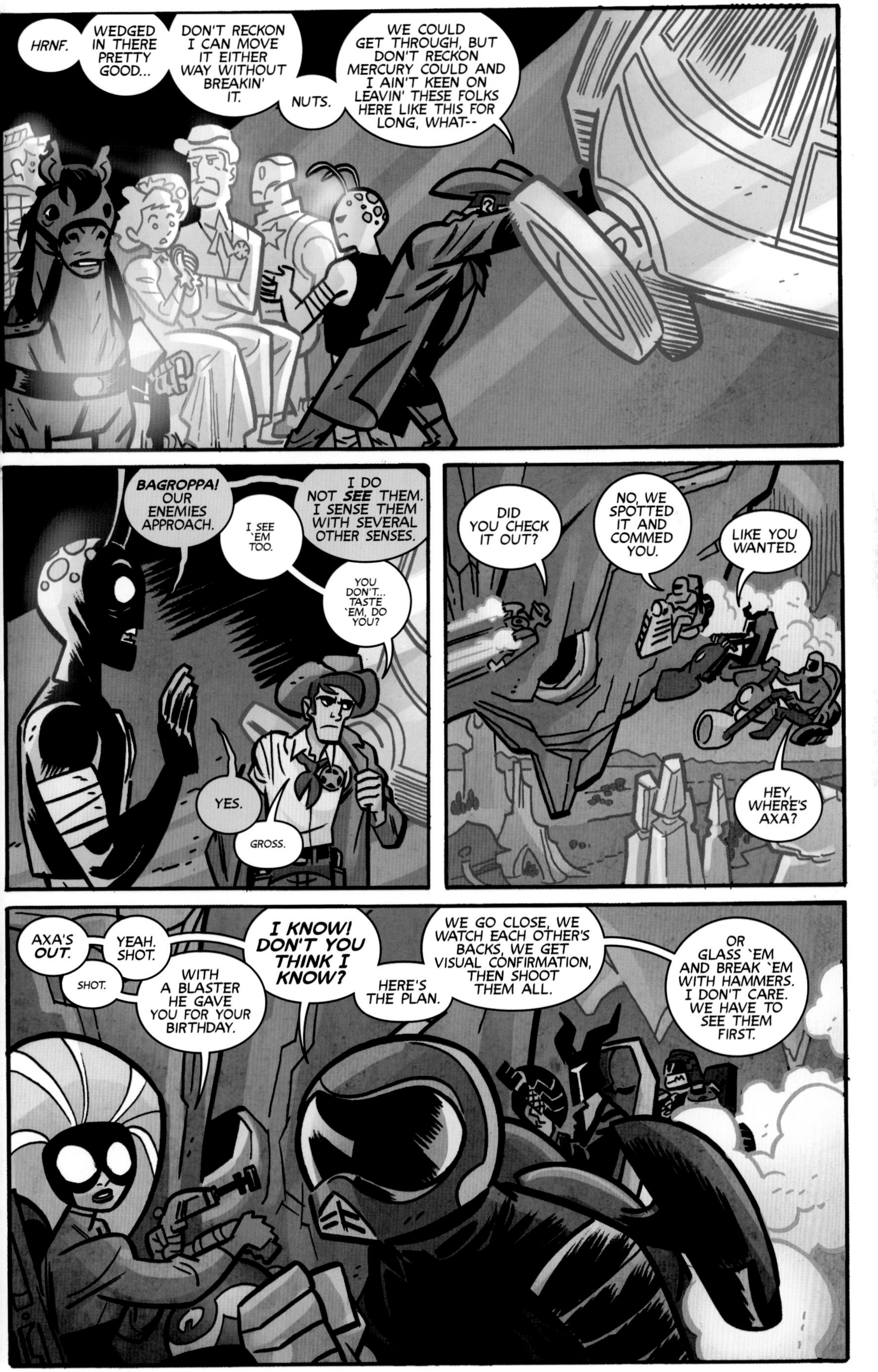
HRNF.
WEDGED IN THERE PRETTY GOOD...
DON'T RECKON I CAN MOVE IT EITHER WAY WITHOUT BREAKIN' IT.
NUTS.
WE COULD GET THROUGH, BUT DON'T RECKON MERCURY COULD AND I AIN'T KEEN ON LEAVIN' THESE FOLKS HERE LIKE THIS FOR LONG, WHAT--
BAGROPPA! OUR ENEMIES APPROACH.
I DO NOT SEE THEM. I SENSE THEM WITH SEVERAL OTHER SENSES.
I SEE `EM TOO.
YOU DON'T... TASTE `EM, DO YOU?
YES.
GROSS.
DID YOU CHECK IT OUT?
NO, WE SPOTTED IT AND COMMED YOU.
LIKE YOU WANTED.
HEY, WHERE'S AXA?
AXA'S OUT.
YEAH. SHOT.
SHOT.
WITH A BLASTER HE GAVE YOU FOR YOUR BIRTHDAY.
I KNOW! DON'T YOU THINK I KNOW?
HERE'S THE PLAN.
WE GO CLOSE, WE WATCH EACH OTHER'S BACKS, WE GET VISUAL CONFIRMATION, THEN SHOOT THEM ALL.
OR GLASS `EM AND BREAK `EM WITH HAMMERS. I DON'T CARE. WE HAVE TO SEE THEM FIRST.

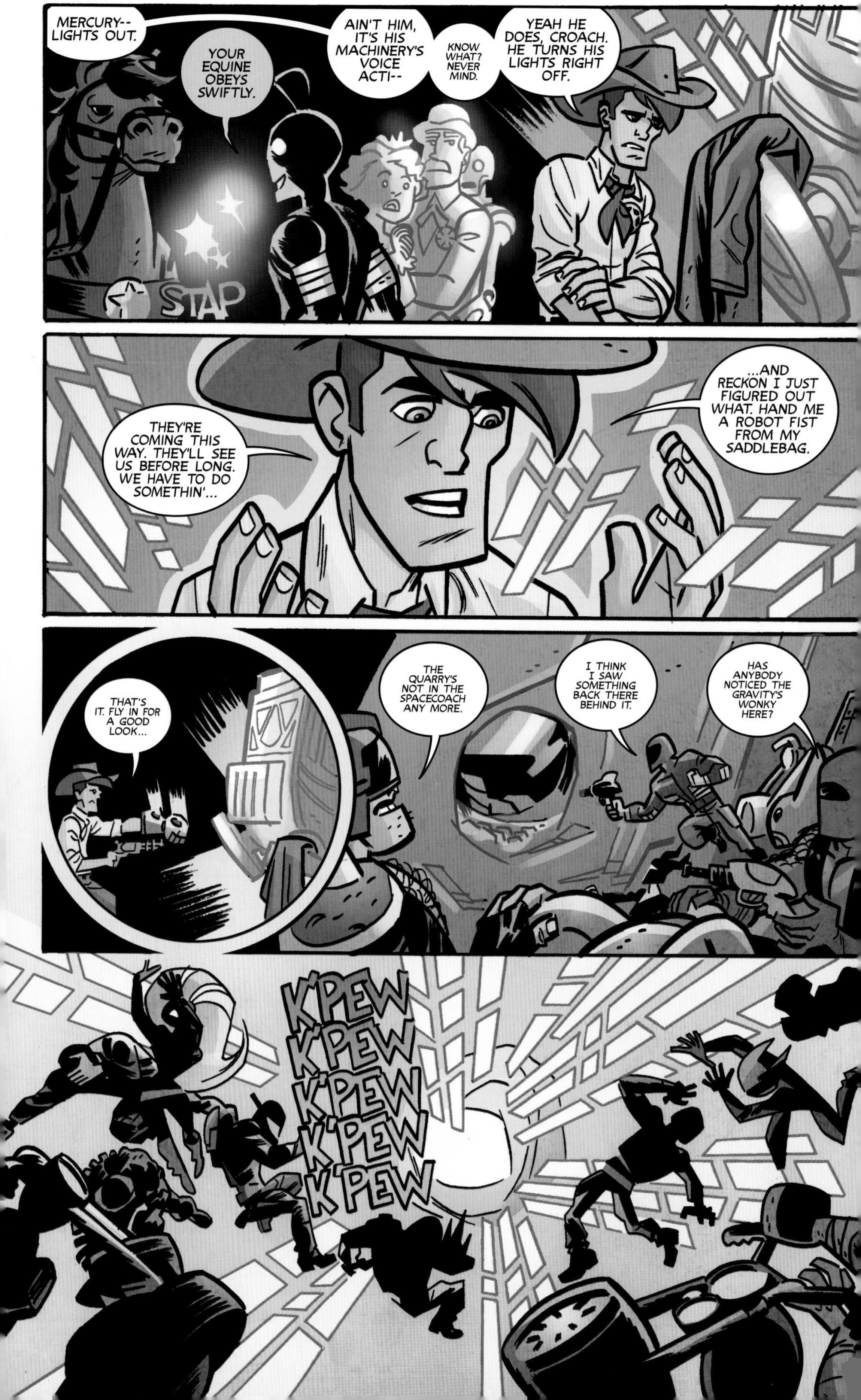
MERCURY--
LIGHTS OUT.
YOUR EQUINE OBEYS SWIFTLY.
AIN'T HIM, IT'S HIS MACHINERY'S VOICE ACTI--
KNOW WHAT? NEVER MIND.
YEAH HE DOES, CROACH. HE TURNS HIS LIGHTS RIGHT OFF.
STAP
THEY'RE COMING THIS WAY. THEY'LL SEE US BEFORE LONG. WE HAVE TO DO SOMETHIN'...
...AND RECKON I JUST FIGURED OUT WHAT. HAND ME A ROBOT FIST FROM MY SADDLEBAG.
THAT'S IT. FLY IN FOR A GOOD LOOK...
THE QUARRY'S NOT IN THE SPACECOACH ANY MORE.
I THINK I SAW SOMETHING BACK THERE BEHIND IT.
HAS ANYBODY NOTICED THE GRAVITY'S WONKY HERE?
K'PEW K'PEW K'PEW K'PEW K'PEW K'PEW

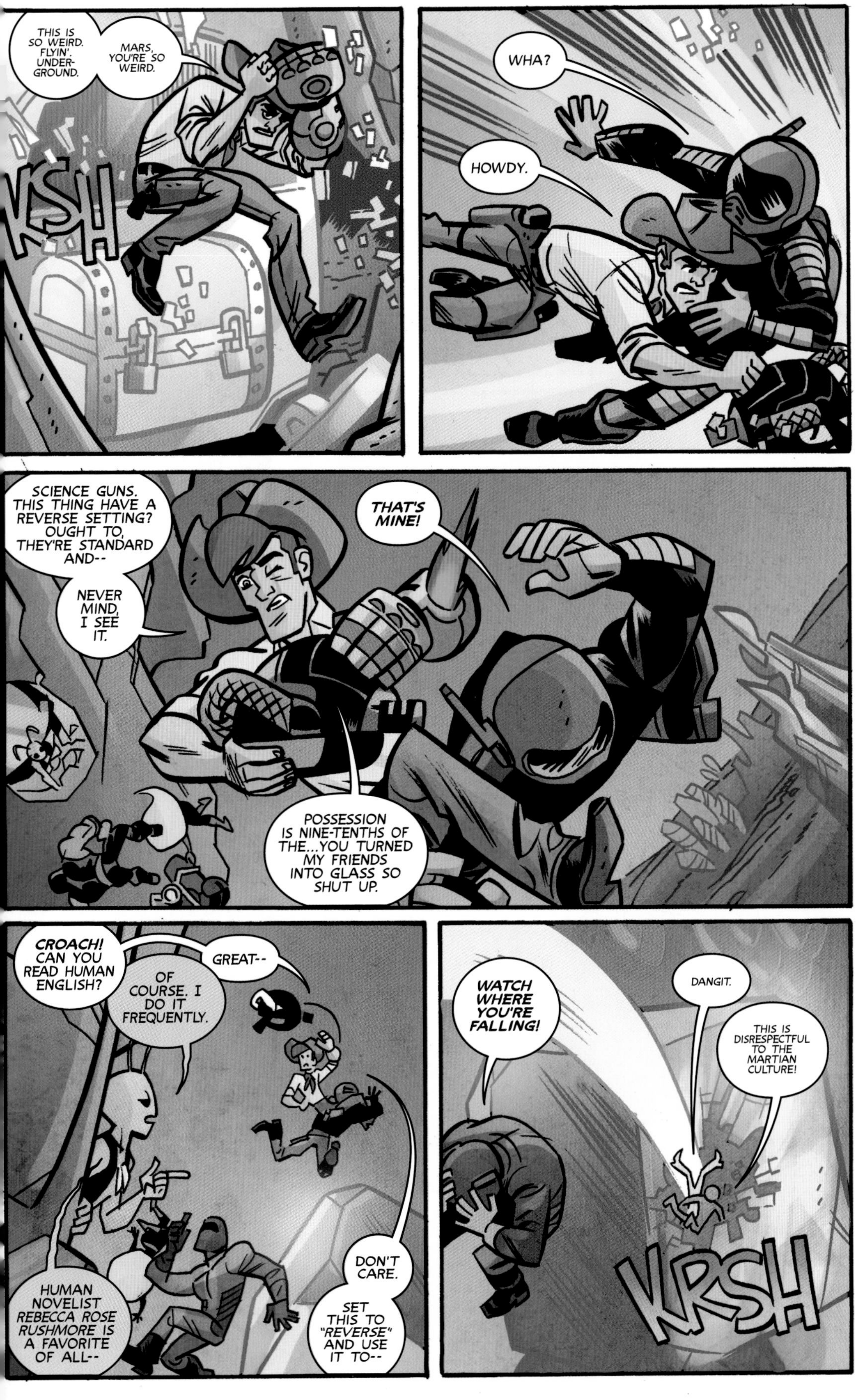

THIS IS SO WEIRD. FLYIN'. UNDER-GROUND.
MARS, YOU'RE SO WEIRD.
KSH
WHA?
HOWDY.
SCIENCE GUNS. THIS THING HAVE A REVERSE SETTING? OUGHT TO, THEY'RE STANDARD AND--
NEVER MIND, I SEE IT.
THAT'S MINE!
POSSESSION IS NINE-TENTHS OF THE...YOU TURNED MY FRIENDS INTO GLASS SO SHUT UP.
CROACH! CAN YOU READ HUMAN ENGLISH?
GREAT--
OF COURSE. I DO IT FREQUENTLY.
HUMAN NOVELIST *REBECCA ROSE RUSHMORE* IS A FAVORITE OF ALL--
DON'T CARE.
SET THIS TO *"REVERSE"* AND USE IT TO--
WATCH WHERE YOU'RE FALLING!
DANGIT.
THIS IS DISRESPECTFUL TO THE MARTIAN CULTURE!
KRSH

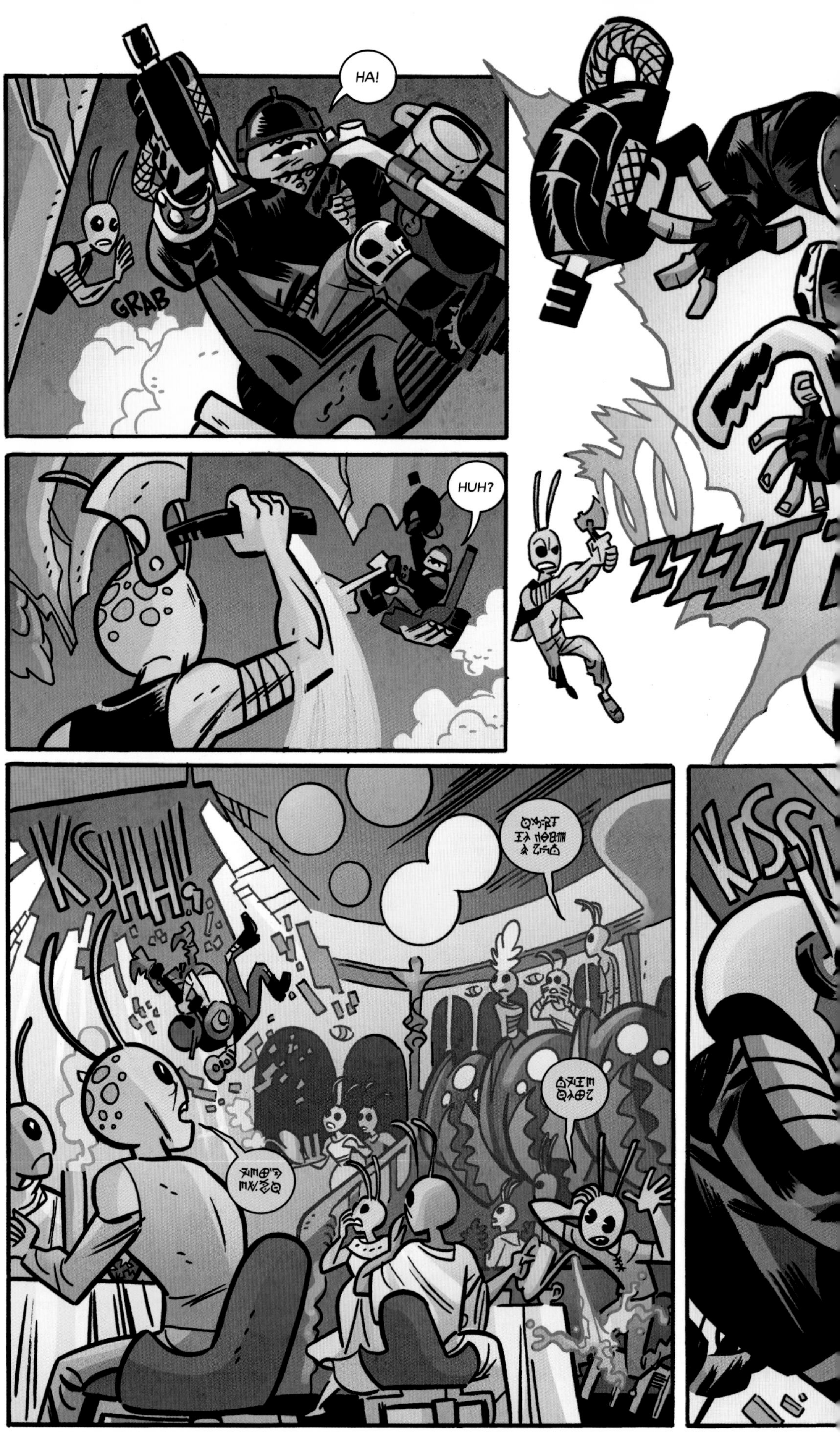
HA!
GRAB
HUH?
ZZZLT
KSHH!
KSS

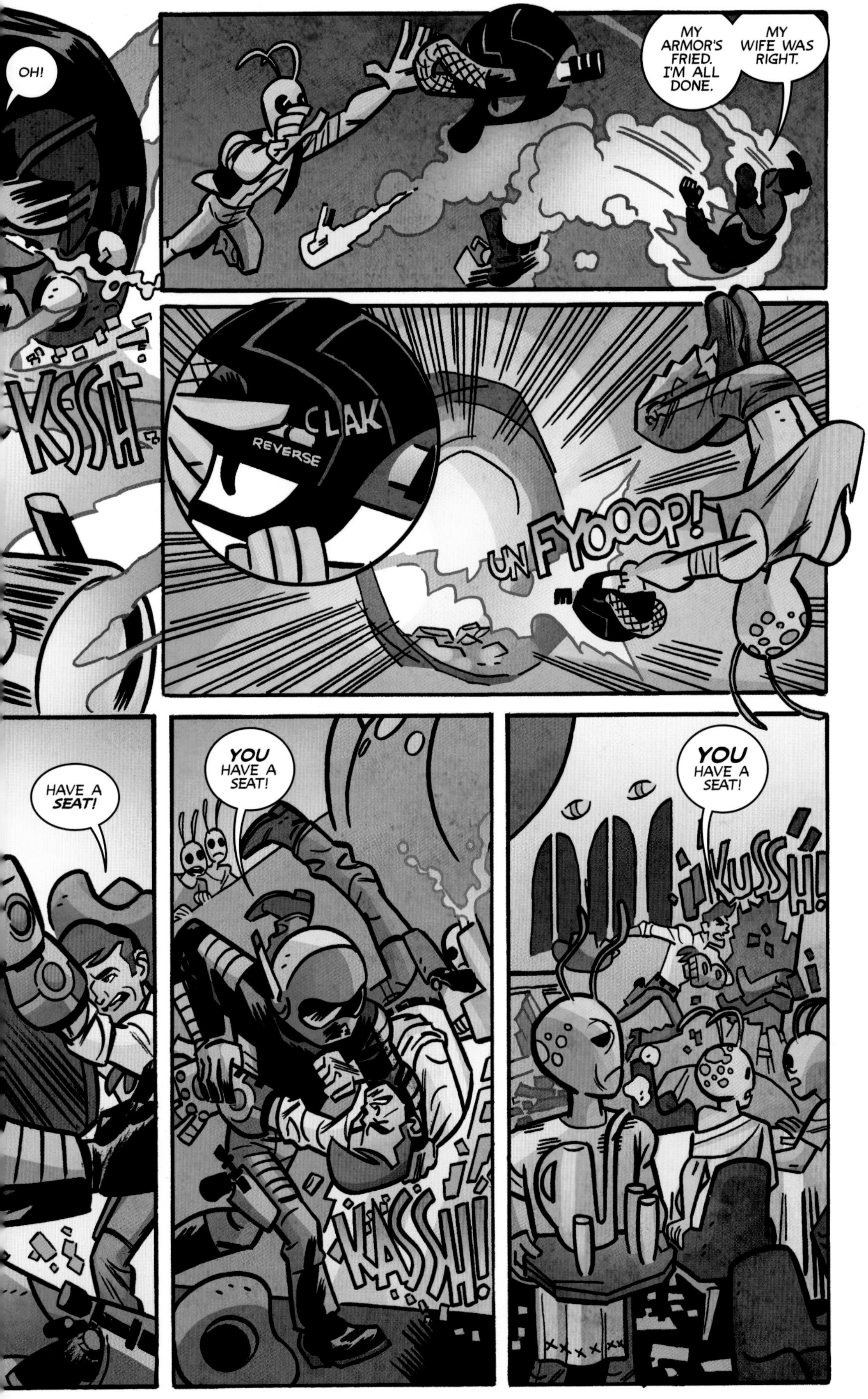
OH!
MY ARMOR'S FRIED. I'M ALL DONE.
MY WIFE WAS RIGHT.
KSSSH
CLAK
REVERSE
UNFYOOOP!
HAVE A *SEAT!*
YOU HAVE A SEAT!
KASSH!
YOU HAVE A SEAT!
KUSSH!

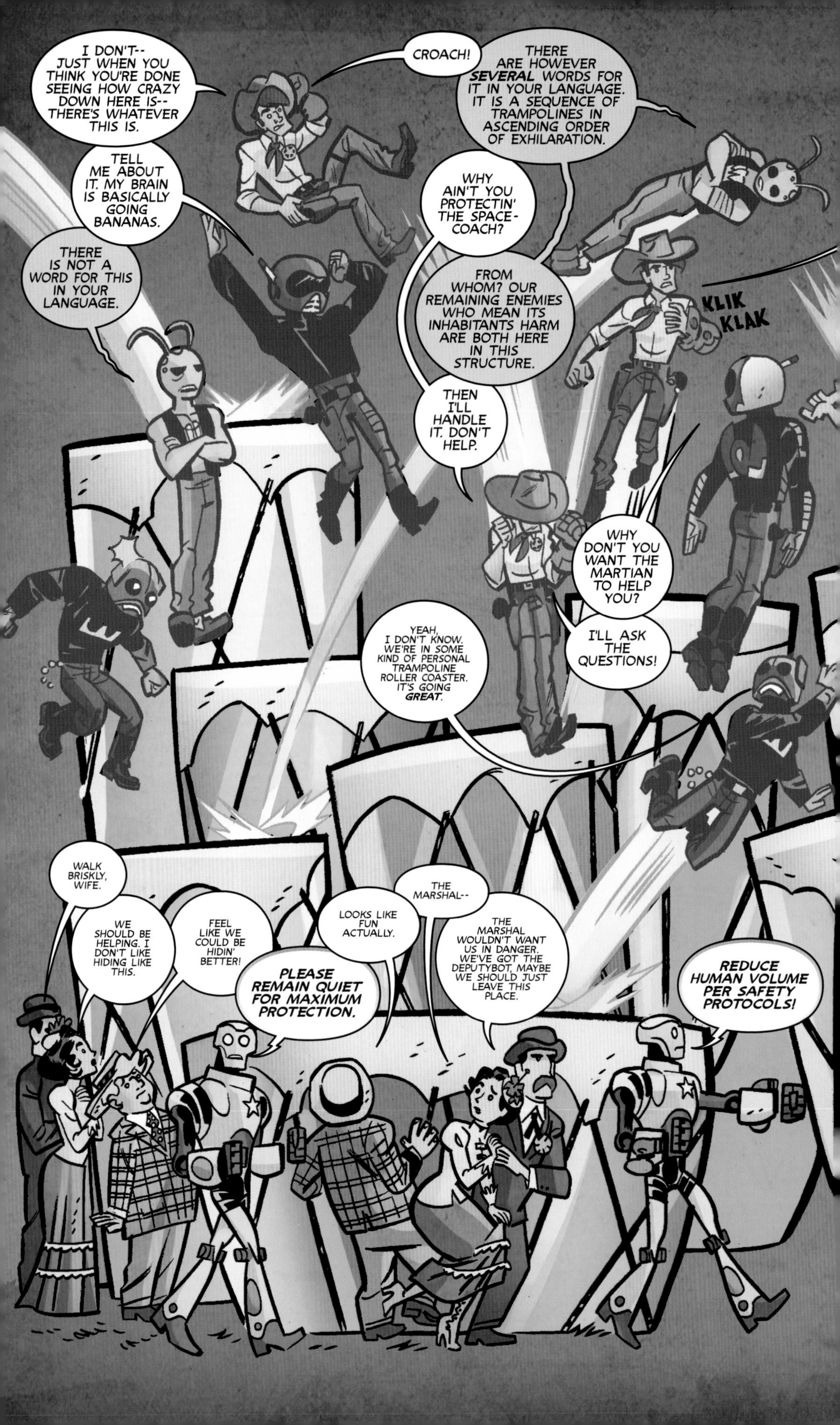

I DON'T-- JUST WHEN YOU THINK YOU'RE DONE SEEING HOW CRAZY DOWN HERE IS-- THERE'S WHATEVER THIS IS.
CROACH!
THERE ARE HOWEVER SEVERAL WORDS FOR IT IN YOUR LANGUAGE. IT IS A SEQUENCE OF TRAMPOLINES IN ASCENDING ORDER OF EXHILARATION.
TELL ME ABOUT IT. MY BRAIN IS BASICALLY GOING BANANAS.
THERE IS NOT A WORD FOR THIS IN YOUR LANGUAGE.
WHY AIN'T YOU PROTECTIN' THE SPACE-COACH?
FROM WHOM? OUR REMAINING ENEMIES WHO MEAN ITS INHABITANTS HARM ARE BOTH HERE IN THIS STRUCTURE.
KLIK KLAK
THEN I'LL HANDLE IT. DON'T HELP.
WHY DON'T YOU WANT THE MARTIAN TO HELP YOU?
I'LL ASK THE QUESTIONS!
YEAH, I DON'T KNOW. WE'RE IN SOME KIND OF PERSONAL TRAMPOLINE ROLLER COASTER. IT'S GOING GREAT.
WALK BRISKLY, WIFE.
WE SHOULD BE HELPING. I DON'T LIKE HIDING LIKE THIS.
FEEL LIKE WE COULD BE HIDIN' BETTER!
PLEASE REMAIN QUIET FOR MAXIMUM PROTECTION.
LOOKS LIKE FUN ACTUALLY.
THE MARSHAL--
THE MARSHAL WOULDN'T WANT US IN DANGER. WE'VE GOT THE DEPUTYBOT, MAYBE WE SHOULD JUST LEAVE THIS PLACE.
REDUCE HUMAN VOLUME PER SAFETY PROTOCOLS!

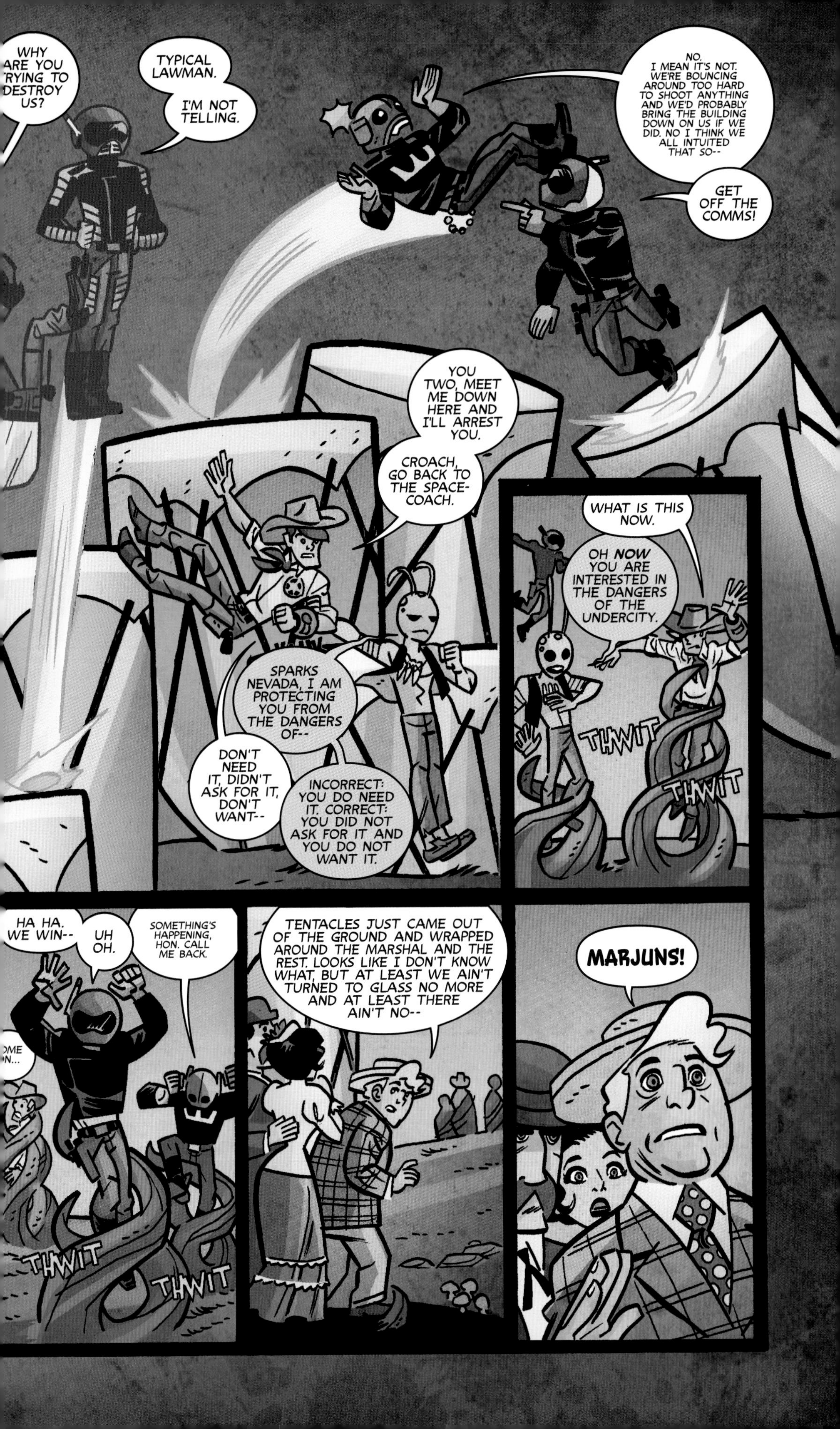
WHY ARE YOU TRYING TO DESTROY US?
TYPICAL LAWMAN.
I'M NOT TELLING.
NO. I MEAN IT'S NOT. WE'RE BOUNCING AROUND TOO HARD TO SHOOT ANYTHING AND WE'D PROBABLY BRING THE BUILDING DOWN ON US IF WE DID. NO I THINK WE ALL INTUITED THAT SO--
GET OFF THE COMMS!
YOU TWO, MEET ME DOWN HERE AND I'LL ARREST YOU.
CROACH, GO BACK TO THE SPACE-COACH.
SPARKS NEVADA, I AM PROTECTING YOU FROM THE DANGERS OF--
DON'T NEED IT, DIDN'T ASK FOR IT, DON'T WANT--
INCORRECT: YOU DO NEED IT. CORRECT: YOU DID NOT ASK FOR IT AND YOU DO NOT WANT IT.
WHAT IS THIS NOW.
OH NOW YOU ARE INTERESTED IN THE DANGERS OF THE UNDERCITY.
THWIT
THWIT
HA HA. WE WIN--
UH OH.
SOMETHING'S HAPPENING, HON. CALL ME BACK.
THWIT
THWIT
TENTACLES JUST CAME OUT OF THE GROUND AND WRAPPED AROUND THE MARSHAL AND THE REST. LOOKS LIKE I DON'T KNOW WHAT, BUT AT LEAST WE AIN'T TURNED TO GLASS NO MORE AND AT LEAST THERE AIN'T NO--
MARJUNS!

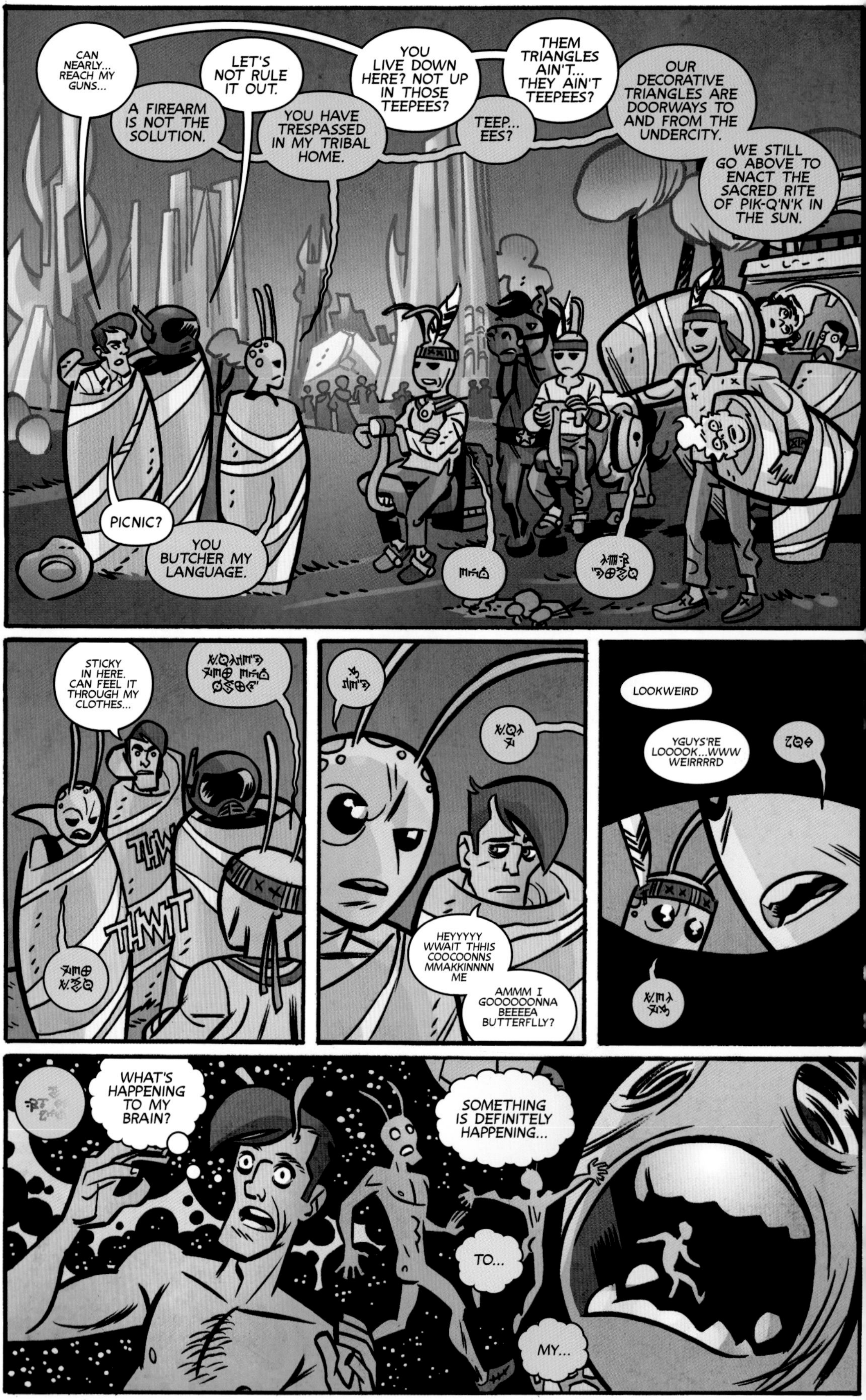
CAN NEARLY... REACH MY GUNS...
A FIREARM IS NOT THE SOLUTION.
LET'S NOT RULE IT OUT.
YOU HAVE TRESPASSED IN MY TRIBAL HOME.
YOU LIVE DOWN HERE? NOT UP IN THOSE TEEPEES?
TEEP... EES?
THEM TRIANGLES AIN'T... THEY AIN'T TEEPEES?
OUR DECORATIVE TRIANGLES ARE DOORWAYS TO AND FROM THE UNDERCITY.
WE STILL GO ABOVE TO ENACT THE SACRED RITE OF PIK-Q'N'K IN THE SUN.
PICNIC?
YOU BUTCHER MY LANGUAGE.
STICKY IN HERE. CAN FEEL IT THROUGH MY CLOTHES...
THWT
THWIT
HEYYYYY WWAIT THHIS COOCOONNS MMAKKINNNN ME
AMMM I GOOOOOONNA BEEEEA BUTTERFLLY?
LOOKWEIRD
YGUYS'RE LOOOOK...WWW WEIRRRRD
WHAT'S HAPPENING TO MY BRAIN?
SOMETHING IS DEFINITELY HAPPENING...
TO...
MY...

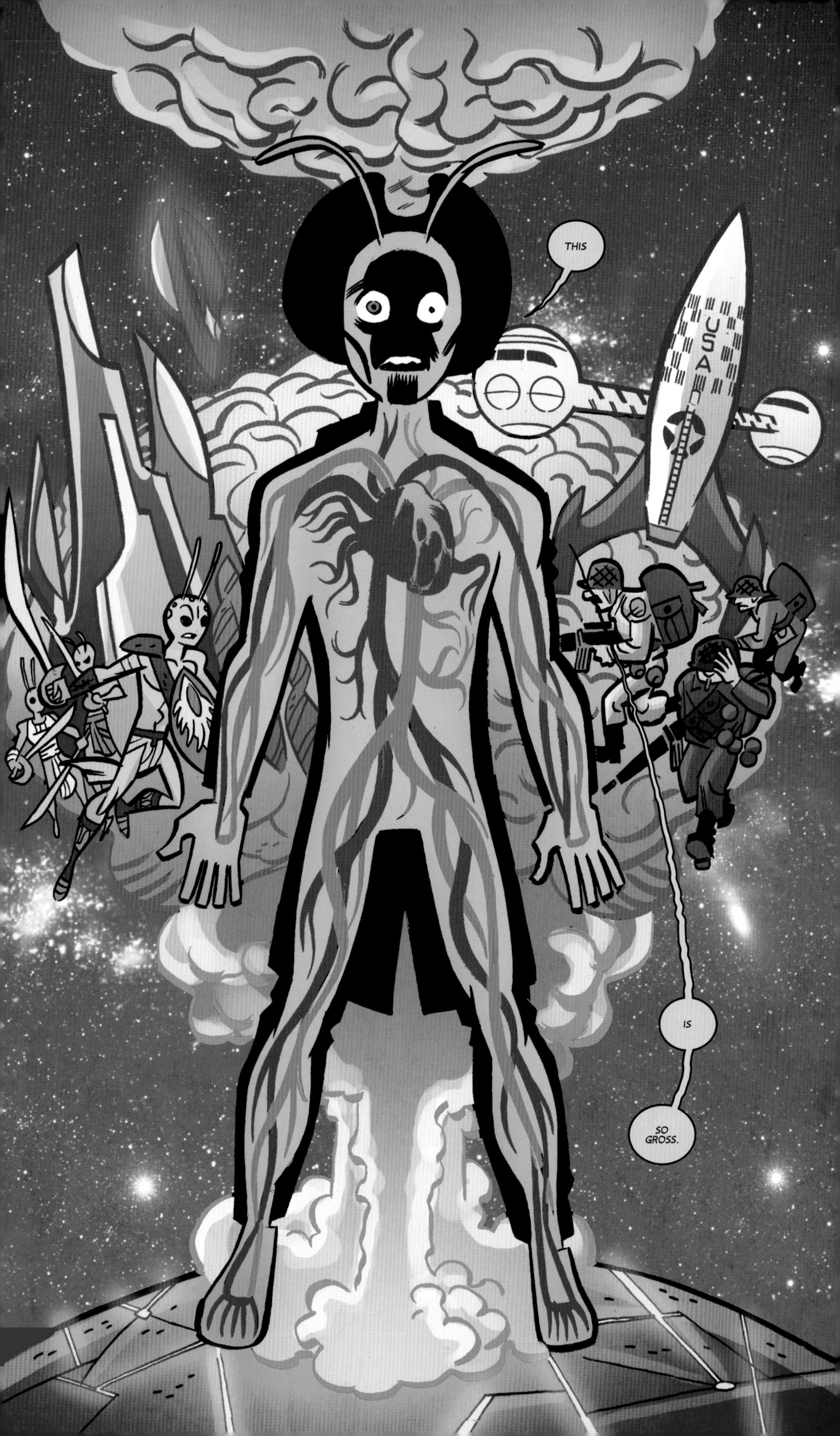
THIS
IS
SO GROSS.

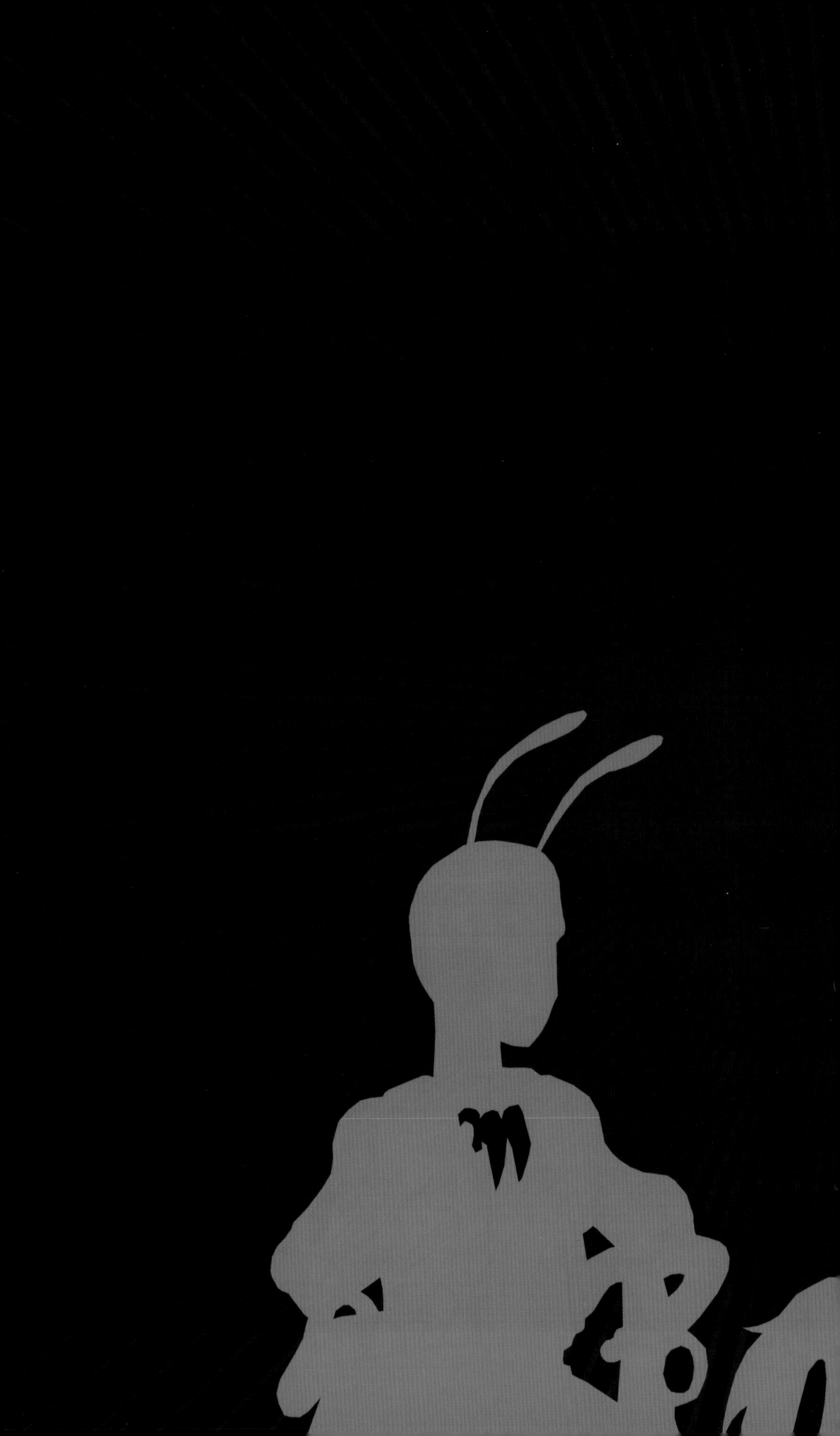

Chapter THREE

Mercenary Roughness

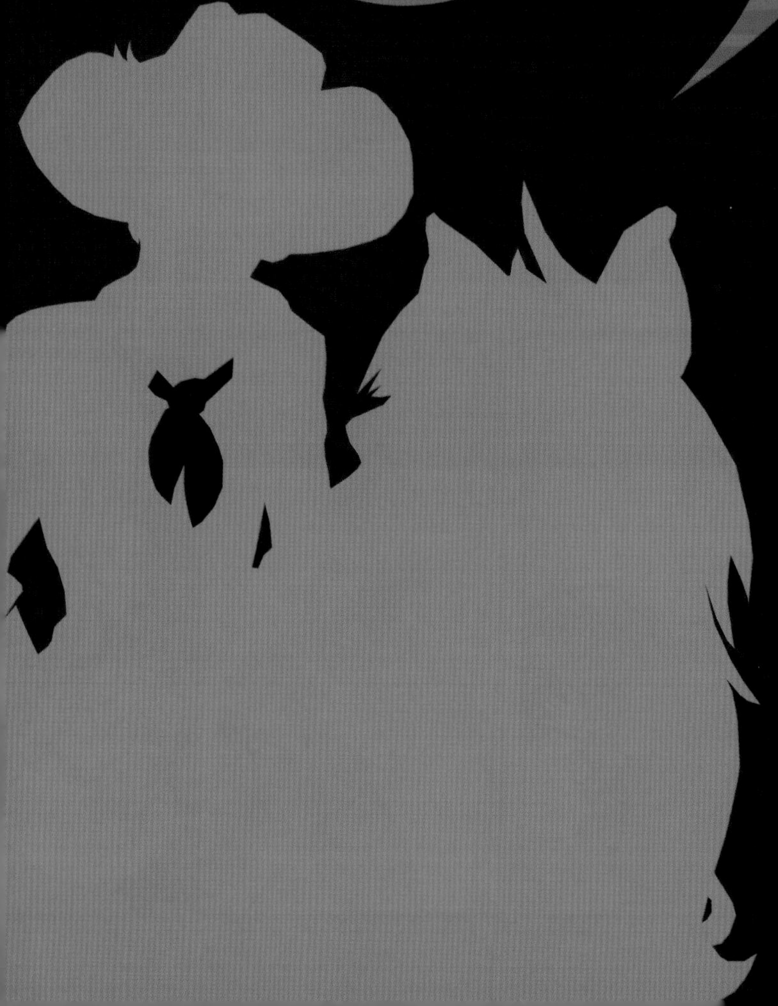

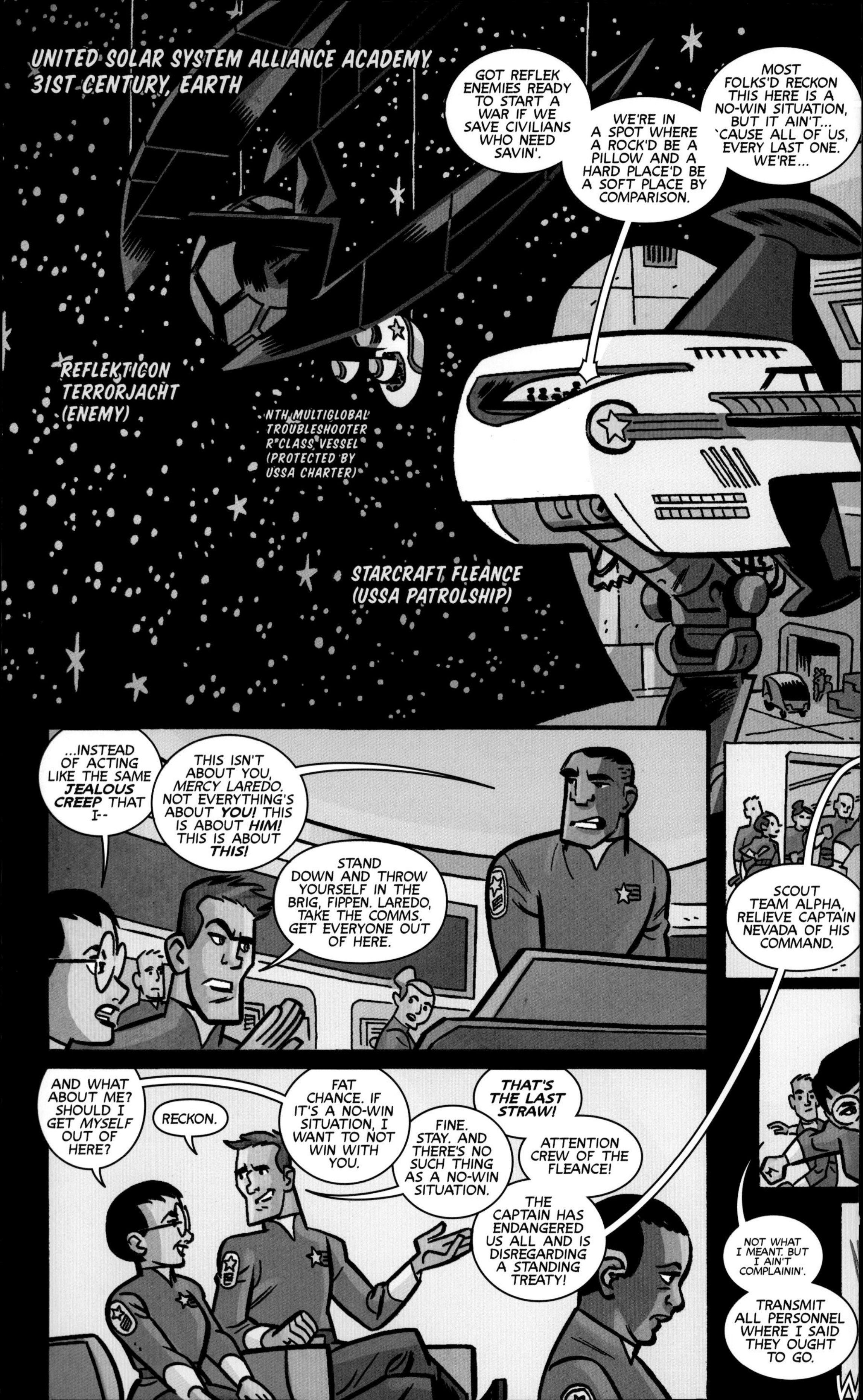

UNITED SOLAR SYSTEM ALLIANCE ACADEMY
31ST CENTURY, EARTH
GOT REFLEK ENEMIES READY TO START A WAR IF WE SAVE CIVILIANS WHO NEED SAVIN'.
WE'RE IN A SPOT WHERE A ROCK'D BE A PILLOW AND A HARD PLACE'D BE A SOFT PLACE BY COMPARISON.
MOST FOLKS'D RECKON THIS HERE IS A NO-WIN SITUATION, BUT IT AIN'T... 'CAUSE ALL OF US, EVERY LAST ONE. WE'RE...
REFLEKTICON TERRORJACHT (ENEMY)
NTH MULTIGLOBAL TROUBLESHOOTER R CLASS VESSEL (PROTECTED BY USSA CHARTER)
STARCRAFT FLEANCE (USSA PATROLSHIP)
...INSTEAD OF ACTING LIKE THE SAME JEALOUS CREEP THAT I--
THIS ISN'T ABOUT YOU, MERCY LAREDO. NOT EVERYTHING'S ABOUT YOU! THIS IS ABOUT HIM! THIS IS ABOUT THIS!
STAND DOWN AND THROW YOURSELF IN THE BRIG, FIPPEN. LAREDO, TAKE THE COMMS. GET EVERYONE OUT OF HERE.
SCOUT TEAM ALPHA, RELIEVE CAPTAIN NEVADA OF HIS COMMAND.
AND WHAT ABOUT ME? SHOULD I GET MYSELF OUT OF HERE?
RECKON.
FAT CHANCE. IF IT'S A NO-WIN SITUATION, I WANT TO NOT WIN WITH YOU.
FINE. STAY. AND THERE'S NO SUCH THING AS A NO-WIN SITUATION.
THAT'S THE LAST STRAW!
ATTENTION CREW OF THE FLEANCE!
THE CAPTAIN HAS ENDANGERED US ALL AND IS DISREGARDING A STANDING TREATY!
NOT WHAT I MEANT. BUT I AIN'T COMPLAININ'.
TRANSMIT ALL PERSONNEL WHERE I SAID THEY OUGHT TO GO.

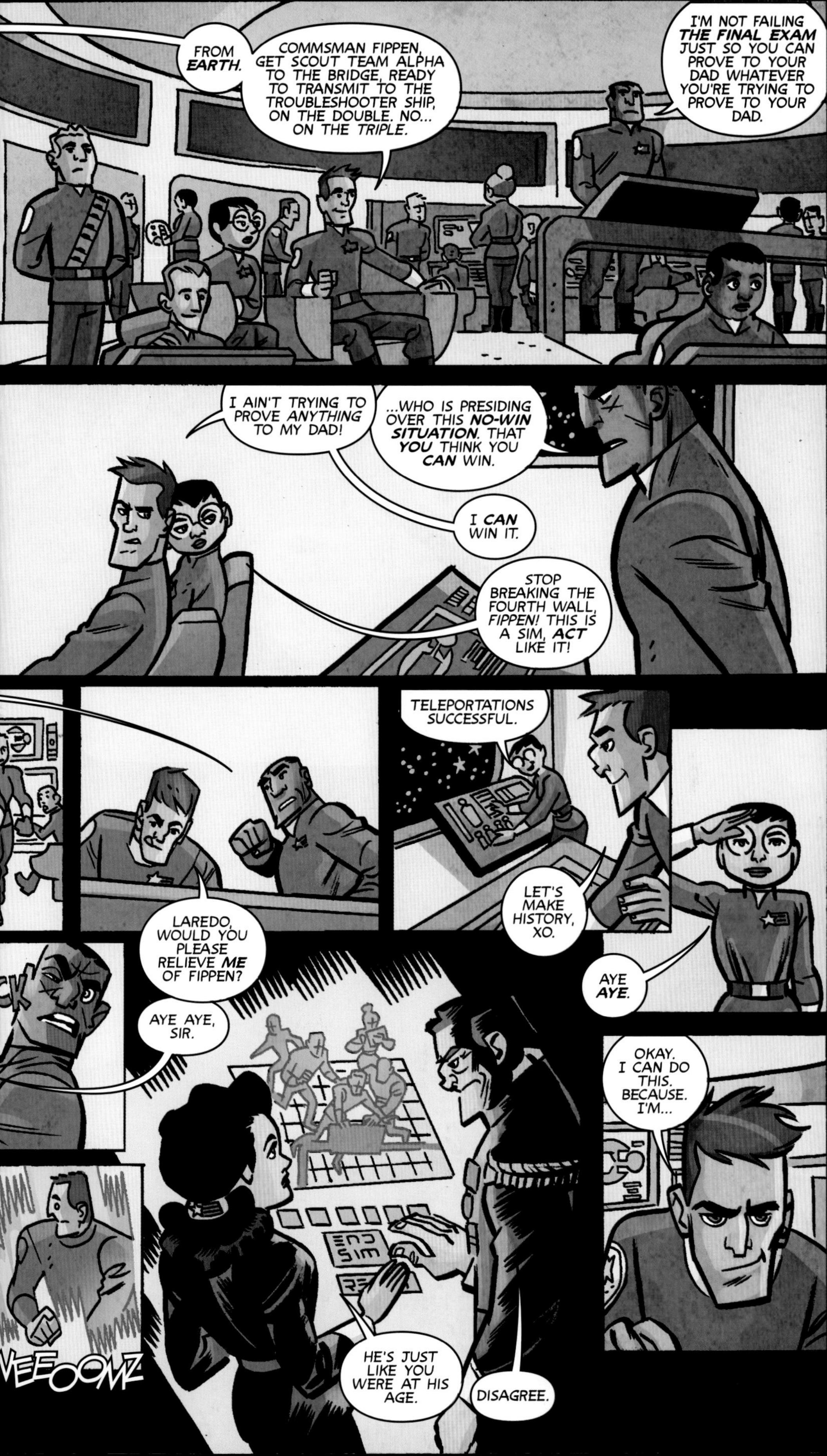
FROM EARTH.
COMMSMAN FIPPEN, GET SCOUT TEAM ALPHA TO THE BRIDGE, READY TO TRANSMIT TO THE TROUBLESHOOTER SHIP, ON THE DOUBLE. NO... ON THE TRIPLE.
I'M NOT FAILING THE FINAL EXAM JUST SO YOU CAN PROVE TO YOUR DAD WHATEVER YOU'RE TRYING TO PROVE TO YOUR DAD.
I AIN'T TRYING TO PROVE ANYTHING TO MY DAD!
...WHO IS PRESIDING OVER THIS NO-WIN SITUATION. THAT YOU THINK YOU CAN WIN.
I CAN WIN IT.
STOP BREAKING THE FOURTH WALL, FIPPEN! THIS IS A SIM, ACT LIKE IT!
LAREDO, WOULD YOU PLEASE RELIEVE ME OF FIPPEN?
AYE AYE, SIR.
TELEPORTATIONS SUCCESSFUL.
LET'S MAKE HISTORY, XO.
AYE AYE.
OKAY. I CAN DO THIS. BECAUSE. I'M...
VEEOOMZ
END SIM
HE'S JUST LIKE YOU WERE AT HIS AGE.
DISAGREE.

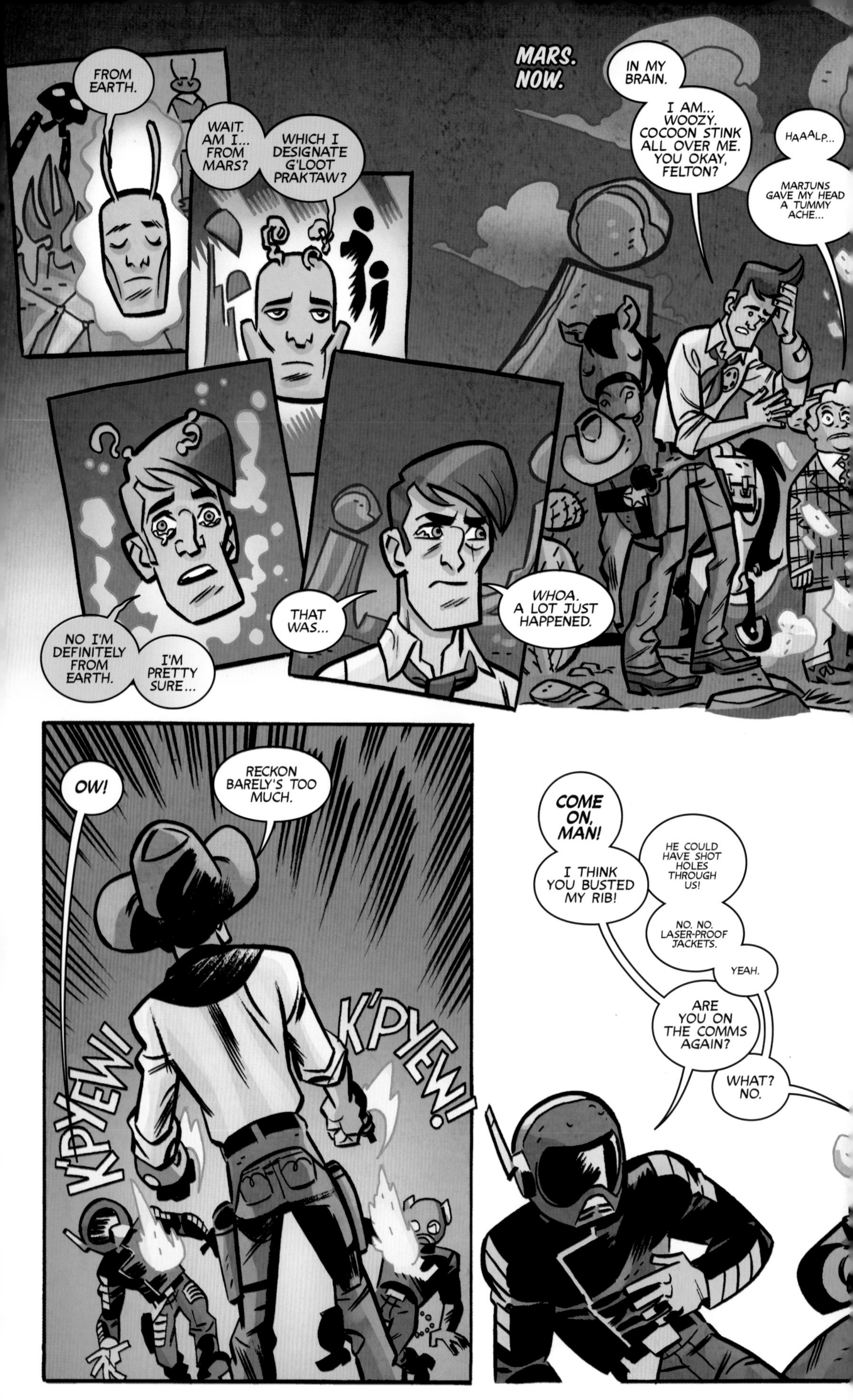

FROM EARTH.
WAIT. AM I... FROM MARS?
WHICH I DESIGNATE G'LOOT PRAKTAW?
NO I'M DEFINITELY FROM EARTH.
I'M PRETTY SURE...
THAT WAS...
WHOA. A LOT JUST HAPPENED.
MARS. NOW.
IN MY BRAIN.
I AM... WOOZY. COCOON STINK ALL OVER ME. YOU OKAY, FELTON?
HAAALP...
MARJUNS GAVE MY HEAD A TUMMY ACHE...
OW!
RECKON BARELY'S TOO MUCH.
K'PYEW!
K'PYEW!
COME ON, MAN!
I THINK YOU BUSTED MY RIB!
HE COULD HAVE SHOT HOLES THROUGH US!
NO. NO. LASER-PROOF JACKETS.
YEAH.
ARE YOU ON THE COMMS AGAIN?
WHAT? NO.

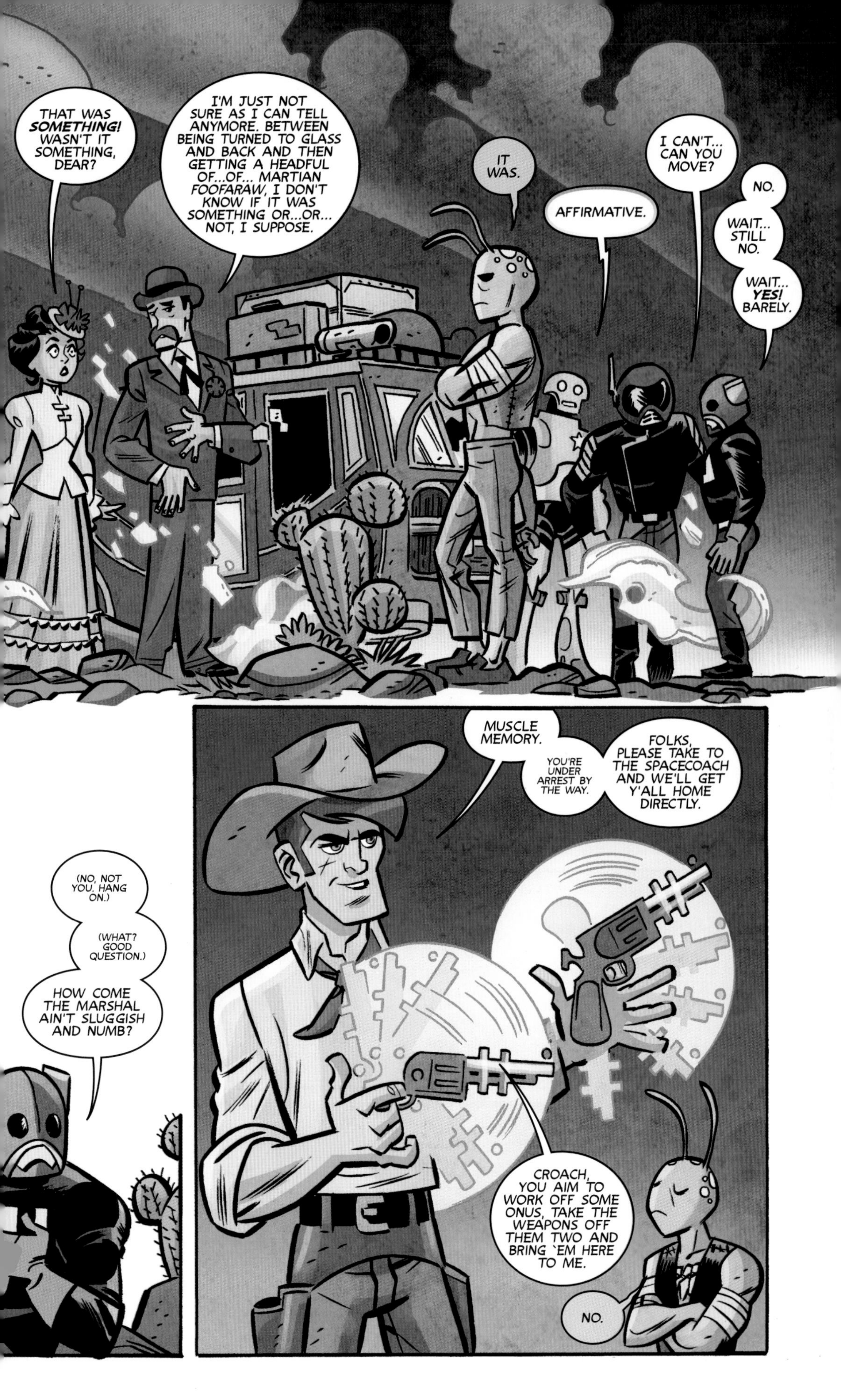
THAT WAS *SOMETHING!* WASN'T IT SOMETHING, DEAR?
I'M JUST NOT SURE AS I CAN TELL ANYMORE. BETWEEN BEING TURNED TO GLASS AND BACK AND THEN GETTING A HEADFUL OF...OF... MARTIAN *FOOFARAW*, I DON'T KNOW IF IT WAS SOMETHING OR...OR... NOT, I SUPPOSE.
IT WAS.
AFFIRMATIVE.
I CAN'T... CAN YOU MOVE?
NO.
WAIT... STILL NO.
WAIT... *YES!* BARELY.
(NO, NOT YOU. HANG ON.)
(WHAT? GOOD QUESTION.)
HOW COME THE MARSHAL AIN'T SLUGGISH AND NUMB?
MUSCLE MEMORY.
YOU'RE UNDER ARREST BY THE WAY.
FOLKS, PLEASE TAKE TO THE SPACECOACH AND WE'LL GET Y'ALL HOME DIRECTLY.
CROACH, YOU AIM TO WORK OFF SOME ONUS, TAKE THE WEAPONS OFF THEM TWO AND BRING `EM HERE TO ME.
NO.

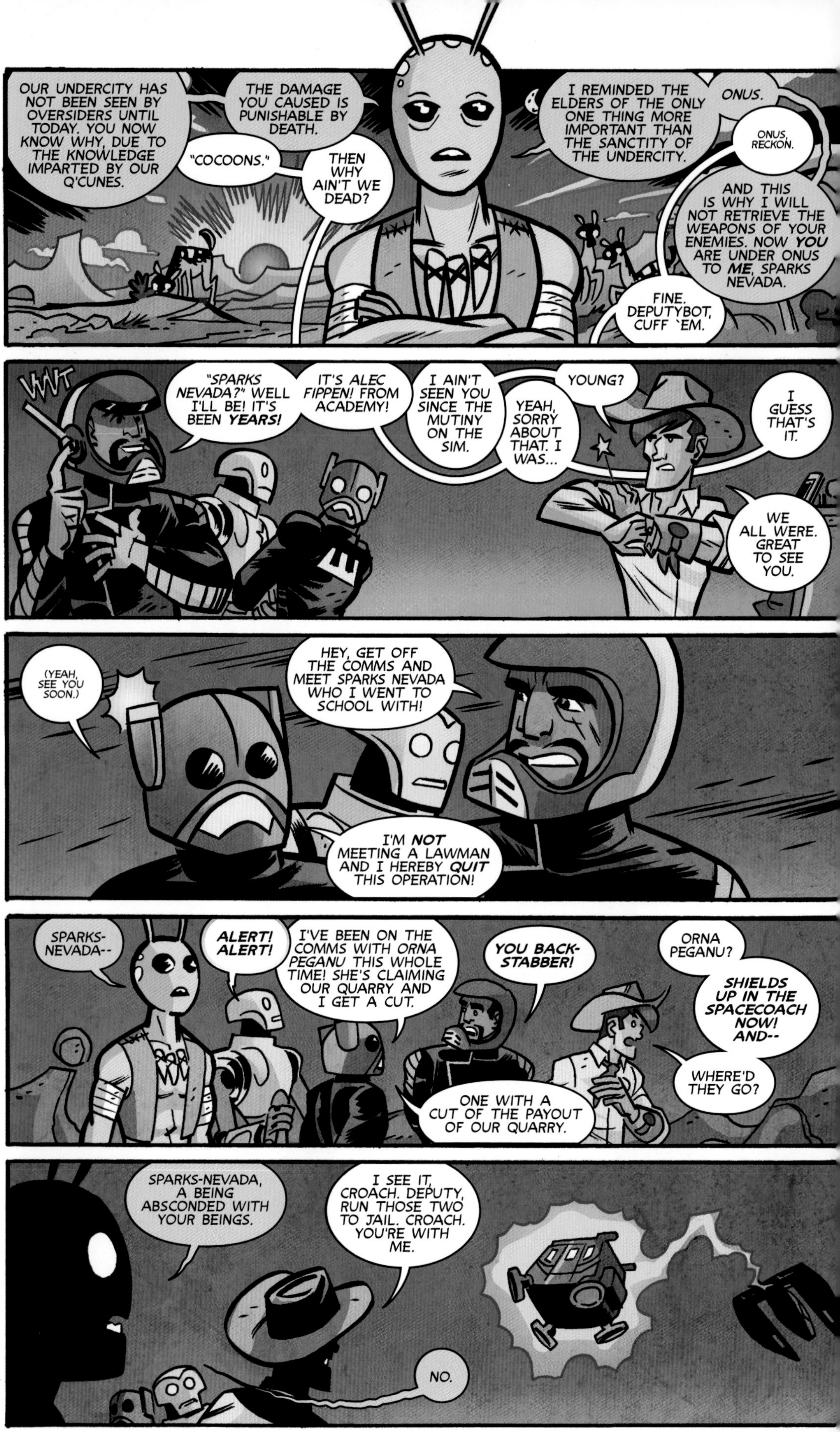
OUR UNDERCITY HAS NOT BEEN SEEN BY OVERSIDERS UNTIL TODAY. YOU NOW KNOW WHY, DUE TO THE KNOWLEDGE IMPARTED BY OUR Q'CUNES.
"COCOONS."
THE DAMAGE YOU CAUSED IS PUNISHABLE BY DEATH.
THEN WHY AIN'T WE DEAD?
I REMINDED THE ELDERS OF THE ONLY ONE THING MORE IMPORTANT THAN THE SANCTITY OF THE UNDERCITY.
ONUS.
ONUS, RECKON.
AND THIS IS WHY I WILL NOT RETRIEVE THE WEAPONS OF YOUR ENEMIES. NOW YOU ARE UNDER ONUS TO ME, SPARKS NEVADA.
FINE. DEPUTYBOT, CUFF `EM.
VVVT
"SPARKS NEVADA?" WELL I'LL BE! IT'S BEEN YEARS!
IT'S ALEC FIPPEN! FROM ACADEMY!
I AIN'T SEEN YOU SINCE THE MUTINY ON THE SIM.
YOUNG?
YEAH, SORRY ABOUT THAT. I WAS...
I GUESS THAT'S IT.
WE ALL WERE. GREAT TO SEE YOU.
(YEAH, SEE YOU SOON.)
HEY, GET OFF THE COMMS AND MEET SPARKS NEVADA WHO I WENT TO SCHOOL WITH!
I'M NOT MEETING A LAWMAN AND I HEREBY QUIT THIS OPERATION!
SPARKS-NEVADA--
ALERT! ALERT!
I'VE BEEN ON THE COMMS WITH ORNA PEGANU THIS WHOLE TIME! SHE'S CLAIMING OUR QUARRY AND I GET A CUT.
YOU BACK-STABBER!
ORNA PEGANU?
SHIELDS UP IN THE SPACECOACH NOW! AND--
ONE WITH A CUT OF THE PAYOUT OF OUR QUARRY.
WHERE'D THEY GO?
SPARKS-NEVADA, A BEING ABSCONDED WITH YOUR BEINGS.
I SEE IT, CROACH. DEPUTY, RUN THOSE TWO TO JAIL. CROACH. YOU'RE WITH ME.
NO.

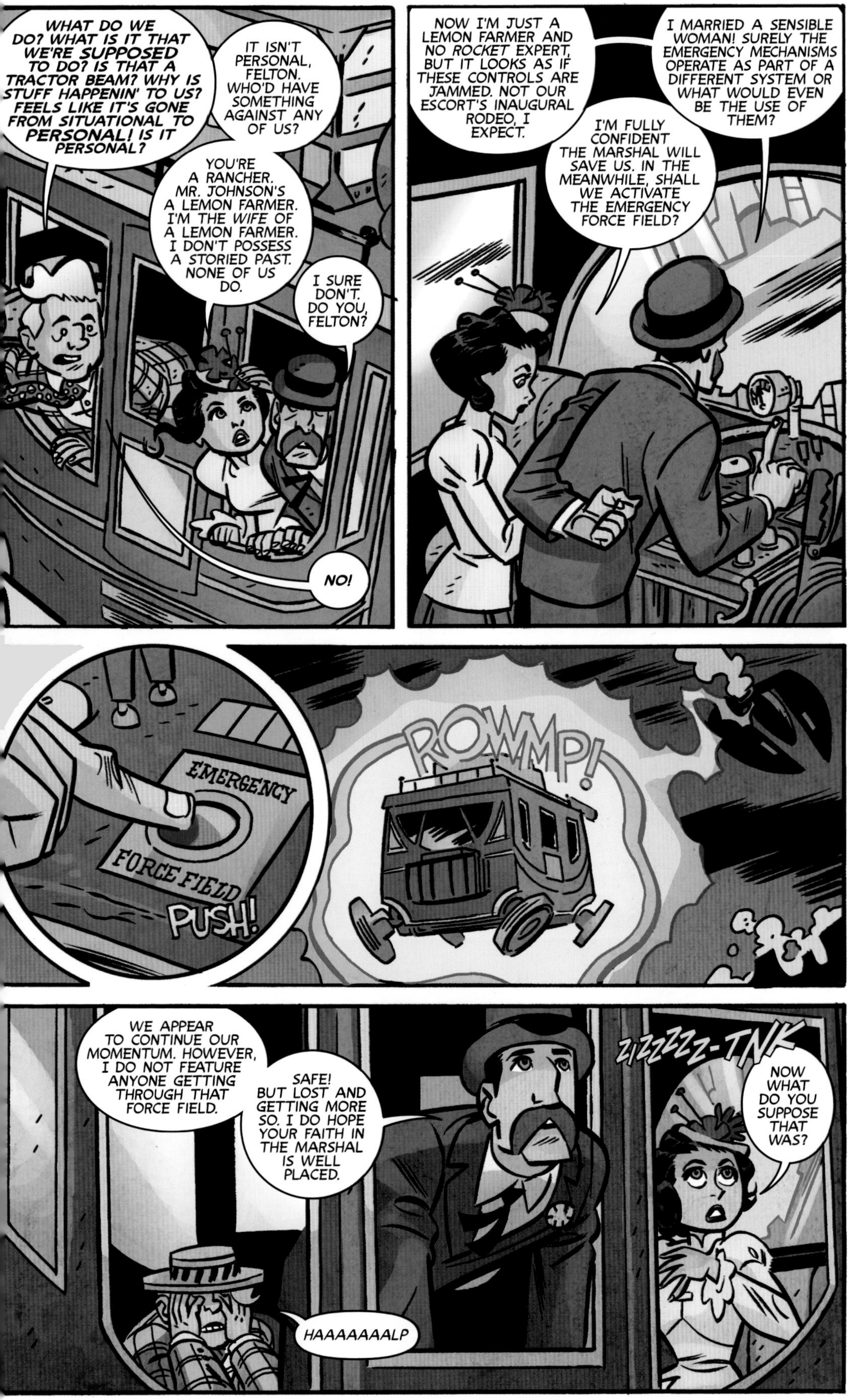
WHAT DO WE DO? WHAT IS IT THAT WE'RE SUPPOSED TO DO? IS THAT A TRACTOR BEAM? WHY IS STUFF HAPPENIN' TO US? FEELS LIKE IT'S GONE FROM SITUATIONAL TO PERSONAL! IS IT PERSONAL?
IT ISN'T PERSONAL, FELTON. WHO'D HAVE SOMETHING AGAINST ANY OF US?
YOU'RE A RANCHER. MR. JOHNSON'S A LEMON FARMER. I'M THE WIFE OF A LEMON FARMER. I DON'T POSSESS A STORIED PAST. NONE OF US DO.
I SURE DON'T. DO YOU, FELTON?
NO!
NOW I'M JUST A LEMON FARMER AND NO ROCKET EXPERT, BUT IT LOOKS AS IF THESE CONTROLS ARE JAMMED. NOT OUR ESCORT'S INAUGURAL RODEO, I EXPECT.
I MARRIED A SENSIBLE WOMAN! SURELY THE EMERGENCY MECHANISMS OPERATE AS PART OF A DIFFERENT SYSTEM OR WHAT WOULD EVEN BE THE USE OF THEM?
I'M FULLY CONFIDENT THE MARSHAL WILL SAVE US. IN THE MEANWHILE, SHALL WE ACTIVATE THE EMERGENCY FORCE FIELD?
EMERGENCY FORCE FIELD PUSH!
ROWMP!
WE APPEAR TO CONTINUE OUR MOMENTUM. HOWEVER, I DO NOT FEATURE ANYONE GETTING THROUGH THAT FORCE FIELD.
SAFE! BUT LOST AND GETTING MORE SO. I DO HOPE YOUR FAITH IN THE MARSHAL IS WELL PLACED.
ZZZZZZZ-TNK
NOW WHAT DO YOU SUPPOSE THAT WAS?
HAAAAAAALP

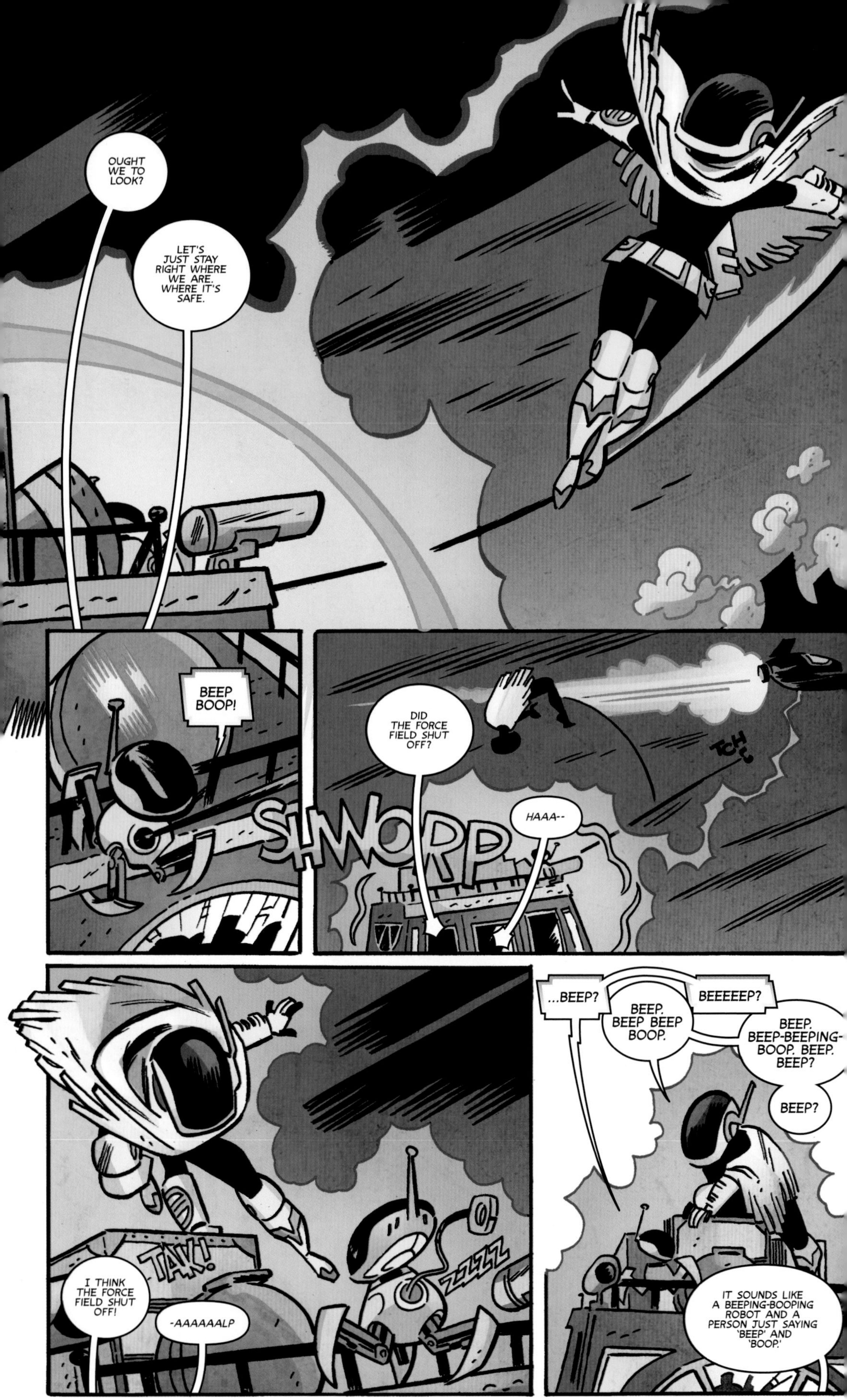
OUGHT WE TO LOOK?
LET'S JUST STAY RIGHT WHERE WE ARE. WHERE IT'S SAFE.
BEEP BOOP!
SHWORP
DID THE FORCE FIELD SHUT OFF?
HAAA--
TCH
TAK!
ZZZZZ
I THINK THE FORCE FIELD SHUT OFF!
-AAAAAALP
...BEEP?
BEEP. BEEP BEEP BOOP.
BEEEEEP?
BEEP. BEEP-BEEPING-BOOP. BEEP. BEEP?
BEEP?
IT SOUNDS LIKE A BEEPING-BOOPING ROBOT AND A PERSON JUST SAYING 'BEEP' AND 'BOOP.'

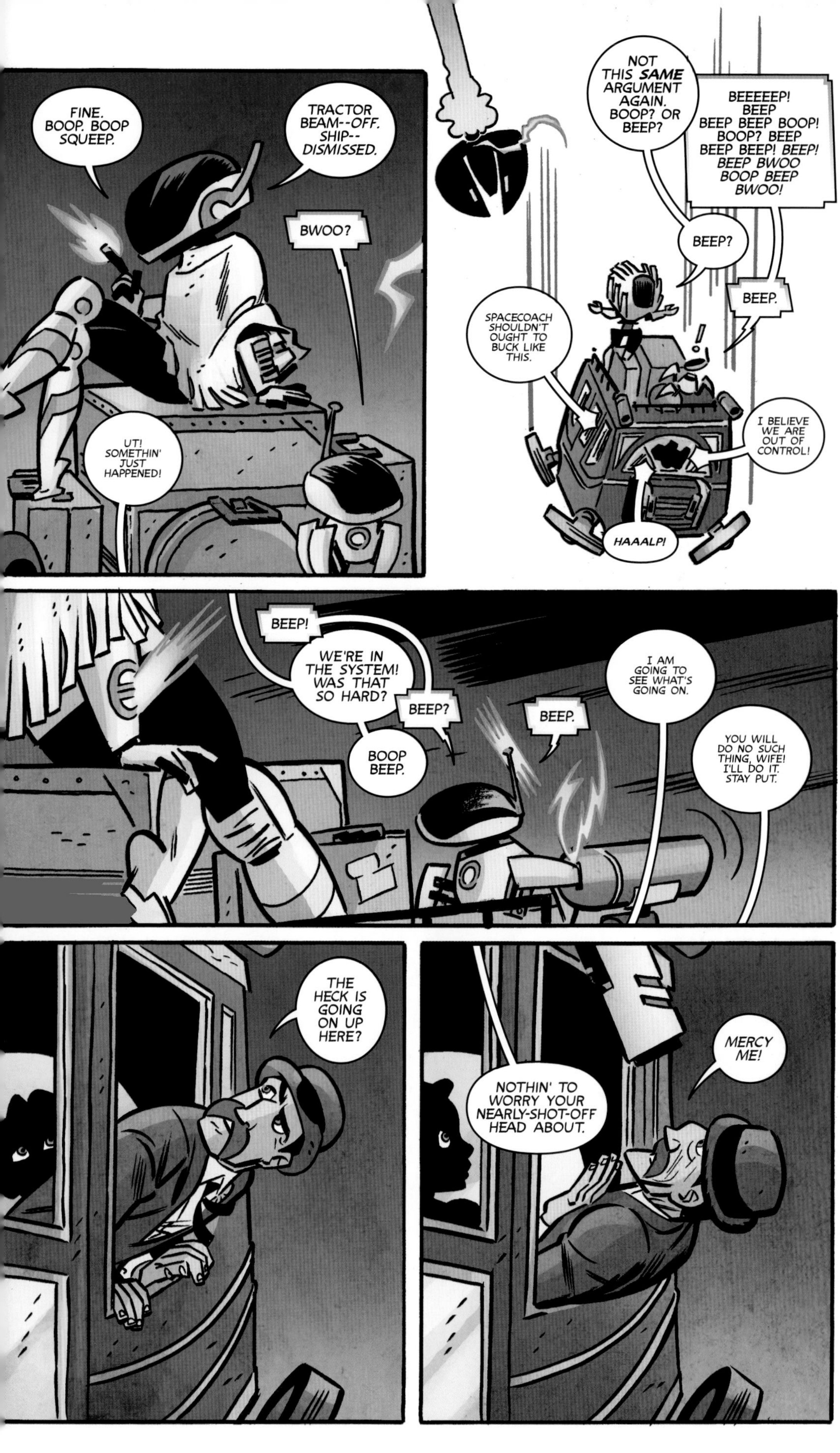
FINE. BOOP. BOOP SQUEEP.
TRACTOR BEAM--OFF. SHIP--DISMISSED.
BWOO?
UT! SOMETHIN' JUST HAPPENED!
NOT THIS SAME ARGUMENT AGAIN. BOOP? OR BEEP?
BEEEEEP! BEEP BEEP BEEP BOOP! BOOP? BEEP BEEP BEEP! BEEP! BEEP BWOO BOOP BEEP BWOO!
BEEP?
BEEP.
SPACECOACH SHOULDN'T OUGHT TO BUCK LIKE THIS.
!
I BELIEVE WE ARE OUT OF CONTROL!
HAAALP!
BEEP!
WE'RE IN THE SYSTEM! WAS THAT SO HARD?
BEEP?
BOOP BEEP.
BEEP.
I AM GOING TO SEE WHAT'S GOING ON.
YOU WILL DO NO SUCH THING, WIFE! I'LL DO IT. STAY PUT.
THE HECK IS GOING ON UP HERE?
NOTHIN' TO WORRY YOUR NEARLY-SHOT-OFF HEAD ABOUT.
MERCY ME!

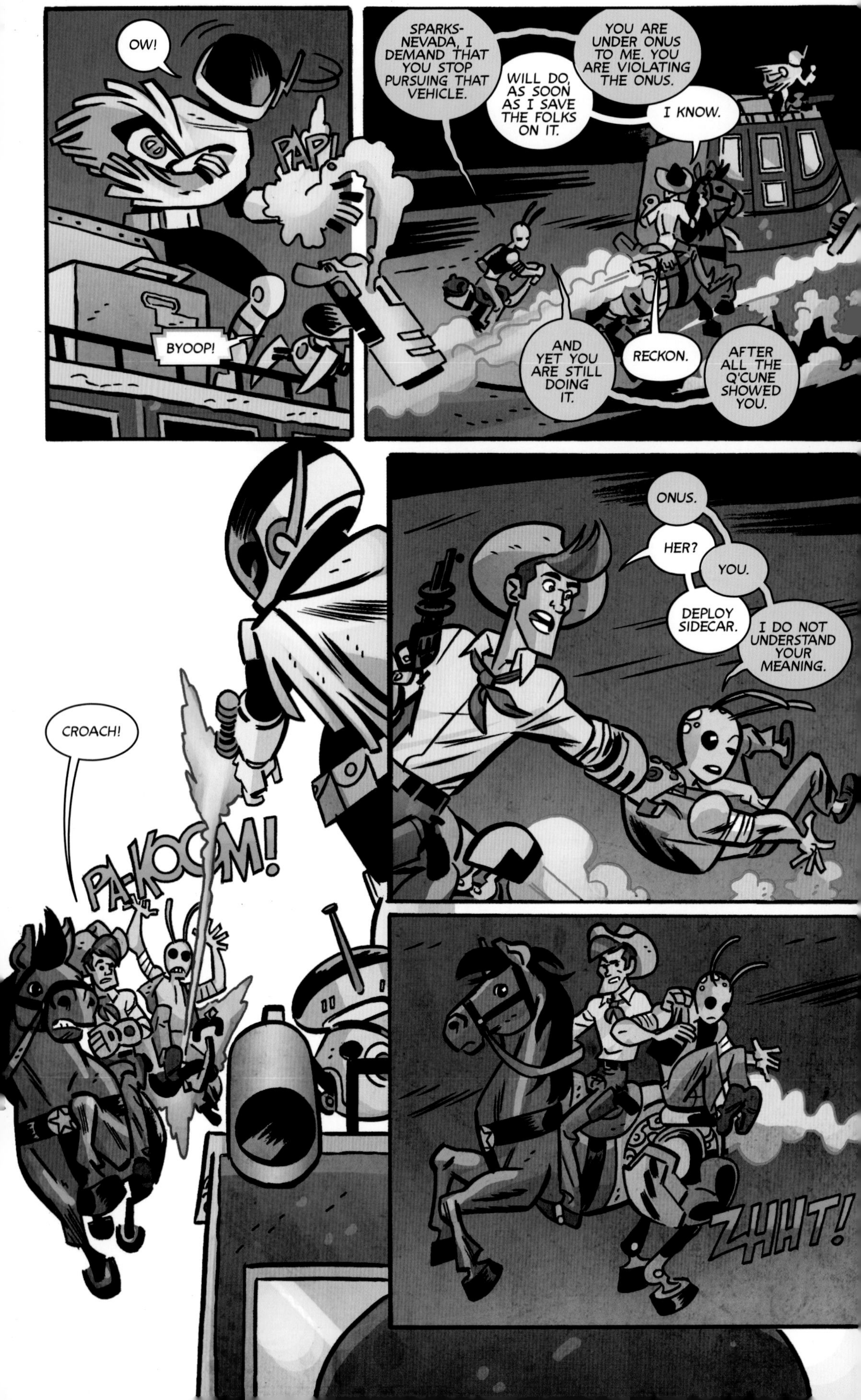
OW!
PAP!
BYOOP!
SPARKS-NEVADA, I DEMAND THAT YOU STOP PURSUING THAT VEHICLE.
WILL DO, AS SOON AS I SAVE THE FOLKS ON IT.
YOU ARE UNDER ONUS TO ME. YOU ARE VIOLATING THE ONUS.
I KNOW.
AND YET YOU ARE STILL DOING IT.
RECKON.
AFTER ALL THE Q'CUNE SHOWED YOU.
CROACH!
PA-KOOM!
ONUS.
HER?
YOU.
DEPLOY SIDECAR.
I DO NOT UNDERSTAND YOUR MEANING.
ZHHT!

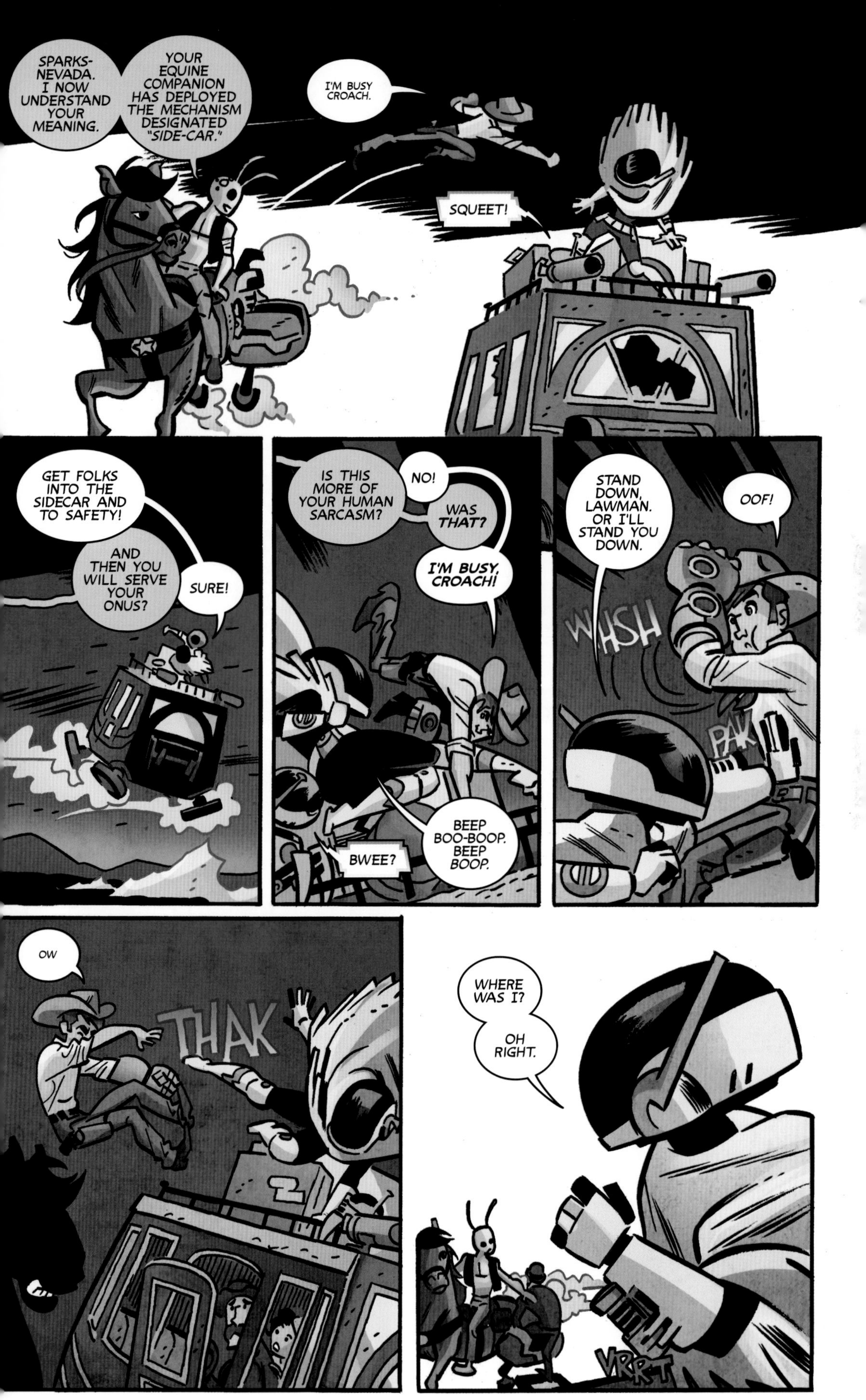
SPARKS-NEVADA. I NOW UNDERSTAND YOUR MEANING.
YOUR EQUINE COMPANION HAS DEPLOYED THE MECHANISM DESIGNATED "SIDE-CAR."
I'M BUSY CROACH.
SQUEET!
GET FOLKS INTO THE SIDECAR AND TO SAFETY!
AND THEN YOU WILL SERVE YOUR ONUS?
SURE!
IS THIS MORE OF YOUR HUMAN SARCASM?
NO!
WAS THAT?
I'M BUSY, CROACH!
BEEP BOO-BOOP. BEEP BOOP.
BWEE?
STAND DOWN, LAWMAN. OR I'LL STAND YOU DOWN.
OOF!
WHSH
PAK
OW
THAK
WHERE WAS I?
OH RIGHT.
VRRT

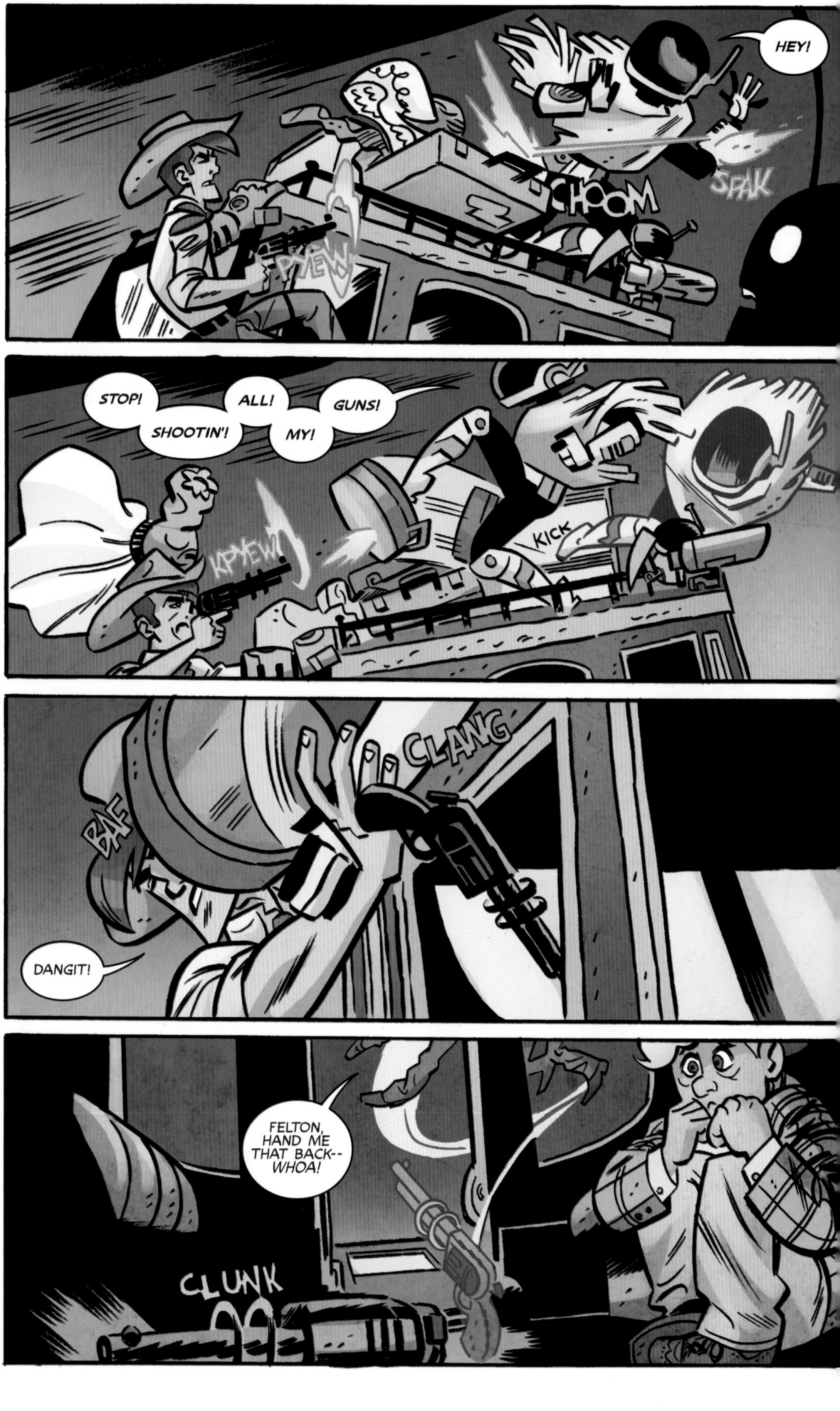
HEY!
CHOOM
SPAK
PYEW
STOP!
SHOOTIN'!
ALL!
MY!
GUNS!
KPYEW
KICK
CLANG
BAF
DANGIT!
FELTON, HAND ME THAT BACK-- WHOA!
CLUNK

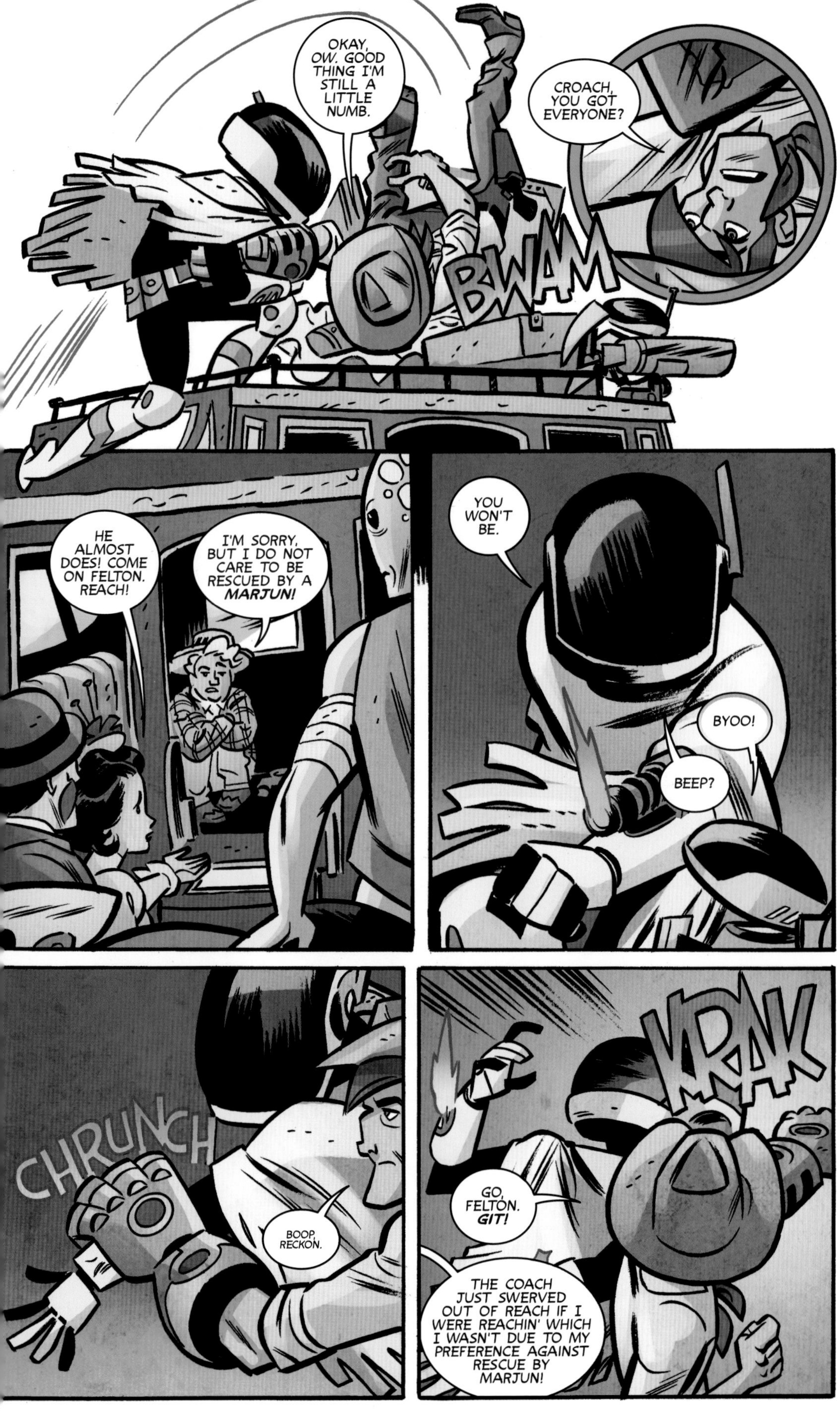
OKAY, OW. GOOD THING I'M STILL A LITTLE NUMB.
CROACH, YOU GOT EVERYONE?
BWAM
HE ALMOST DOES! COME ON FELTON. REACH!
I'M SORRY, BUT I DO NOT CARE TO BE RESCUED BY A ***MARJUN!***
YOU WON'T BE.
BYOO!
BEEP?
CHRUNCH
BOOP, RECKON.
VRAK
GO, FELTON. ***GIT!***
THE COACH JUST SWERVED OUT OF REACH IF I WERE REACHIN' WHICH I WASN'T DUE TO MY PREFERENCE AGAINST RESCUE BY MARJUN!

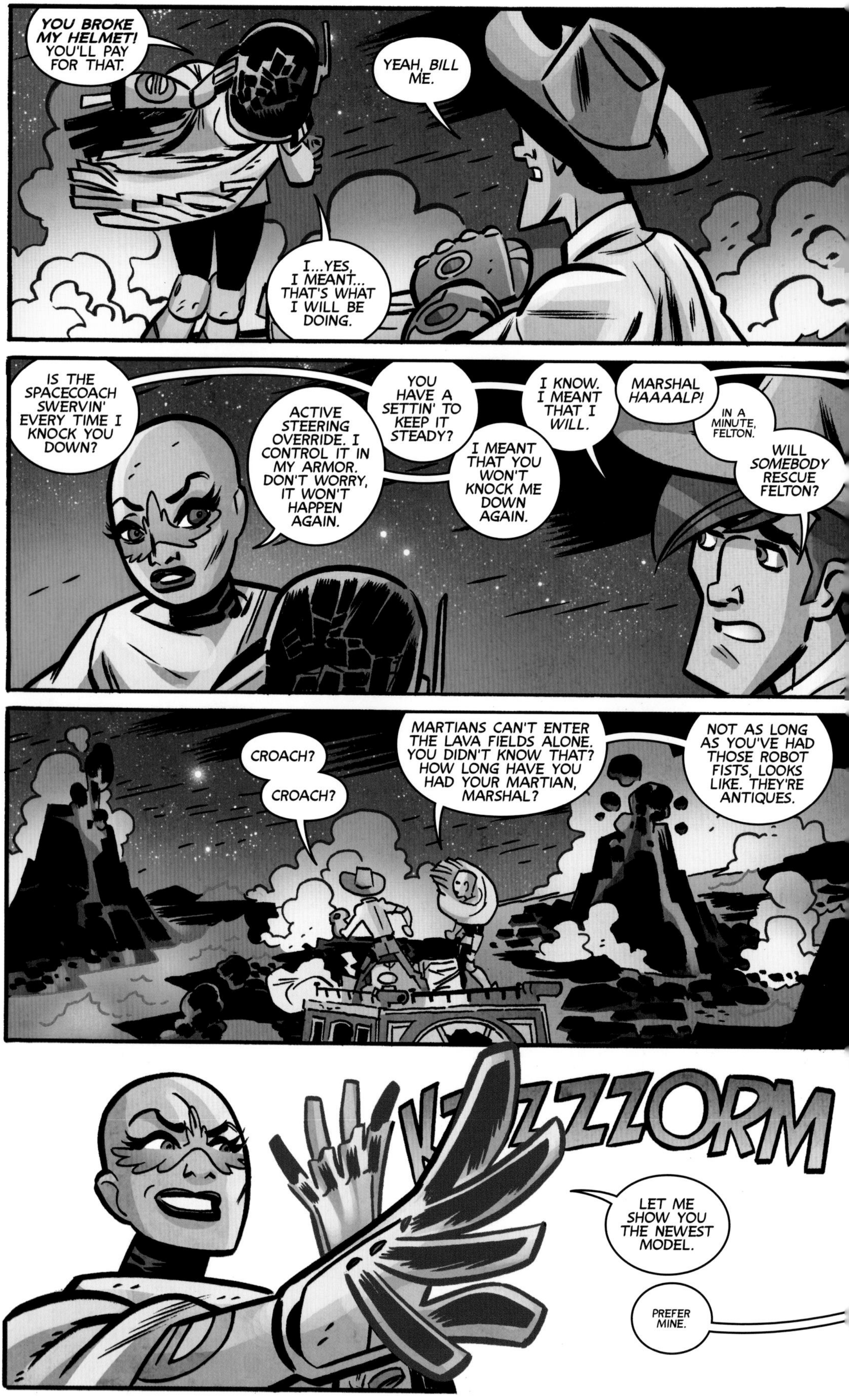

YOU BROKE MY HELMET! YOU'LL PAY FOR THAT.
YEAH, BILL ME.
I...YES, I MEANT... THAT'S WHAT I WILL BE DOING.
IS THE SPACECOACH SWERVIN' EVERY TIME I KNOCK YOU DOWN?
ACTIVE STEERING OVERRIDE. I CONTROL IT IN MY ARMOR. DON'T WORRY, IT WON'T HAPPEN AGAIN.
YOU HAVE A SETTIN' TO KEEP IT STEADY?
I MEANT THAT YOU WON'T KNOCK ME DOWN AGAIN.
I KNOW. I MEANT THAT I WILL.
MARSHAL HAAAALP!
IN A MINUTE, FELTON.
WILL SOMEBODY RESCUE FELTON?
CROACH?
CROACH?
MARTIANS CAN'T ENTER THE LAVA FIELDS ALONE. YOU DIDN'T KNOW THAT? HOW LONG HAVE YOU HAD YOUR MARTIAN, MARSHAL?
NOT AS LONG AS YOU'VE HAD THOSE ROBOT FISTS, LOOKS LIKE. THEY'RE ANTIQUES.
VZZZZORM
LET ME SHOW YOU THE NEWEST MODEL.
PREFER MINE.

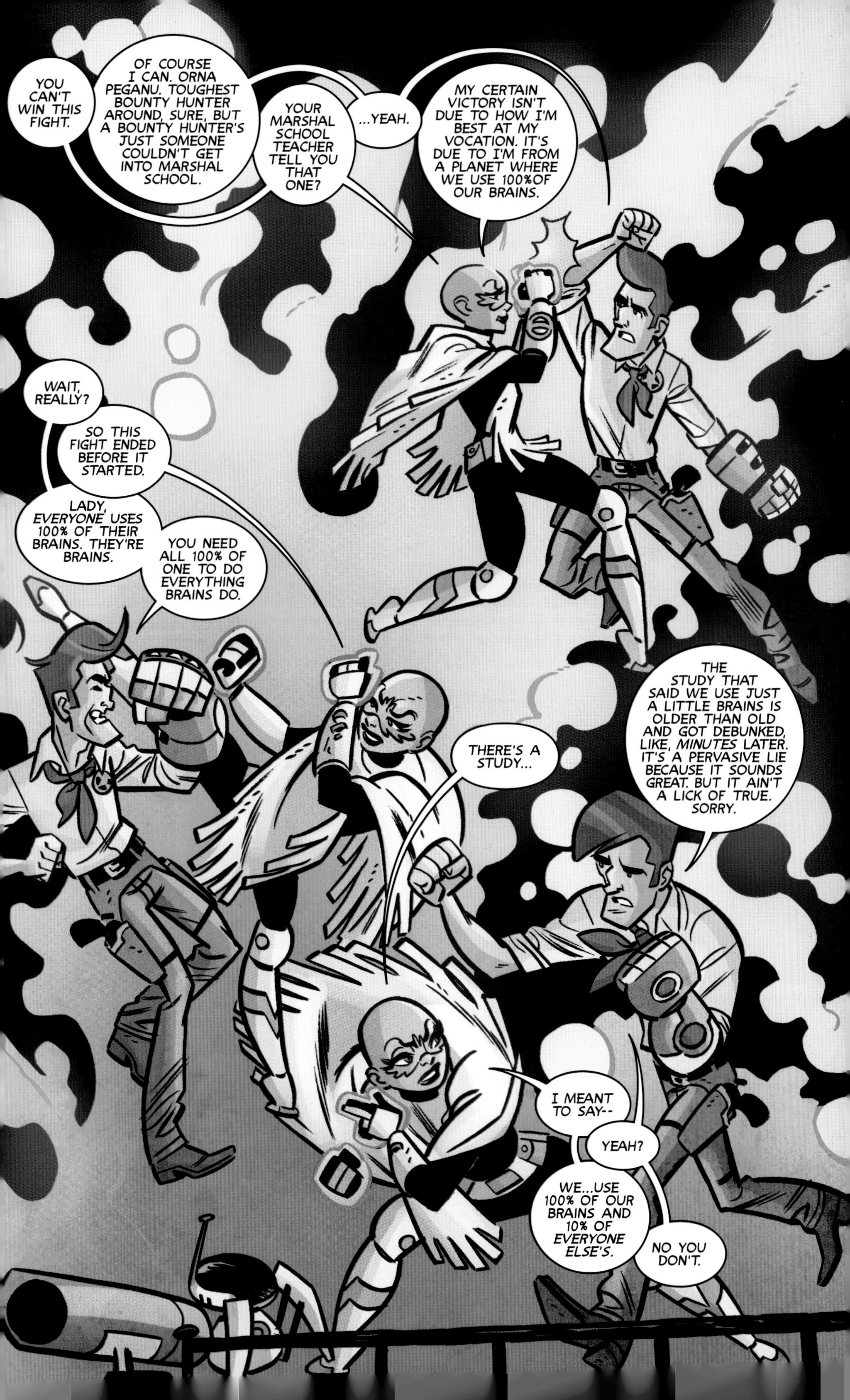

YOU CAN'T WIN THIS FIGHT.
OF COURSE I CAN. ORNA PEGANU. TOUGHEST BOUNTY HUNTER AROUND, SURE, BUT A BOUNTY HUNTER'S JUST SOMEONE COULDN'T GET INTO MARSHAL SCHOOL.
YOUR MARSHAL SCHOOL TEACHER TELL YOU THAT ONE?
...YEAH.
MY CERTAIN VICTORY ISN'T DUE TO HOW I'M BEST AT MY VOCATION. IT'S DUE TO I'M FROM A PLANET WHERE WE USE 100%OF OUR BRAINS.
WAIT, REALLY?
SO THIS FIGHT ENDED BEFORE IT STARTED.
LADY, EVERYONE USES 100% OF THEIR BRAINS. THEY'RE BRAINS.
YOU NEED ALL 100% OF ONE TO DO EVERYTHING BRAINS DO.
THERE'S A STUDY...
THE STUDY THAT SAID WE USE JUST A LITTLE BRAINS IS OLDER THAN OLD AND GOT DEBUNKED, LIKE, MINUTES LATER. IT'S A PERVASIVE LIE BECAUSE IT SOUNDS GREAT. BUT IT AIN'T A LICK OF TRUE. SORRY.
I MEANT TO SAY--
YEAH?
WE...USE 100% OF OUR BRAINS AND 10% OF EVERYONE ELSE'S.
NO YOU DON'T.

YOU ARE SAFE NOW, HUMANS DESIGNATED MISTERJOHNSON AND MISSISJOHNSON AND EQUINE HYBRID DESIGNATED MERCURY.

THE ONUS OF MY TRIBE FULFILLED, I CAN RETURN TO THE UNDERCITY.

GOOD-BYE, BEINGS. IT HAS BEEN AN ONUS TO ENCOUNTER YOU.

THANK YOU FOR HELPING KEEP MY WIFE AND ME SAFE. YOU EVER NEED LEMONS, COME TO JOHNSON'S LEMON ORCHARD. IT'S BEING DELIVERED FROM THE MOON PRESENTLY, BUT WE SHOULD BE UP AND RUNNING IN THE NEXT WEEK OR TWO.

BEST LEMONS IN THE SECTOR, THAT'S THE JOHNSON PROMISE. TELL HIM, DEAR.

YOU *CAN'T* GO, CROACH! THE MARSHAL'S OUT THERE! AND FELTON TOO!

THEY MAY BE IN DANGER! YOU HAVE TO *HELP* THEM!

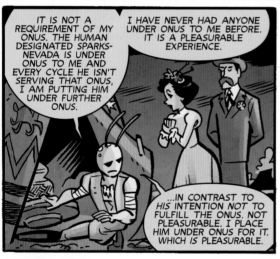

IT IS NOT A REQUIREMENT OF MY ONUS. THE HUMAN DESIGNATED SPARKS-NEVADA IS UNDER ONUS TO ME AND EVERY CYCLE HE ISN'T SERVING THAT ONUS, I AM PUTTING HIM UNDER FURTHER ONUS.

I HAVE NEVER HAD ANYONE UNDER ONUS TO ME BEFORE. IT IS A PLEASURABLE EXPERIENCE.

...IN CONTRAST TO *HIS* INTENTION *NOT* TO FULFILL THE ONUS. NOT PLEASURABLE. I PLACE HIM UNDER ONUS FOR IT. WHICH *IS* PLEASURABLE.

THE MARSHAL'S FIGHTING A BOUNTY HUNTER SO DANGEROUS SHE'S FAMOUS! WHAT IF HE DIES?

THEN HE WILL NO LONGER BE UNDER ONUS TO ME. IF HE POSSESSES OFFSPRING, THEY WILL ASSUME HIS ONUS.

WOULDN'T YOU ENJOY FOR *HIM* TO FULFILL HIS ONUS?

I WOULD, HOWEVER, IT HAS LITTLE CHANCE OF EVENTUATING. I REITERATE THE SALUTARY ACKNOWLEDGEMENT OF MY DEPARTURE: GOOD-BYE.

YOURS IS THE BIGGEST HEART ON MARS, WENDY JOHNSON!

NOW I'D BE "UNDER ONUS" TO YOU IF WE GOT A MOVE ON AWAY FROM ALL THIS WILDERNESS AND TO TOWN.

I COULD USE A HOT BATH AND A HOT MEAL. WHAT DO YOU SAY?

LOOK, COMETBUGS!

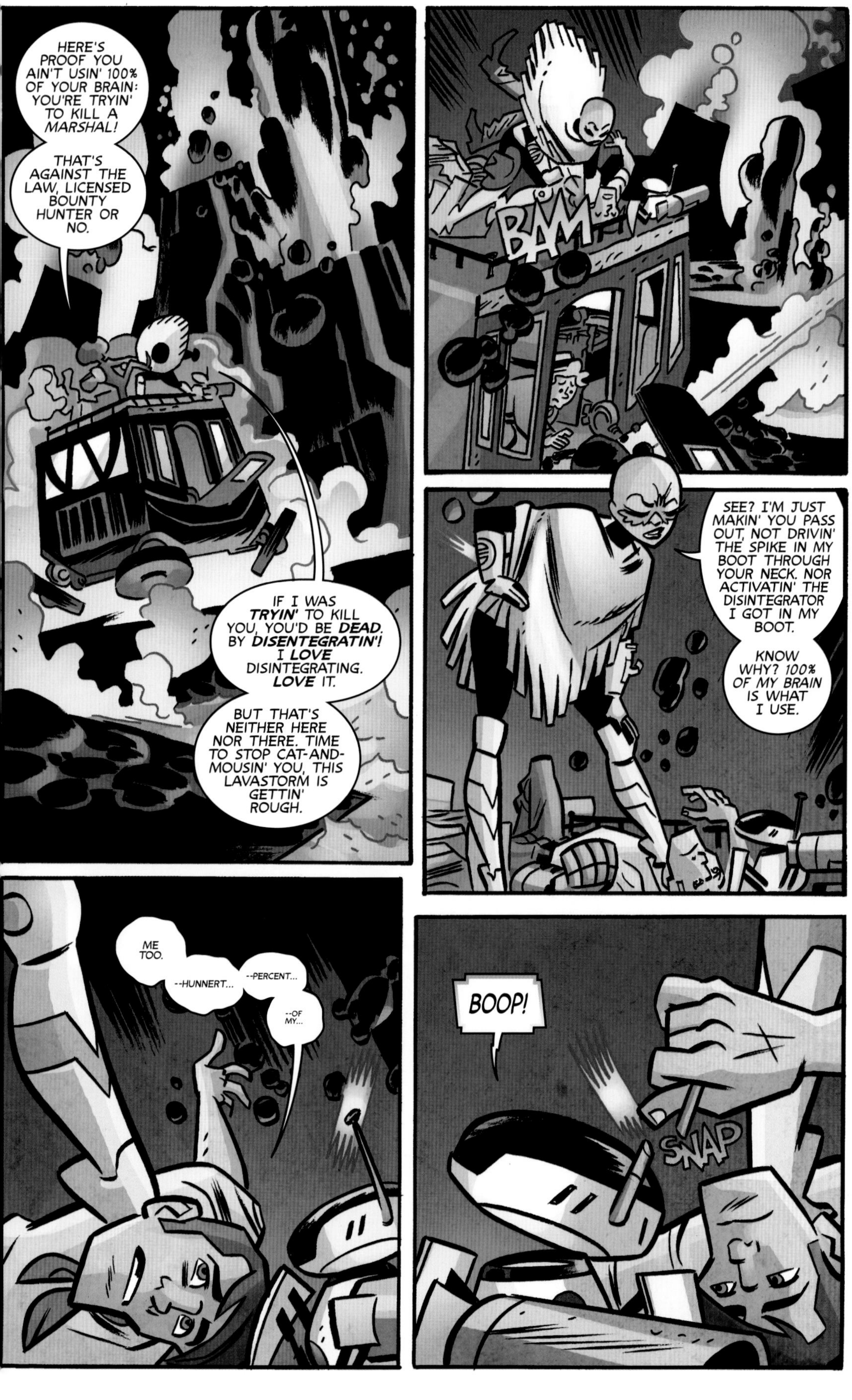
HERE'S PROOF YOU AIN'T USIN' 100% OF YOUR BRAIN: YOU'RE TRYIN' TO KILL A *MARSHAL!*
THAT'S AGAINST THE LAW, LICENSED BOUNTY HUNTER OR NO.
IF I WAS ***TRYIN'*** TO KILL YOU, YOU'D BE ***DEAD***. BY ***DISENTEGRATIN'!*** I ***LOVE*** DISINTEGRATING. ***LOVE*** IT.
BUT THAT'S NEITHER HERE NOR THERE. TIME TO STOP CAT-AND-MOUSIN' YOU, THIS LAVASTORM IS GETTIN' ROUGH.
BAM
SEE? I'M JUST MAKIN' YOU PASS OUT, NOT DRIVIN' THE SPIKE IN MY BOOT THROUGH YOUR NECK. NOR ACTIVATIN' THE DISINTEGRATOR I GOT IN MY BOOT.
KNOW WHY? *100%* OF MY BRAIN IS WHAT I USE.
ME TOO.
--HUNNERT...
--PERCENT...
--OF MY...
BOOP!
SNAP

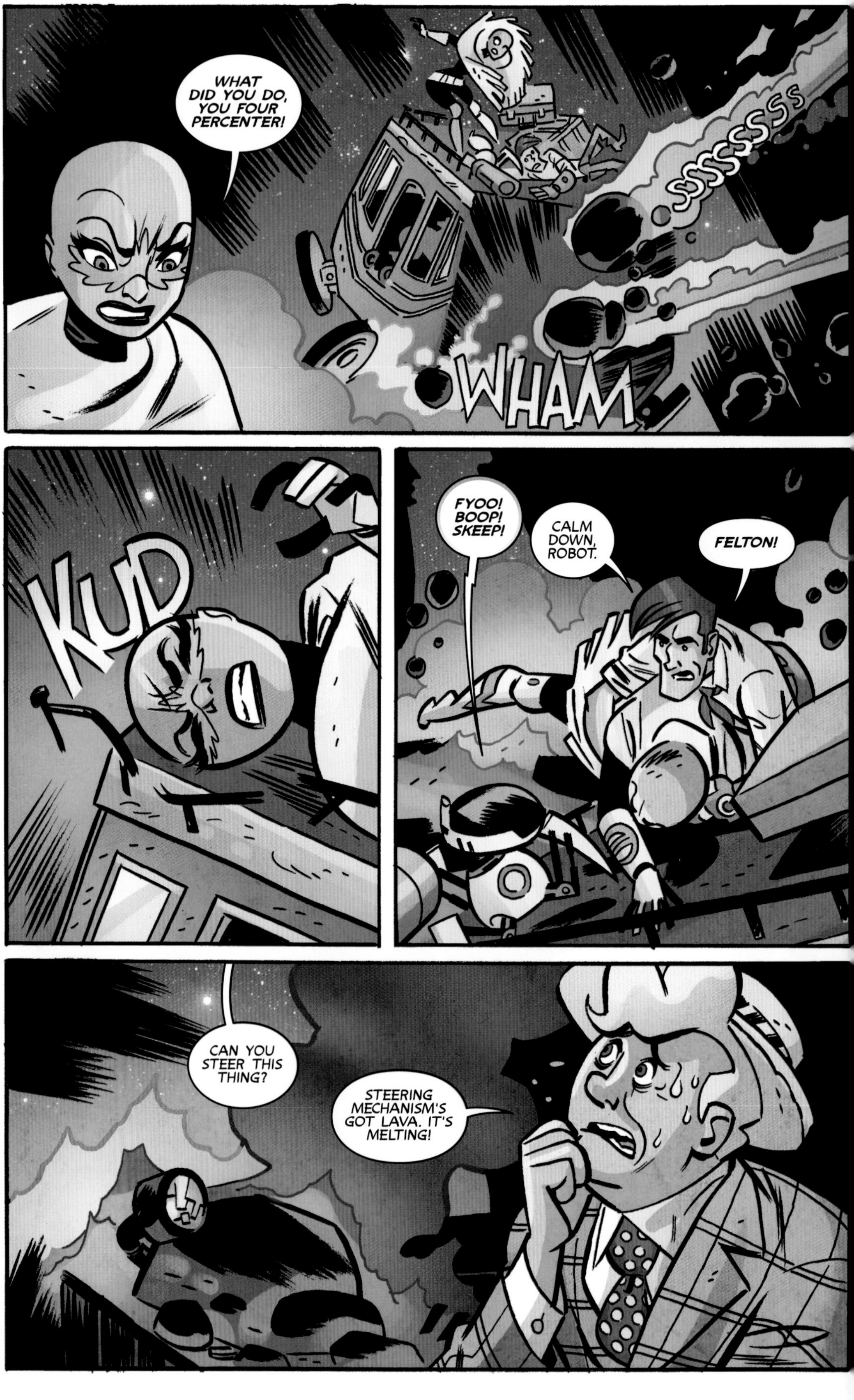
WHAT DID YOU DO, YOU FOUR PERCENTER!
SSSSSSSS
WHAM
KUD
FYOO! BOOP! SKEEP!
CALM DOWN, ROBOT.
FELTON!
CAN YOU STEER THIS THING?
STEERING MECHANISM'S GOT LAVA. IT'S MELTING!

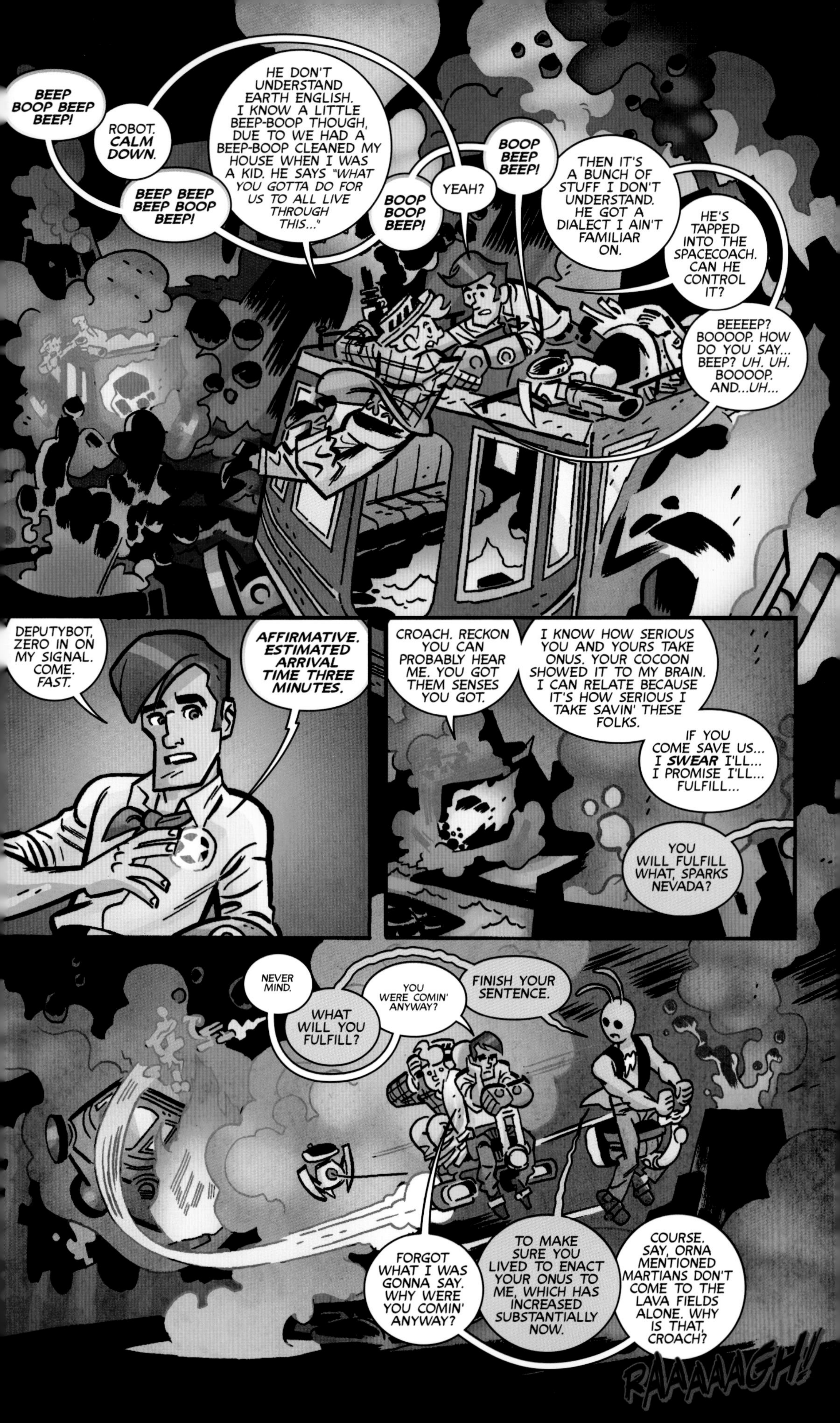
BEEP BOOP BEEP BEEP!
ROBOT. CALM DOWN.
BEEP BEEP BEEP BOOP BEEP!
HE DON'T UNDERSTAND EARTH ENGLISH. I KNOW A LITTLE BEEP-BOOP THOUGH, DUE TO WE HAD A BEEP-BOOP CLEANED MY HOUSE WHEN I WAS A KID. HE SAYS "WHAT YOU GOTTA DO FOR US TO ALL LIVE THROUGH THIS..."
BOOP BOOP BEEP!
YEAH?
BOOP BEEP BEEP!
THEN IT'S A BUNCH OF STUFF I DON'T UNDERSTAND. HE GOT A DIALECT I AIN'T FAMILIAR ON.
HE'S TAPPED INTO THE SPACECOACH. CAN HE CONTROL IT?
BEEEEP? BOOOOP. HOW DO YOU SAY... BEEP? UH. UH. BOOOOP. AND...UH...
DEPUTYBOT, ZERO IN ON MY SIGNAL. COME. FAST.
AFFIRMATIVE. ESTIMATED ARRIVAL TIME THREE MINUTES.
CROACH. RECKON YOU CAN PROBABLY HEAR ME. YOU GOT THEM SENSES YOU GOT.
I KNOW HOW SERIOUS YOU AND YOURS TAKE ONUS. YOUR COCOON SHOWED IT TO MY BRAIN. I CAN RELATE BECAUSE IT'S HOW SERIOUS I TAKE SAVIN' THESE FOLKS.
IF YOU COME SAVE US... I SWEAR I'LL... I PROMISE I'LL... FULFILL...
YOU WILL FULFILL WHAT, SPARKS NEVADA?
FINISH YOUR SENTENCE.
WHAT WILL YOU FULFILL?
NEVER MIND.
YOU WERE COMIN' ANYWAY?
FORGOT WHAT I WAS GONNA SAY. WHY WERE YOU COMIN' ANYWAY?
TO MAKE SURE YOU LIVED TO ENACT YOUR ONUS TO ME, WHICH HAS INCREASED SUBSTANTIALLY NOW.
COURSE. SAY, ORNA MENTIONED MARTIANS DON'T COME TO THE LAVA FIELDS ALONE. WHY IS THAT, CROACH?
RAAAAAGH!!

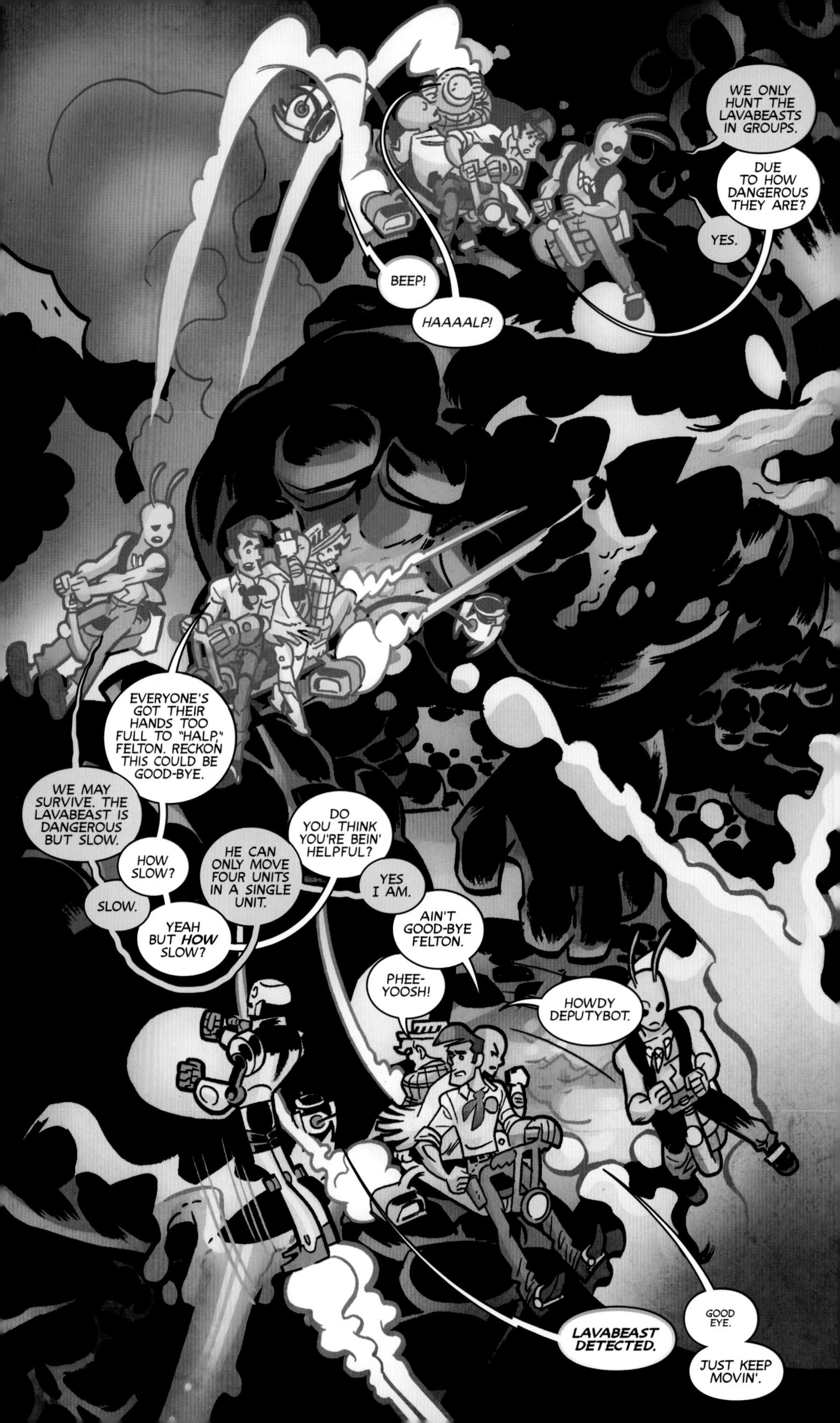
WE ONLY HUNT THE LAVABEASTS IN GROUPS.
DUE TO HOW DANGEROUS THEY ARE?
YES.
BEEP!
HAAAALP!
EVERYONE'S GOT THEIR HANDS TOO FULL TO "HALP," FELTON. RECKON THIS COULD BE GOOD-BYE.
WE MAY SURVIVE. THE LAVABEAST IS DANGEROUS BUT SLOW.
HOW SLOW?
SLOW.
YEAH BUT *HOW* SLOW?
HE CAN ONLY MOVE FOUR UNITS IN A SINGLE UNIT.
DO YOU THINK YOU'RE BEIN' HELPFUL?
YES I AM.
AIN'T GOOD-BYE FELTON.
PHEE-YOOSH!
HOWDY DEPUTYBOT.
LAVABEAST DETECTED.
GOOD EYE.
JUST KEEP MOVIN'.

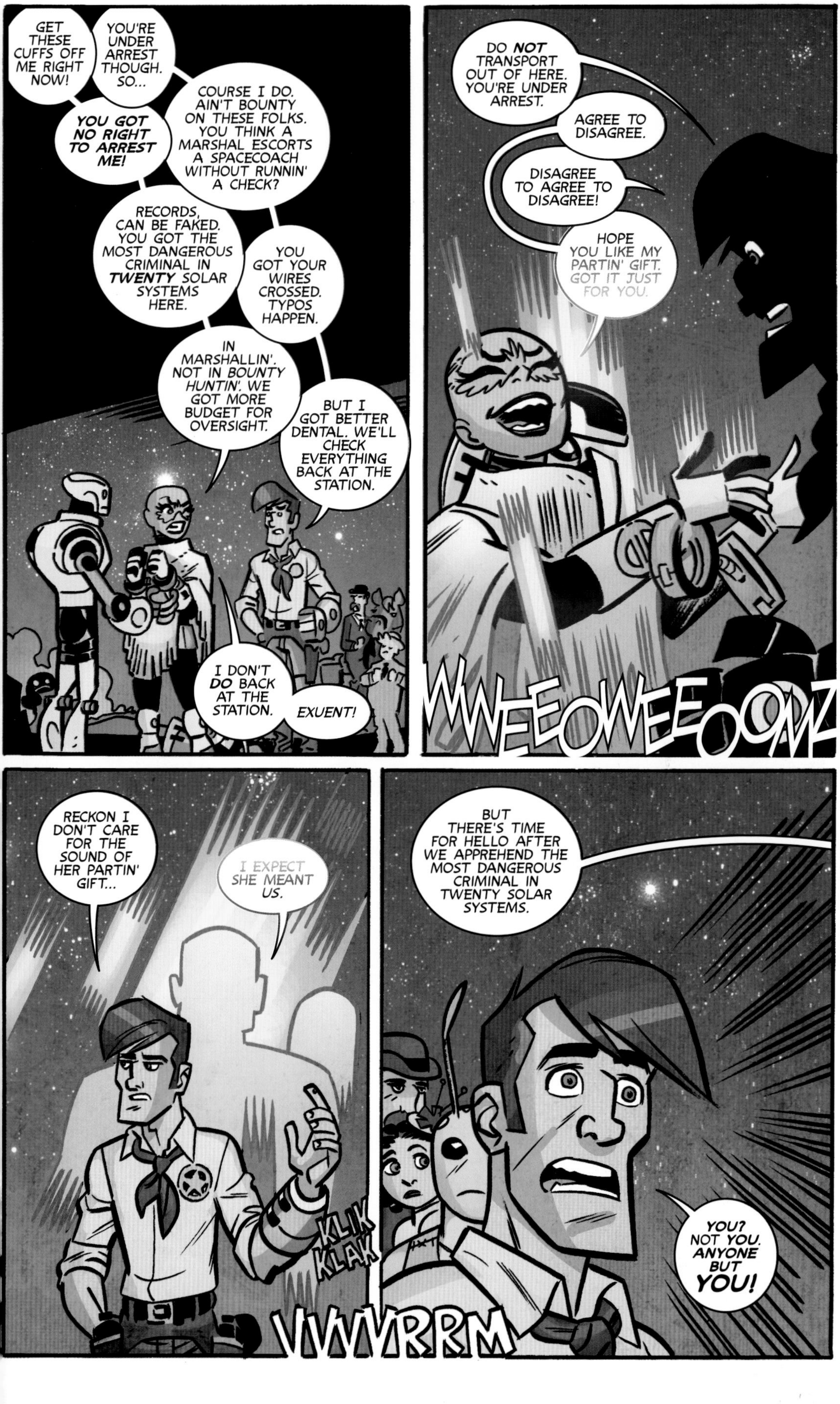
GET THESE CUFFS OFF ME RIGHT NOW!
YOU'RE UNDER ARREST THOUGH. SO...
YOU GOT NO RIGHT TO ARREST ME!
COURSE I DO. AIN'T BOUNTY ON THESE FOLKS. YOU THINK A MARSHAL ESCORTS A SPACECOACH WITHOUT RUNNIN' A CHECK?
RECORDS, CAN BE FAKED. YOU GOT THE MOST DANGEROUS CRIMINAL IN TWENTY SOLAR SYSTEMS HERE.
YOU GOT YOUR WIRES CROSSED. TYPOS HAPPEN.
IN MARSHALLIN'. NOT IN BOUNTY HUNTIN'. WE GOT MORE BUDGET FOR OVERSIGHT.
BUT I GOT BETTER DENTAL. WE'LL CHECK EVERYTHING BACK AT THE STATION.
I DON'T DO BACK AT THE STATION.
EXUENT!
DO NOT TRANSPORT OUT OF HERE. YOU'RE UNDER ARREST.
AGREE TO DISAGREE.
DISAGREE TO AGREE TO DISAGREE!
HOPE YOU LIKE MY PARTIN' GIFT. GOT IT JUST FOR YOU.
WWEEOWEEOOMZ
RECKON I DON'T CARE FOR THE SOUND OF HER PARTIN' GIFT...
I EXPECT SHE MEANT US.
KLIK KLAK
VVVVRRM
BUT THERE'S TIME FOR HELLO AFTER WE APPREHEND THE MOST DANGEROUS CRIMINAL IN TWENTY SOLAR SYSTEMS.
YOU? NOT YOU. ANYONE BUT YOU!

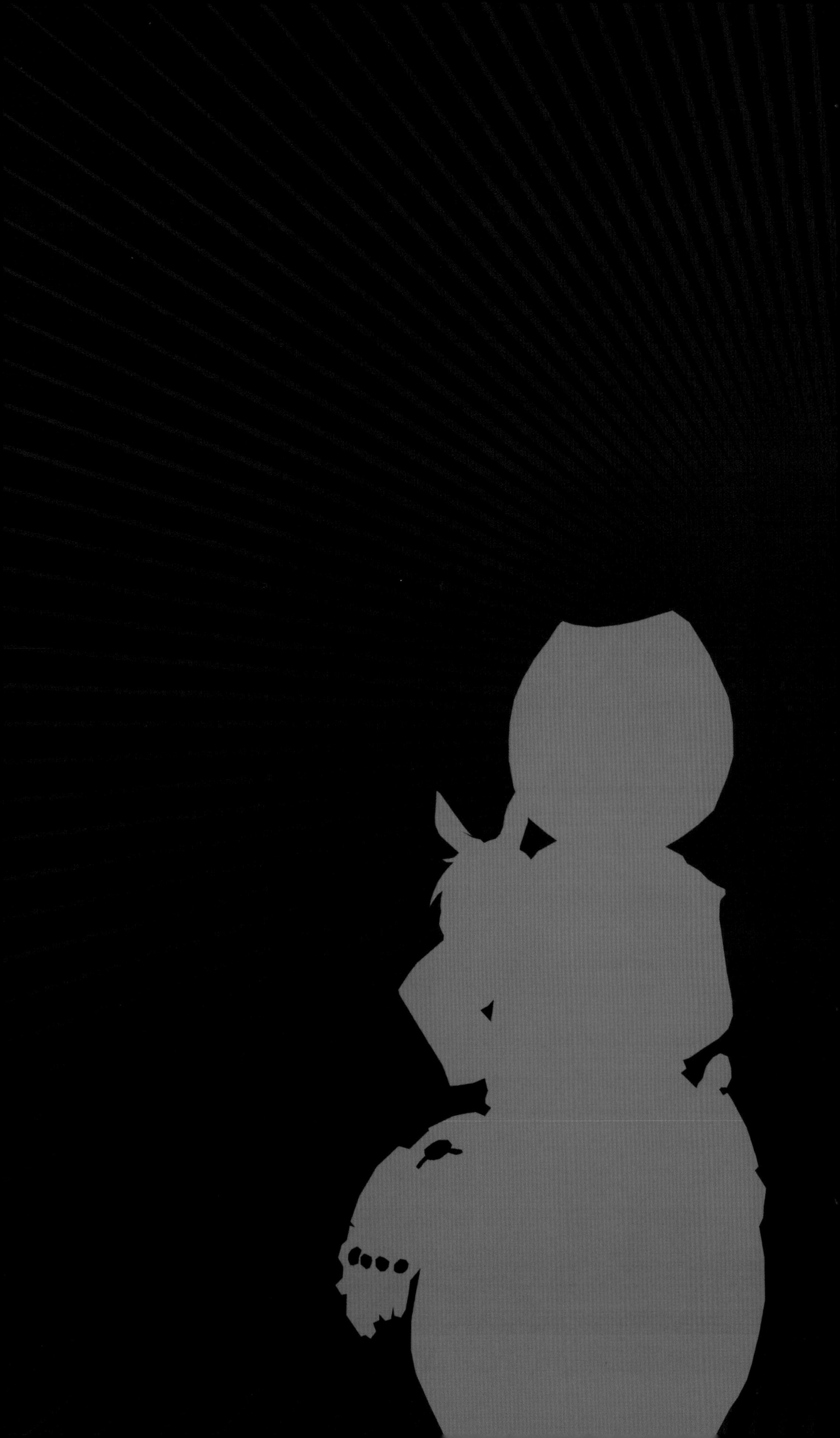

Chapter

FOUR

The Widow Johnson's Sad Sad Song

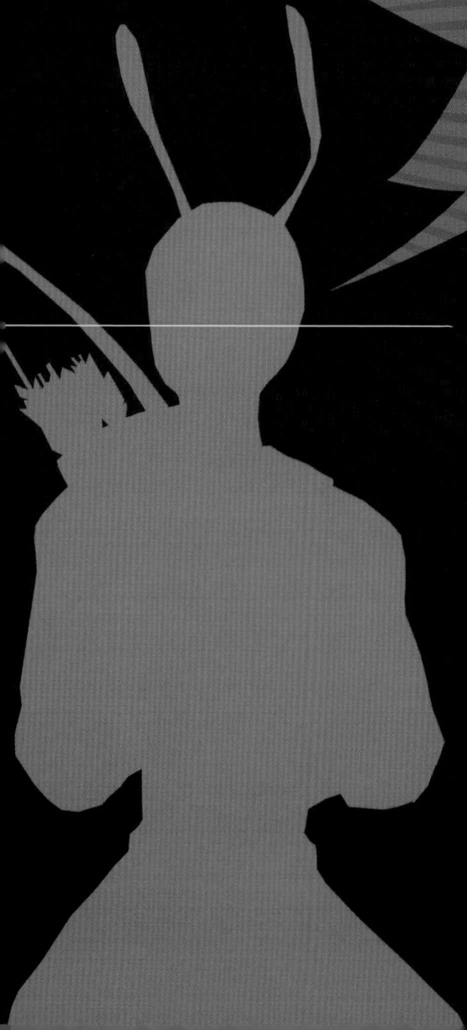

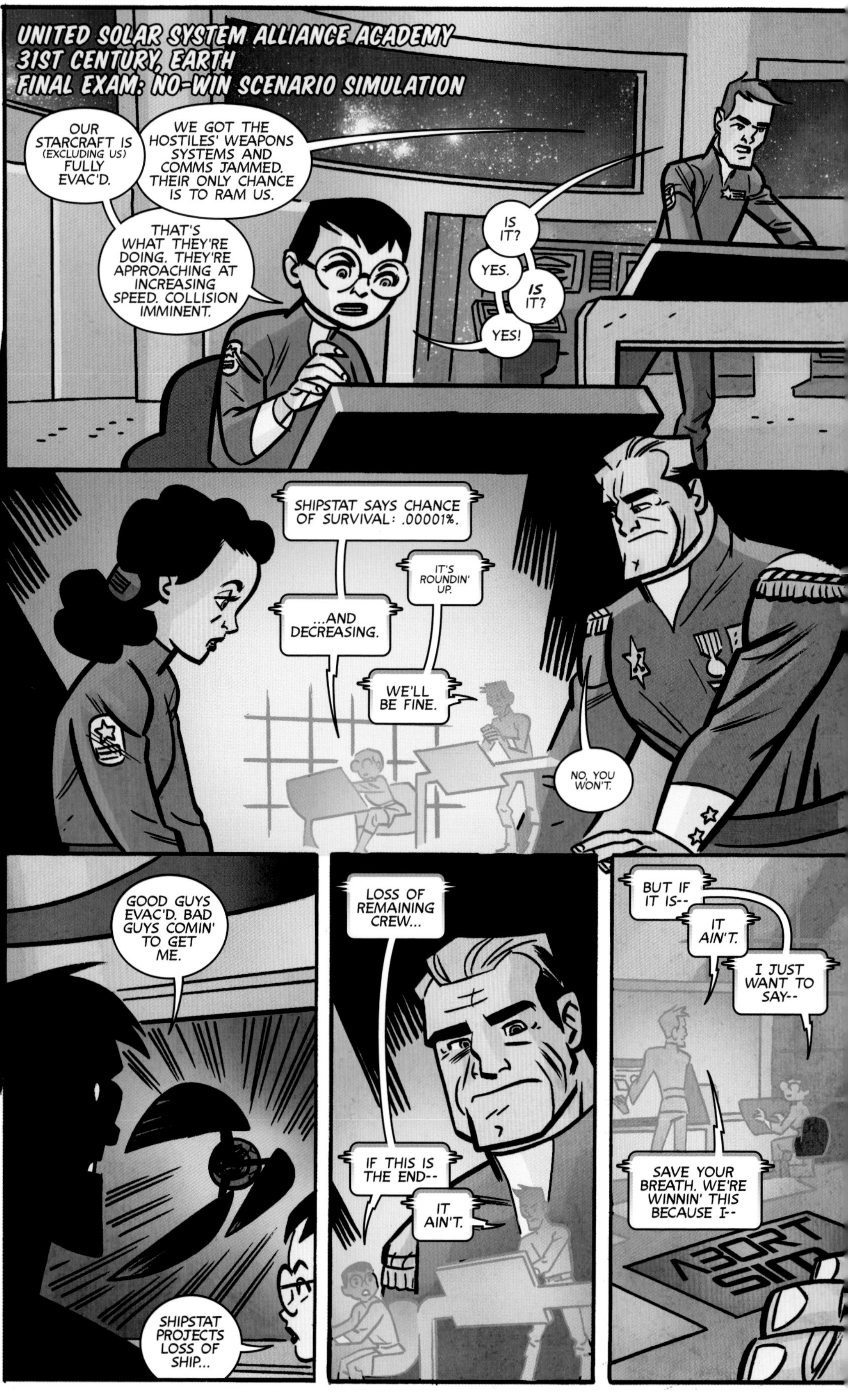
UNITED SOLAR SYSTEM ALLIANCE ACADEMY
31ST CENTURY, EARTH
FINAL EXAM: NO-WIN SCENARIO SIMULATION
OUR STARCRAFT IS (EXCLUDING US) FULLY EVAC'D.
WE GOT THE HOSTILES' WEAPONS SYSTEMS AND COMMS JAMMED. THEIR ONLY CHANCE IS TO RAM US.
THAT'S WHAT THEY'RE DOING. THEY'RE APPROACHING AT INCREASING SPEED. COLLISION IMMINENT.
IS IT?
YES.
IS IT?
YES!
SHIPSTAT SAYS CHANCE OF SURVIVAL: .00001%.
IT'S ROUNDIN' UP.
...AND DECREASING.
WE'LL BE FINE.
NO, YOU WON'T.
GOOD GUYS EVAC'D. BAD GUYS COMIN' TO GET ME.
SHIPSTAT PROJECTS LOSS OF SHIP...
LOSS OF REMAINING CREW...
IF THIS IS THE END--
IT AIN'T.
BUT IF IT IS--
IT AIN'T.
I JUST WANT TO SAY--
SAVE YOUR BREATH. WE'RE WINNIN' THIS BECAUSE I--

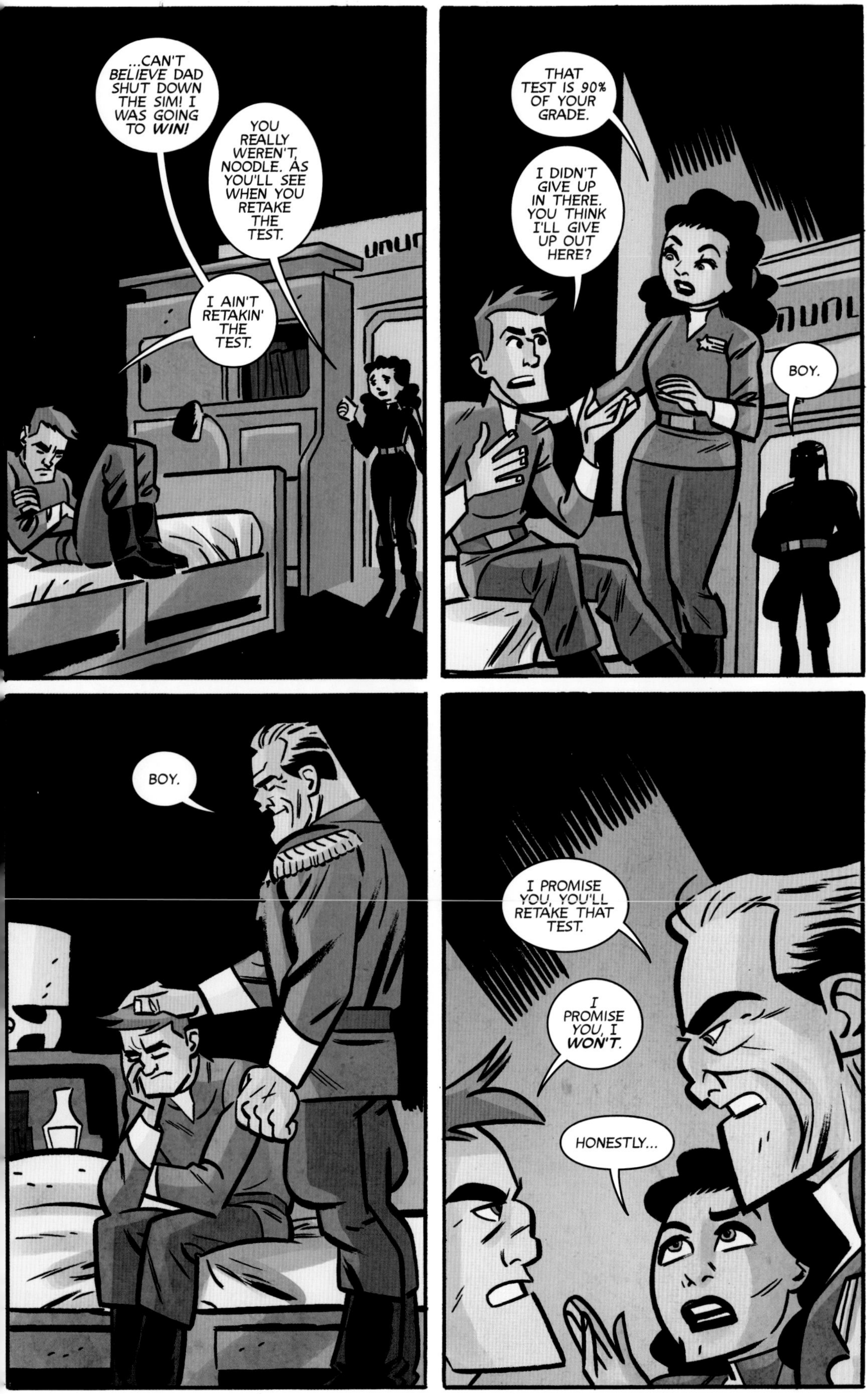
...CAN'T *BELIEVE* DAD SHUT DOWN THE SIM! I WAS GOING TO ***WIN!***
YOU REALLY WEREN'T, NOODLE. AS YOU'LL SEE WHEN YOU RETAKE THE TEST.
I AIN'T RETAKIN' THE TEST.
THAT TEST IS 90% OF YOUR GRADE.
I DIDN'T GIVE UP IN THERE. YOU THINK I'LL GIVE UP OUT HERE?
BOY.
BOY.
I PROMISE YOU, YOU'LL RETAKE THAT TEST.
I PROMISE *YOU*, I ***WON'T***.
HONESTLY...

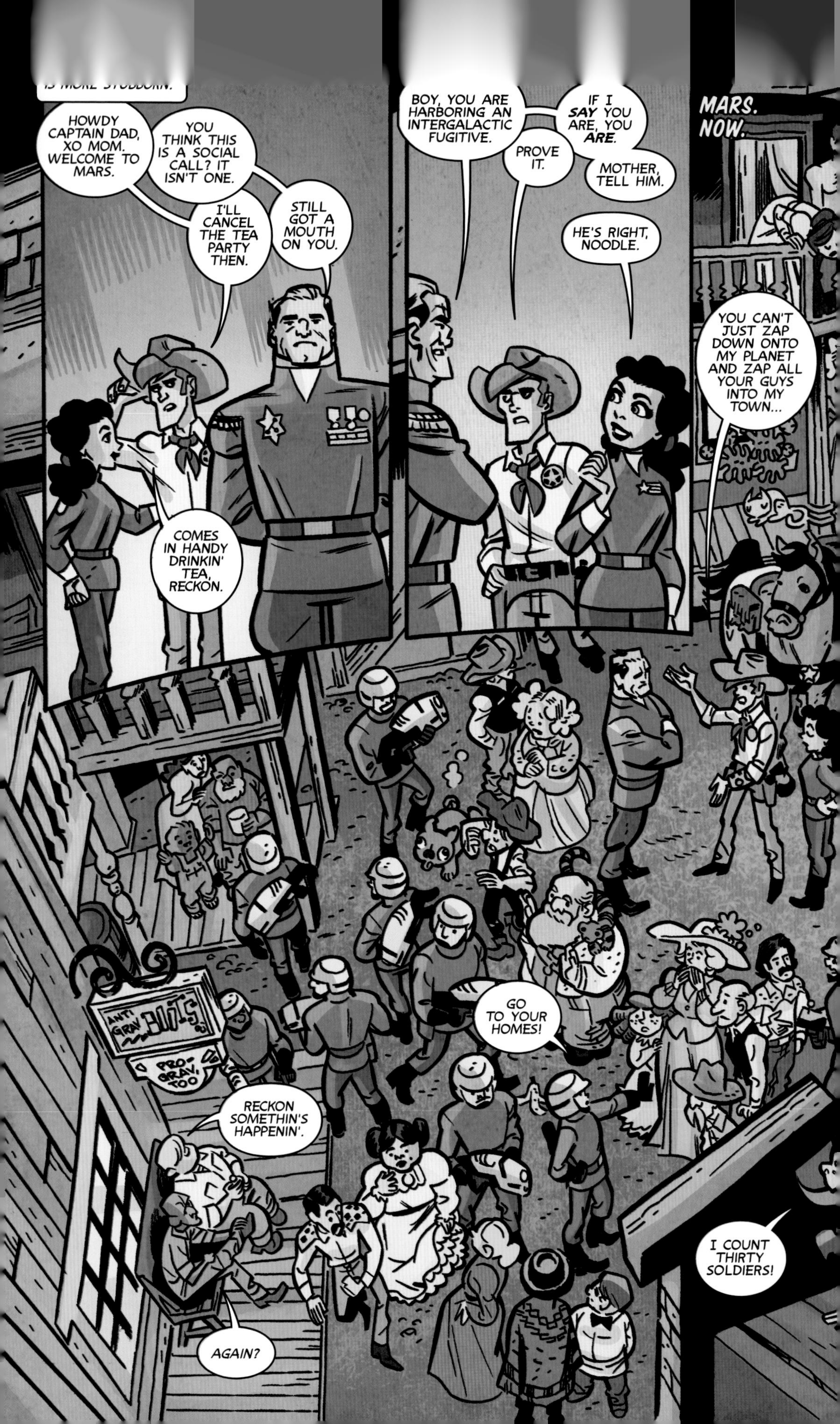
HOWDY CAPTAIN DAD, XO MOM. WELCOME TO MARS.
YOU THINK THIS IS A SOCIAL CALL? IT ISN'T ONE.
I'LL CANCEL THE TEA PARTY THEN.
STILL GOT A MOUTH ON YOU.
COMES IN HANDY DRINKIN' TEA, RECKON.
BOY, YOU ARE HARBORING AN INTERGALACTIC FUGITIVE.
PROVE IT.
IF I SAY YOU ARE, YOU ARE.
MOTHER, TELL HIM.
HE'S RIGHT, NOODLE.
MARS. NOW.
YOU CAN'T JUST ZAP DOWN ONTO MY PLANET AND ZAP ALL YOUR GUYS INTO MY TOWN...
ANTI GRAV BUTS
PRO-GRAV, TOO
GO TO YOUR HOMES!
RECKON SOMETHIN'S HAPPENIN'.
AGAIN?
I COUNT THIRTY SOLDIERS!

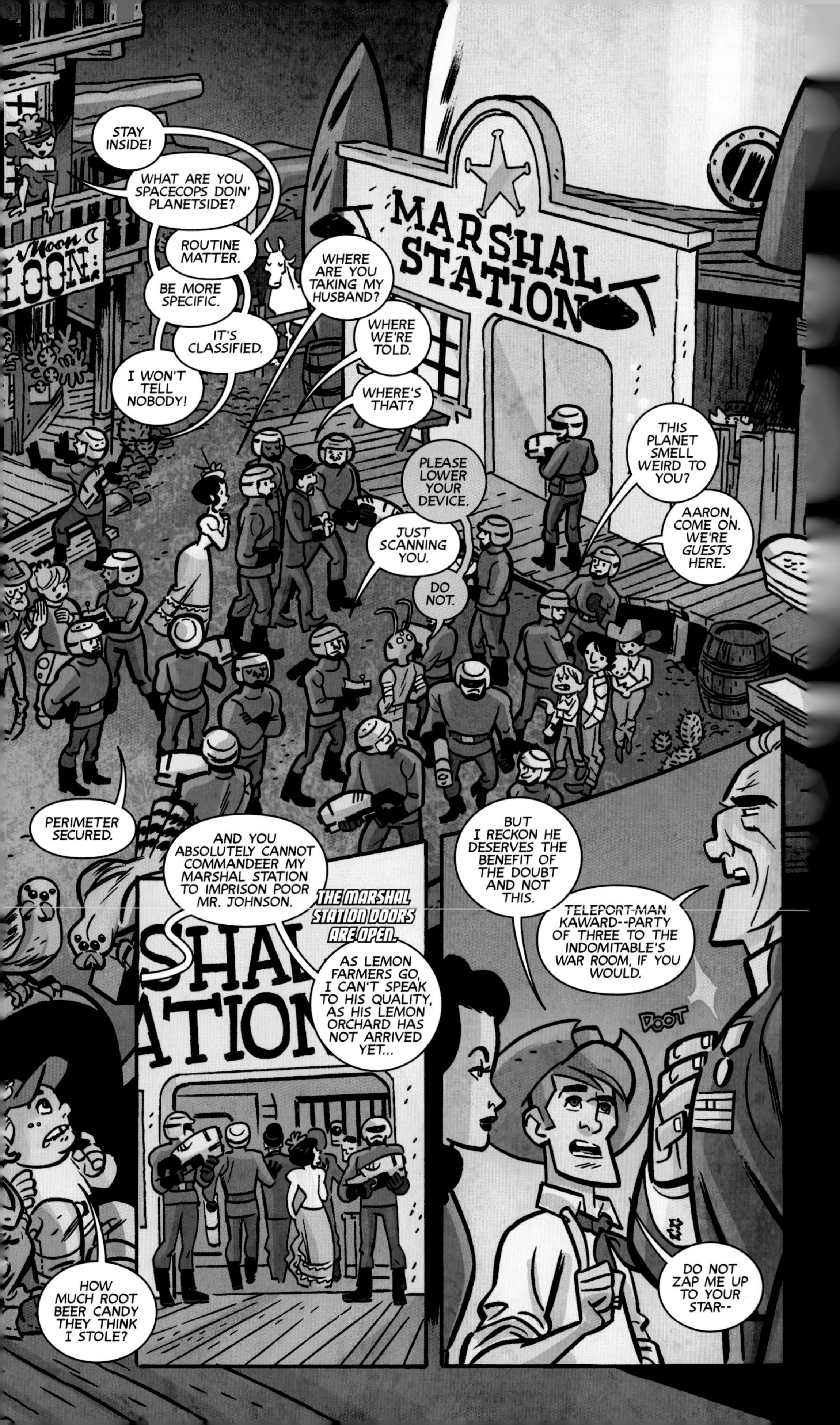
MARSHAL STATION
Moon
LOON
STAY INSIDE!
WHAT ARE YOU SPACECOPS DOIN' PLANETSIDE?
ROUTINE MATTER.
BE MORE SPECIFIC.
IT'S CLASSIFIED.
I WON'T TELL NOBODY!
WHERE ARE YOU TAKING MY HUSBAND?
WHERE WE'RE TOLD.
WHERE'S THAT?
PLEASE LOWER YOUR DEVICE.
JUST SCANNING YOU.
DO NOT.
THIS PLANET SMELL WEIRD TO YOU?
AARON, COME ON. WE'RE *GUESTS* HERE.
PERIMETER SECURED.
AND YOU ABSOLUTELY CANNOT COMMANDEER MY MARSHAL STATION TO IMPRISON POOR MR. JOHNSON.
THE MARSHAL STATION DOORS ARE OPEN.
SHAL
ATION
AS LEMON FARMERS GO, I CAN'T SPEAK TO HIS QUALITY, AS HIS LEMON ORCHARD HAS NOT ARRIVED YET...
HOW MUCH ROOT BEER CANDY THEY THINK I STOLE?
BUT I RECKON HE DESERVES THE BENEFIT OF THE DOUBT AND NOT THIS.
TELEPORT-MAN KAWARD--PARTY OF THREE TO THE INDOMITABLE'S WAR ROOM, IF YOU WOULD.
DOOT
DO NOT ZAP ME UP TO YOUR STAR--

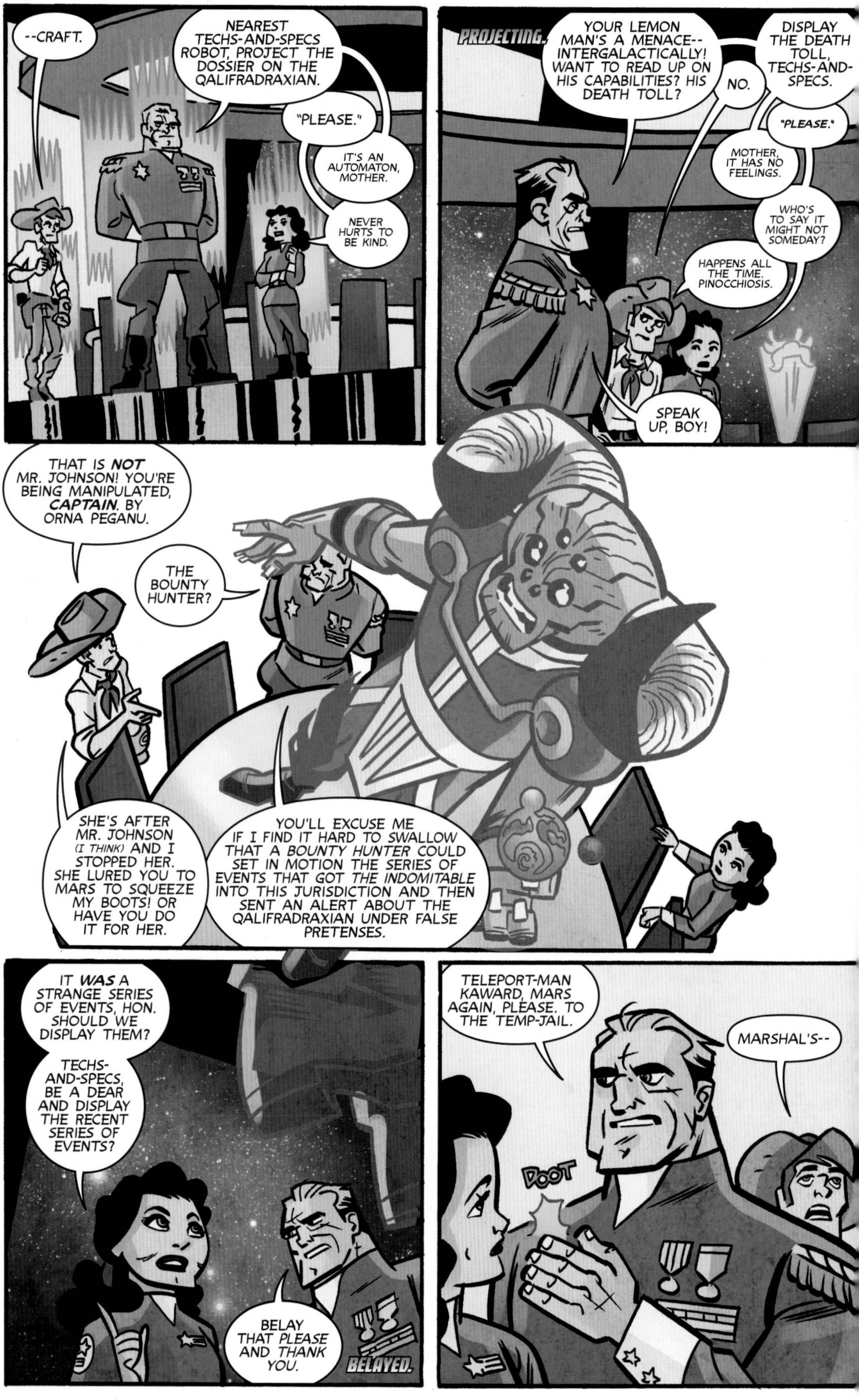
--CRAFT.
NEAREST TECHS-AND-SPECS ROBOT, PROJECT THE DOSSIER ON THE QALIFRADRAXIAN.
"PLEASE."
IT'S AN AUTOMATON, MOTHER.
NEVER HURTS TO BE KIND.
PROJECTING.
YOUR LEMON MAN'S A MENACE-- INTERGALACTICALLY! WANT TO READ UP ON HIS CAPABILITIES? HIS DEATH TOLL?
NO.
DISPLAY THE DEATH TOLL, TECHS-AND-SPECS.
"PLEASE."
MOTHER, IT HAS NO FEELINGS.
WHO'S TO SAY IT MIGHT NOT SOMEDAY?
HAPPENS ALL THE TIME. PINOCCHIOSIS.
SPEAK UP, BOY!
THAT IS NOT MR. JOHNSON! YOU'RE BEING MANIPULATED, CAPTAIN. BY ORNA PEGANU.
THE BOUNTY HUNTER?
SHE'S AFTER MR. JOHNSON (I THINK) AND I STOPPED HER. SHE LURED YOU TO MARS TO SQUEEZE MY BOOTS! OR HAVE YOU DO IT FOR HER.
YOU'LL EXCUSE ME IF I FIND IT HARD TO SWALLOW THAT A BOUNTY HUNTER COULD SET IN MOTION THE SERIES OF EVENTS THAT GOT THE INDOMITABLE INTO THIS JURISDICTION AND THEN SENT AN ALERT ABOUT THE QALIFRADRAXIAN UNDER FALSE PRETENSES.
IT WAS A STRANGE SERIES OF EVENTS, HON. SHOULD WE DISPLAY THEM?
TECHS-AND-SPECS, BE A DEAR AND DISPLAY THE RECENT SERIES OF EVENTS?
BELAY THAT PLEASE AND THANK YOU.
BELAYED.
TELEPORT-MAN KAWARD, MARS AGAIN, PLEASE. TO THE TEMP-JAIL.
MARSHAL'S--
DOOT

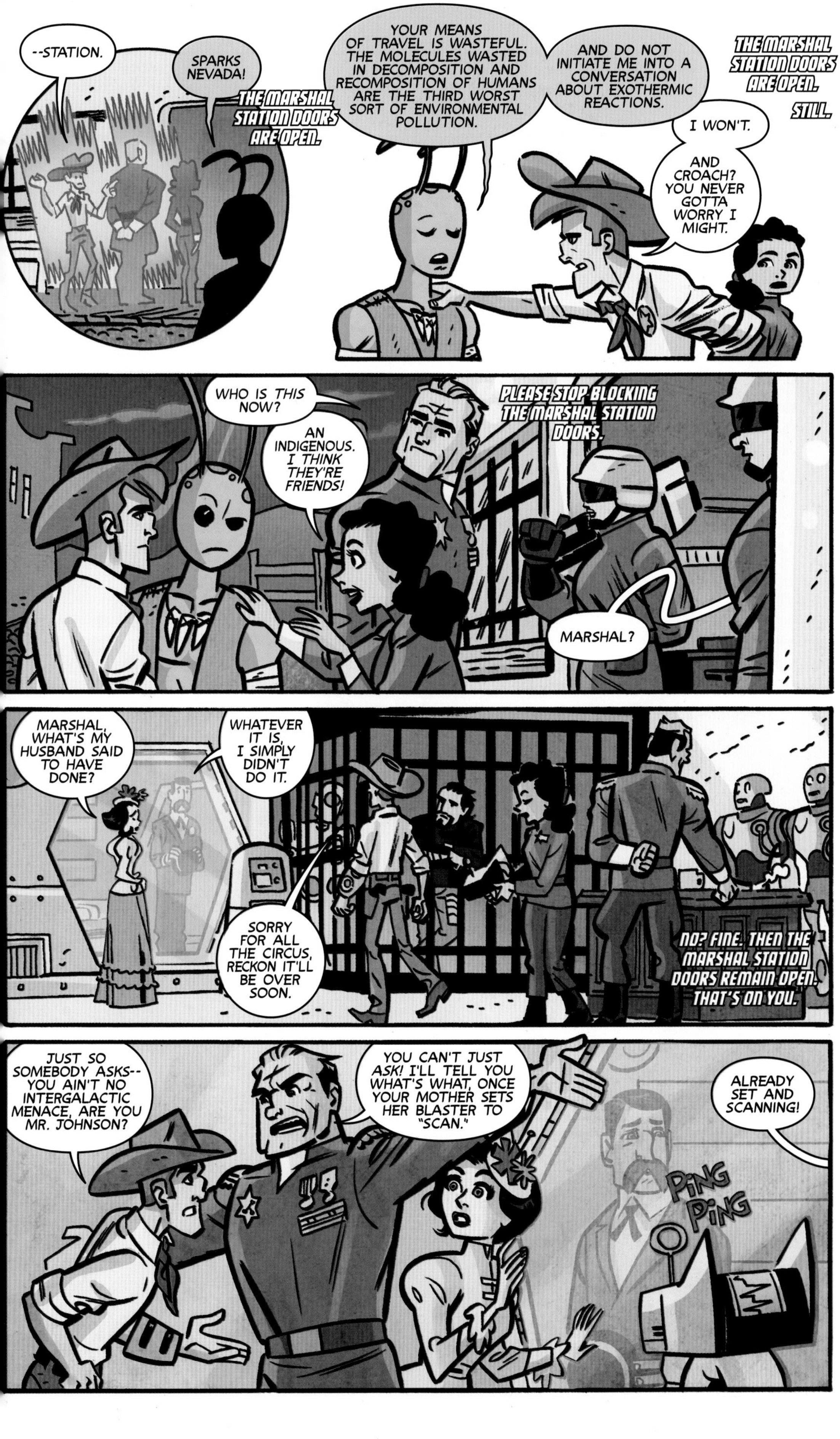
--STATION.
SPARKS NEVADA!
THE MARSHAL STATION DOORS ARE OPEN.
YOUR MEANS OF TRAVEL IS WASTEFUL. THE MOLECULES WASTED IN DECOMPOSITION AND RECOMPOSITION OF HUMANS ARE THE THIRD WORST SORT OF ENVIRONMENTAL POLLUTION.
AND DO NOT INITIATE ME INTO A CONVERSATION ABOUT EXOTHERMIC REACTIONS.
THE MARSHAL STATION DOORS ARE OPEN.
STILL.
I WON'T.
AND CROACH? YOU NEVER GOTTA WORRY I MIGHT.
WHO IS THIS NOW?
AN INDIGENOUS. I THINK THEY'RE FRIENDS!
PLEASE STOP BLOCKING THE MARSHAL STATION DOORS.
MARSHAL?
MARSHAL, WHAT'S MY HUSBAND SAID TO HAVE DONE?
WHATEVER IT IS, I SIMPLY DIDN'T DO IT.
SORRY FOR ALL THE CIRCUS, RECKON IT'LL BE OVER SOON.
NO? FINE. THEN THE MARSHAL STATION DOORS REMAIN OPEN. THAT'S ON YOU.
JUST SO SOMEBODY ASKS-- YOU AIN'T NO INTERGALACTIC MENACE, ARE YOU MR. JOHNSON?
YOU CAN'T JUST ASK! I'LL TELL YOU WHAT'S WHAT, ONCE YOUR MOTHER SETS HER BLASTER TO "SCAN."
ALREADY SET AND SCANNING!
PING PING

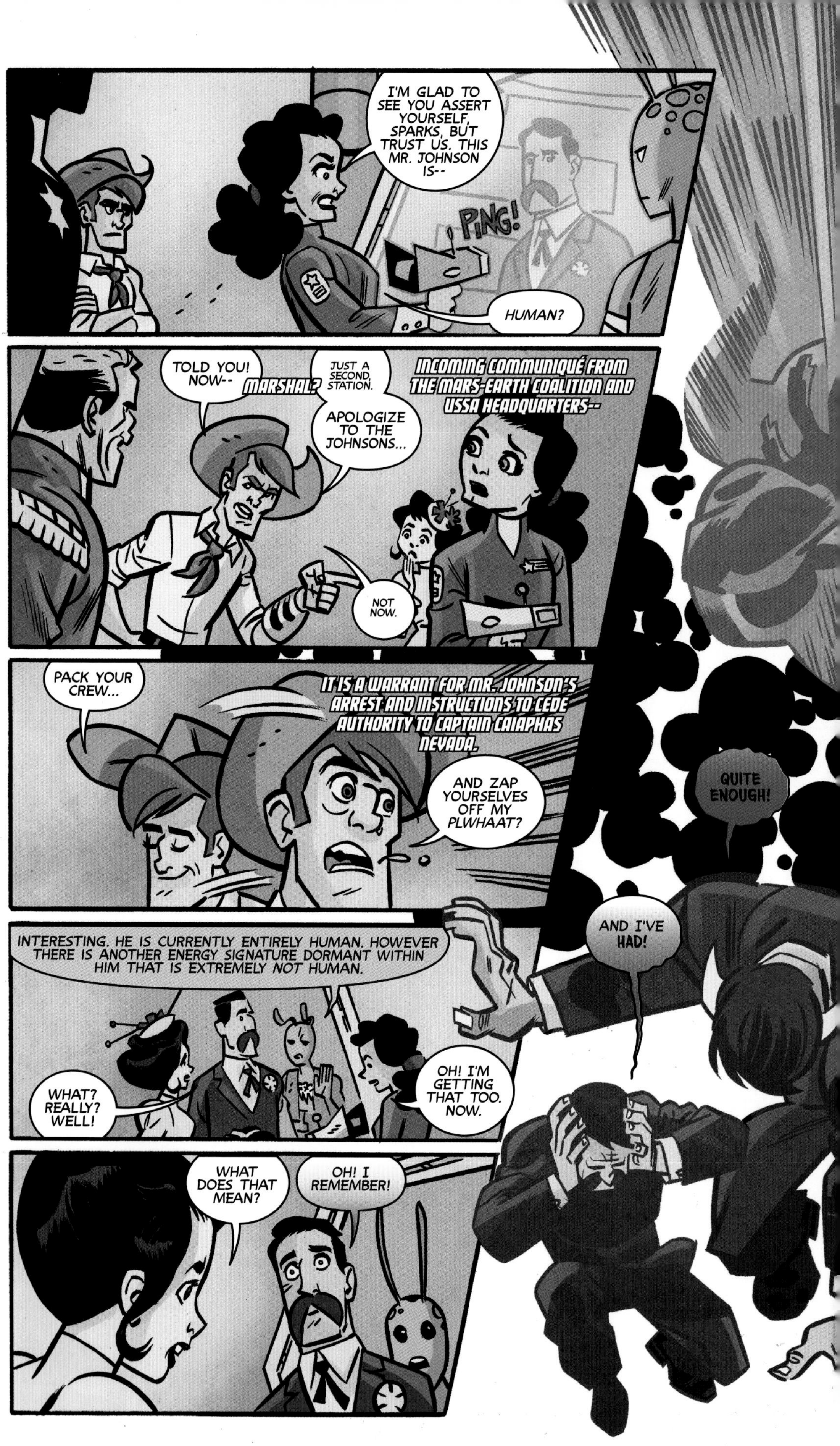
I'M GLAD TO SEE YOU ASSERT YOURSELF, SPARKS, BUT TRUST US. THIS MR. JOHNSON IS--
PING!
HUMAN?
TOLD YOU! NOW--
MARSHAL?
JUST A SECOND, STATION.
APOLOGIZE TO THE JOHNSONS...
INCOMING COMMUNIQUÉ FROM THE MARS-EARTH COALITION AND USSA HEADQUARTERS--
NOT NOW.
PACK YOUR CREW...
IT IS A WARRANT FOR MR. JOHNSON'S ARREST AND INSTRUCTIONS TO CEDE AUTHORITY TO CAPTAIN CAIAPHAS NEVADA.
AND ZAP YOURSELVES OFF MY PLWHAAT?
QUITE ENOUGH!
INTERESTING. HE IS CURRENTLY ENTIRELY HUMAN. HOWEVER THERE IS ANOTHER ENERGY SIGNATURE DORMANT WITHIN HIM THAT IS EXTREMELY NOT HUMAN.
AND I'VE HAD!
WHAT? REALLY? WELL!
OH! I'M GETTING THAT TOO. NOW.
WHAT DOES THAT MEAN?
OH! I REMEMBER!

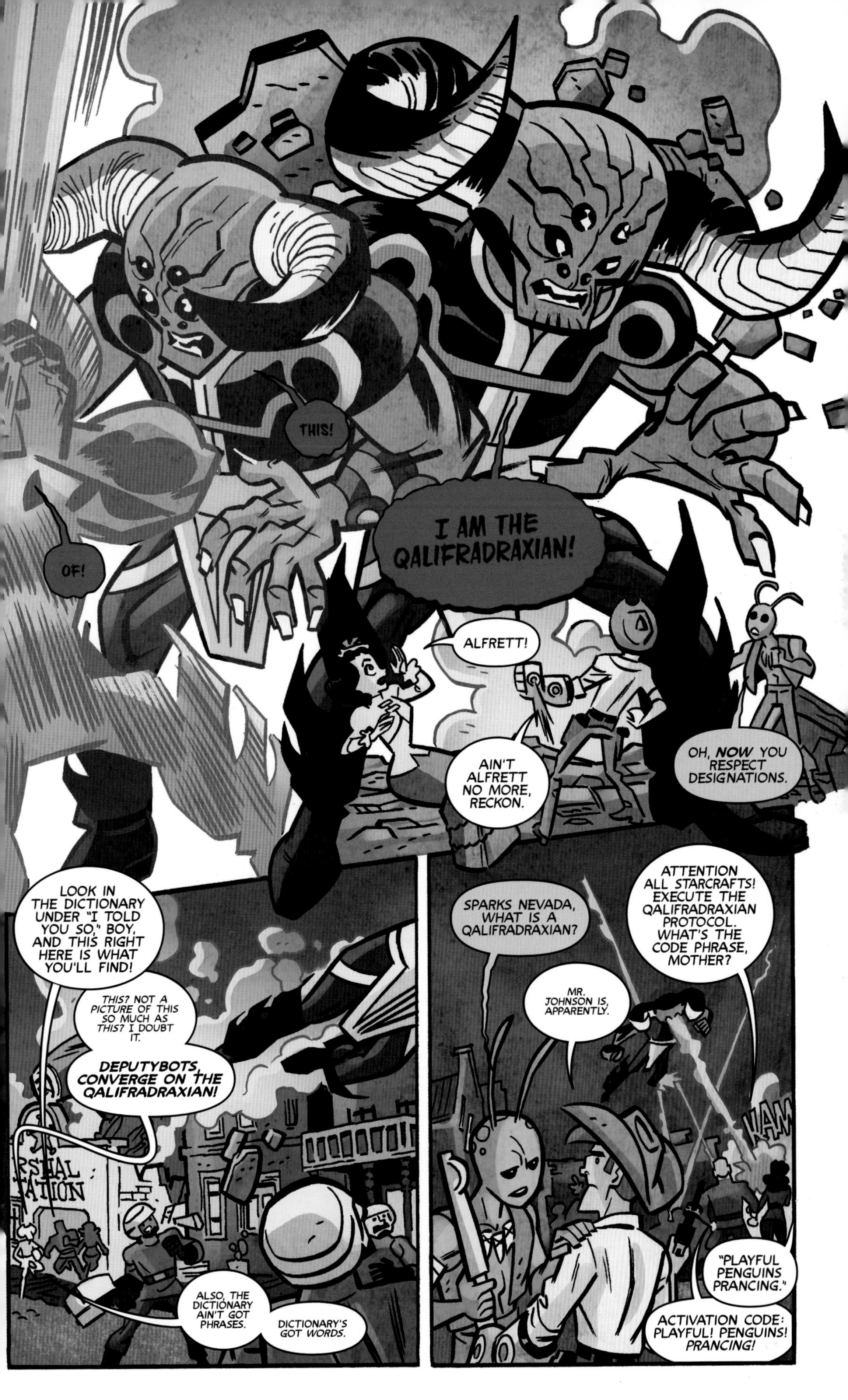

THIS!
OF!
I AM THE QALIFRADRAXIAN!
ALFRETT!
AIN'T ALFRETT NO MORE, RECKON.
OH, NOW YOU RESPECT DESIGNATIONS.
LOOK IN THE DICTIONARY UNDER "I TOLD YOU SO," BOY, AND THIS RIGHT HERE IS WHAT YOU'LL FIND!
THIS? NOT A PICTURE OF THIS SO MUCH AS THIS? I DOUBT IT.
DEPUTYBOTS, CONVERGE ON THE QALIFRADRAXIAN!
ALSO, THE DICTIONARY AIN'T GOT PHRASES.
DICTIONARY'S GOT WORDS.
SPARKS NEVADA, WHAT IS A QALIFRADRAXIAN?
MR. JOHNSON IS, APPARENTLY.
ATTENTION ALL STARCRAFTS! EXECUTE THE QALIFRADRAXIAN PROTOCOL. WHAT'S THE CODE PHRASE, MOTHER?
"PLAYFUL PENGUINS PRANCING."
ACTIVATION CODE: PLAYFUL! PENGUINS! PRANCING!

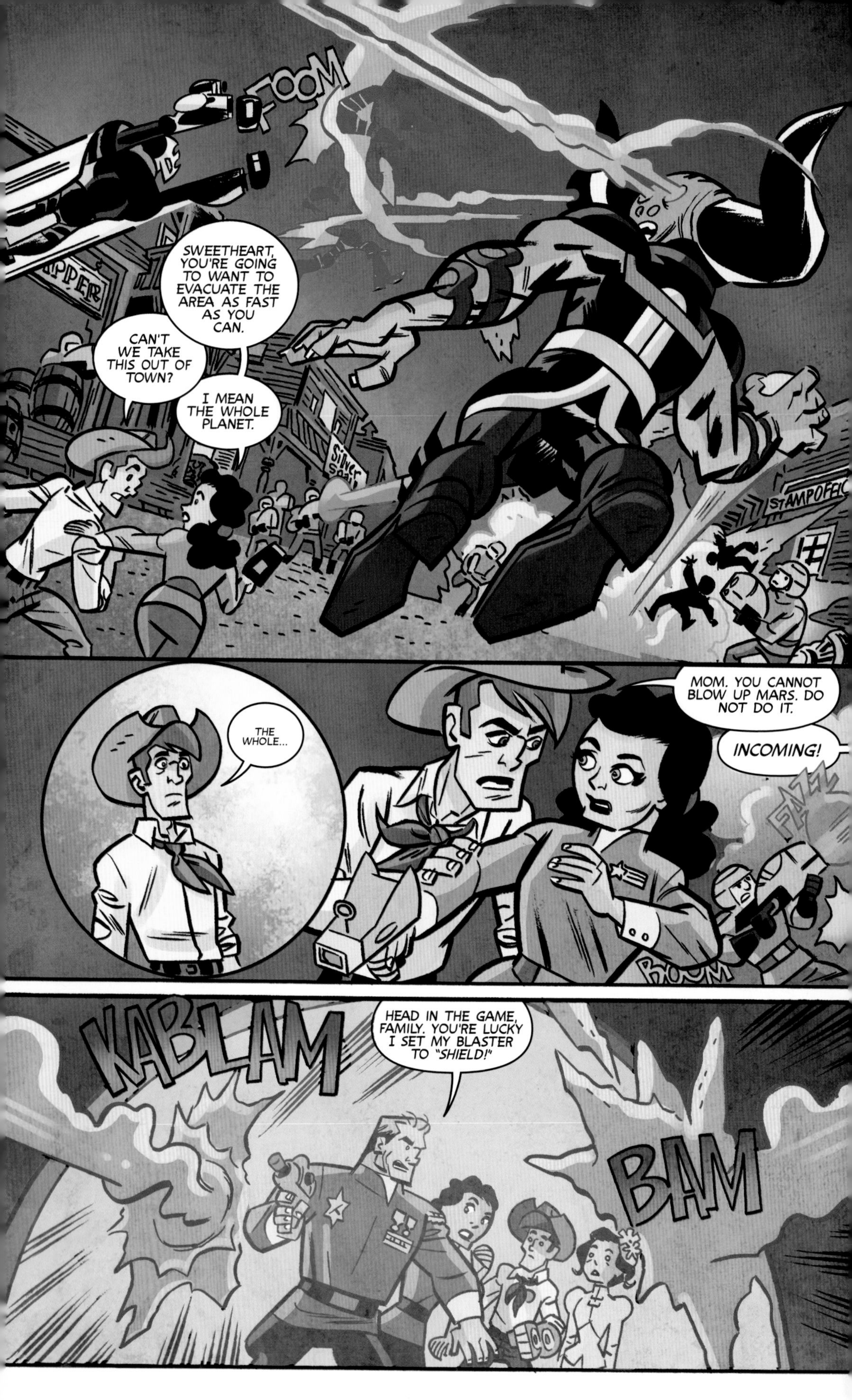

FOOM
SWEETHEART, YOU'RE GOING TO WANT TO EVACUATE THE AREA AS FAST AS YOU CAN.
CAN'T WE TAKE THIS OUT OF TOWN?
I MEAN THE WHOLE PLANET.
STAMPOFFIC
THE WHOLE...
MOM. YOU CANNOT BLOW UP MARS. DO NOT DO IT.
INCOMING!
BOOM
KABLAM
HEAD IN THE GAME, FAMILY. YOU'RE LUCKY I SET MY BLASTER TO "SHIELD!"
BAM

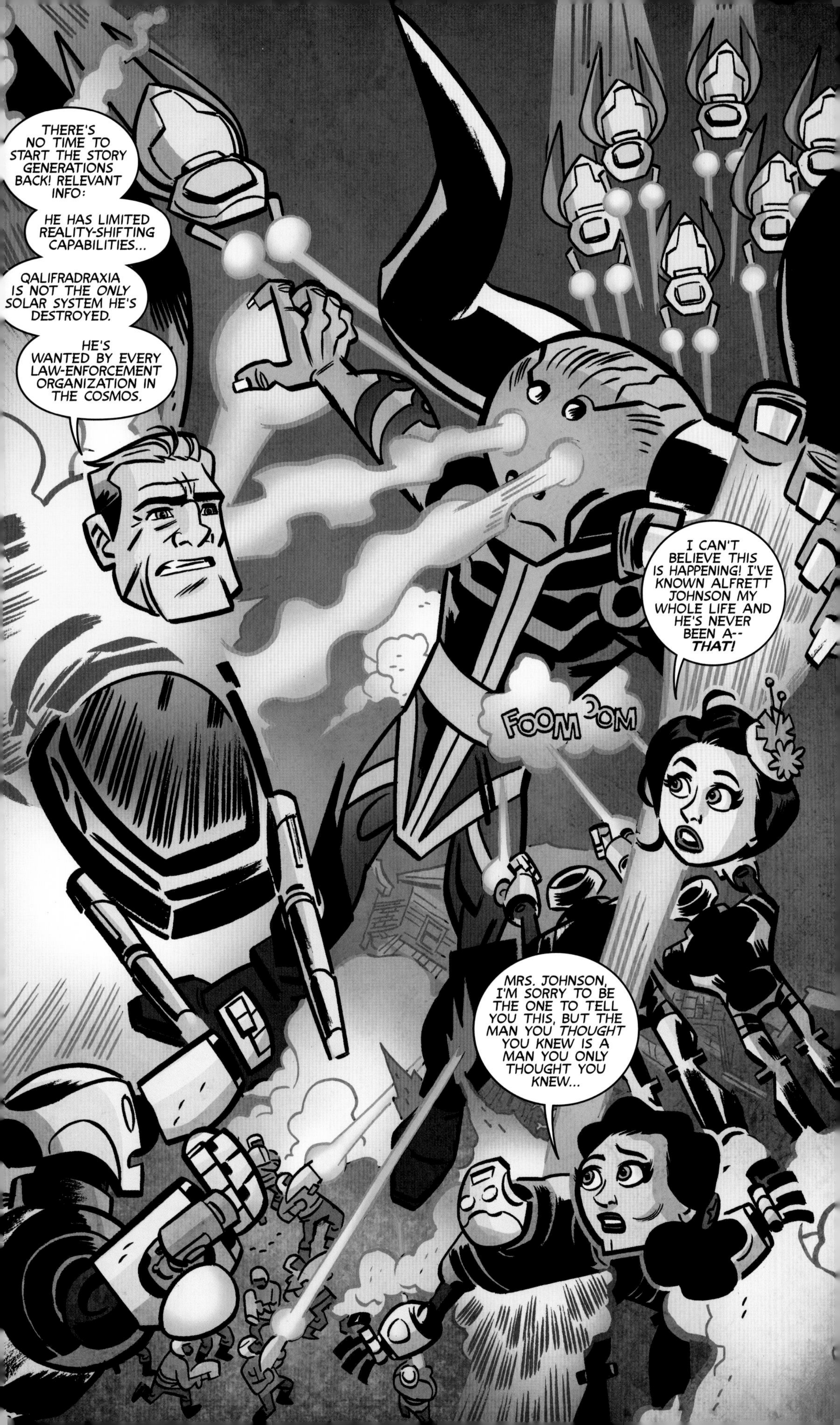
THERE'S NO TIME TO START THE STORY GENERATIONS BACK! RELEVANT INFO:
HE HAS LIMITED REALITY-SHIFTING CAPABILITIES...
QALIFRADRAXIA IS NOT THE ONLY SOLAR SYSTEM HE'S DESTROYED.
HE'S WANTED BY EVERY LAW-ENFORCEMENT ORGANIZATION IN THE COSMOS.
I CAN'T BELIEVE THIS IS HAPPENING! I'VE KNOWN ALFRETT JOHNSON MY WHOLE LIFE AND HE'S NEVER BEEN A-- *THAT!*
FOOM
FOOM
MRS. JOHNSON, I'M SORRY TO BE THE ONE TO TELL YOU THIS, BUT THE MAN YOU *THOUGHT* YOU KNEW IS A MAN YOU ONLY THOUGHT YOU KNEW...

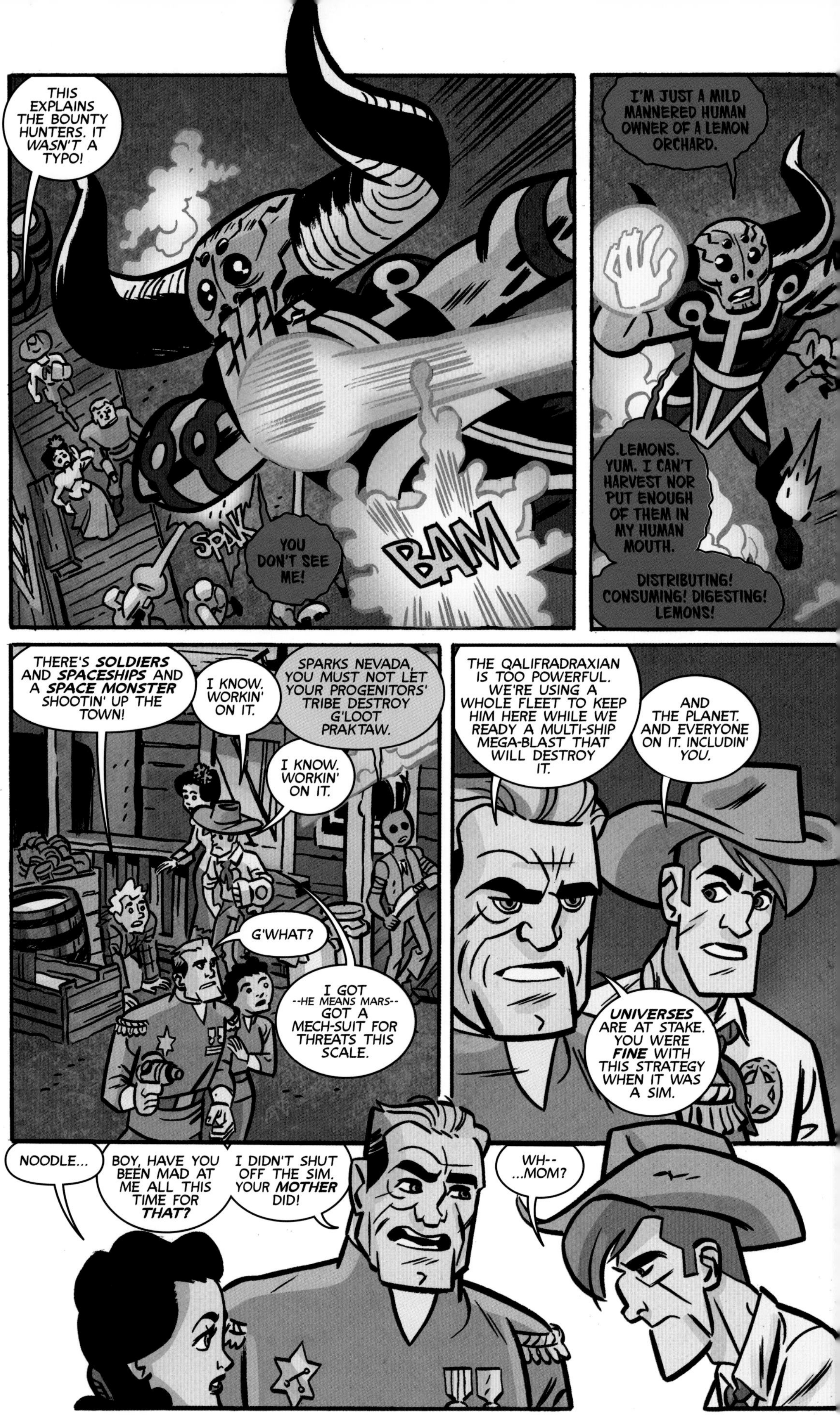
THIS EXPLAINS THE BOUNTY HUNTERS. IT WASN'T A TYPO!
SPAK
YOU DON'T SEE ME!
BAM
I'M JUST A MILD MANNERED HUMAN OWNER OF A LEMON ORCHARD.
LEMONS. YUM. I CAN'T HARVEST NOR PUT ENOUGH OF THEM IN MY HUMAN MOUTH.
DISTRIBUTING! CONSUMING! DIGESTING! LEMONS!
THERE'S SOLDIERS AND SPACESHIPS AND A SPACE MONSTER SHOOTIN' UP THE TOWN!
I KNOW. WORKIN' ON IT.
SPARKS NEVADA, YOU MUST NOT LET YOUR PROGENITORS' TRIBE DESTROY G'LOOT PRAKTAW.
I KNOW. WORKIN' ON IT.
G'WHAT?
I GOT --HE MEANS MARS-- GOT A MECH-SUIT FOR THREATS THIS SCALE.
THE QALIFRADRAXIAN IS TOO POWERFUL. WE'RE USING A WHOLE FLEET TO KEEP HIM HERE WHILE WE READY A MULTI-SHIP MEGA-BLAST THAT WILL DESTROY IT.
AND THE PLANET. AND EVERYONE ON IT. INCLUDIN' YOU.
UNIVERSES ARE AT STAKE. YOU WERE FINE WITH THIS STRATEGY WHEN IT WAS A SIM.
NOODLE...
BOY, HAVE YOU BEEN MAD AT ME ALL THIS TIME FOR THAT?
I DIDN'T SHUT OFF THE SIM. YOUR MOTHER DID!
WH-- ...MOM?

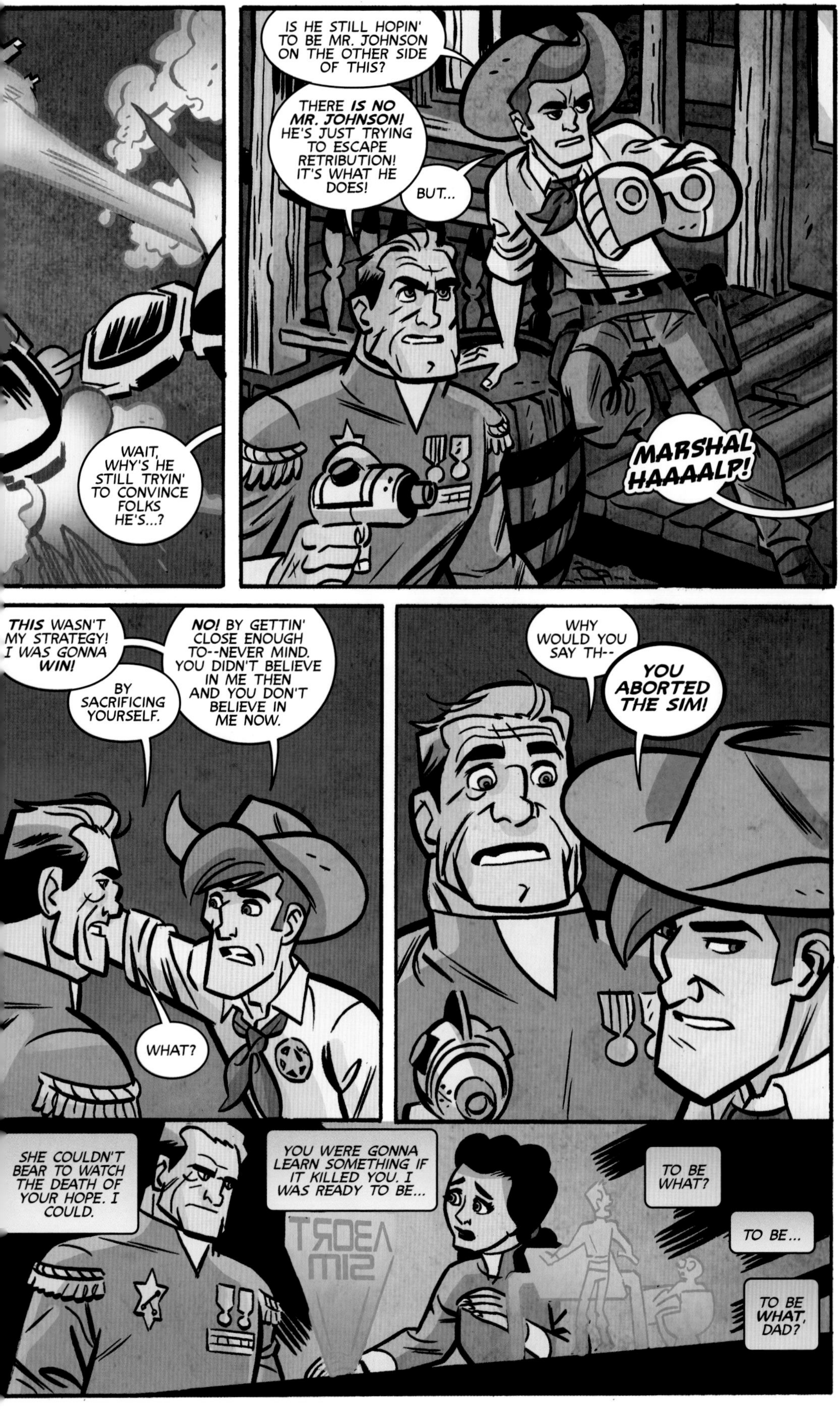
WAIT, WHY'S HE STILL TRYIN' TO CONVINCE FOLKS HE'S...?
IS HE STILL HOPIN' TO BE MR. JOHNSON ON THE OTHER SIDE OF THIS?
THERE **IS NO MR. JOHNSON!** HE'S JUST TRYING TO ESCAPE RETRIBUTION! IT'S WHAT HE DOES!
BUT...
MARSHAL HAAAALP!
THIS *WASN'T MY STRATEGY! I WAS GONNA* ***WIN!***
BY SACRIFICING YOURSELF.
NO! BY GETTIN' CLOSE ENOUGH TO--NEVER MIND. YOU DIDN'T BELIEVE IN ME THEN AND YOU DON'T BELIEVE IN ME NOW.
WHAT?
WHY WOULD YOU SAY TH--
YOU ABORTED THE SIM!
SHE COULDN'T BEAR TO WATCH THE DEATH OF YOUR HOPE. I COULD.
YOU WERE GONNA LEARN SOMETHING IF IT KILLED YOU. I WAS READY TO BE...
ABORT SIM
TO BE WHAT?
TO BE...
TO BE ***WHAT,*** *DAD?*

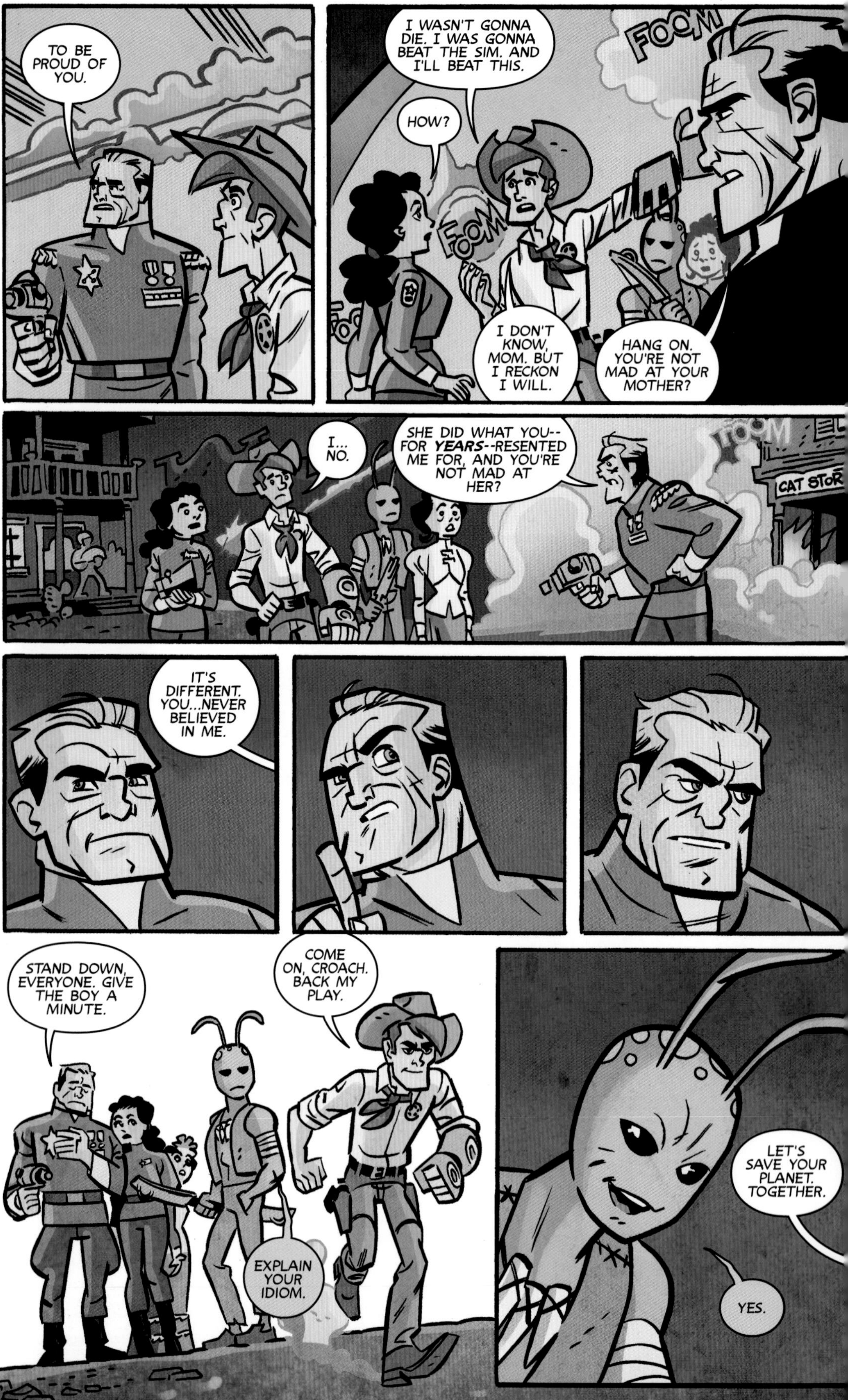
TO BE PROUD OF YOU.
FOOM
I WASN'T GONNA DIE. I WAS GONNA BEAT THE SIM. AND I'LL BEAT THIS.
HOW?
FOOM
I DON'T KNOW, MOM. BUT I RECKON I WILL.
HANG ON. YOU'RE NOT MAD AT YOUR MOTHER?
I... NO.
SHE DID WHAT YOU--FOR ***YEARS***--RESENTED ME FOR, AND YOU'RE NOT MAD AT HER?
FOOM
CAT STOR
IT'S DIFFERENT. YOU...NEVER BELIEVED IN ME.
STAND DOWN, EVERYONE. GIVE THE BOY A MINUTE.
COME ON, CROACH. BACK MY PLAY.
EXPLAIN YOUR IDIOM.
LET'S SAVE YOUR PLANET. TOGETHER.
YES.

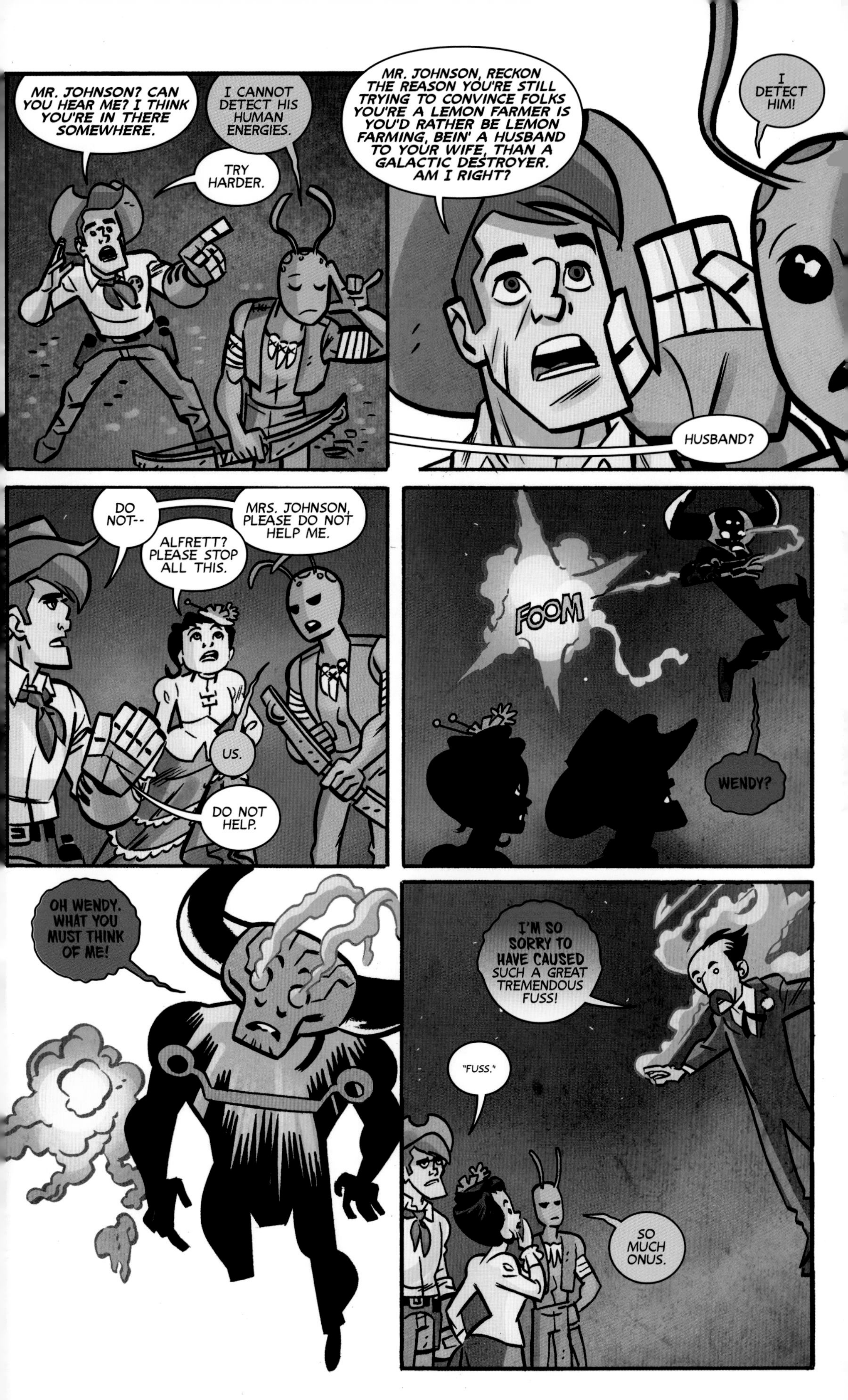
MR. JOHNSON? CAN YOU HEAR ME? I THINK YOU'RE IN THERE SOMEWHERE.
I CANNOT DETECT HIS HUMAN ENERGIES.
TRY HARDER.
MR. JOHNSON, RECKON THE REASON YOU'RE STILL TRYING TO CONVINCE FOLKS YOU'RE A LEMON FARMER IS YOU'D RATHER BE LEMON FARMING, BEIN' A HUSBAND TO YOUR WIFE, THAN A GALACTIC DESTROYER. AM I RIGHT?
I DETECT HIM!
HUSBAND?
DO NOT--
MRS. JOHNSON, PLEASE DO NOT HELP ME.
ALFRETT? PLEASE STOP ALL THIS.
US.
DO NOT HELP.
FOOM
WENDY?
OH WENDY. WHAT YOU MUST THINK OF ME!
I'M SO SORRY TO HAVE CAUSED SUCH A GREAT TREMENDOUS FUSS!
"FUSS."
SO MUCH ONUS.

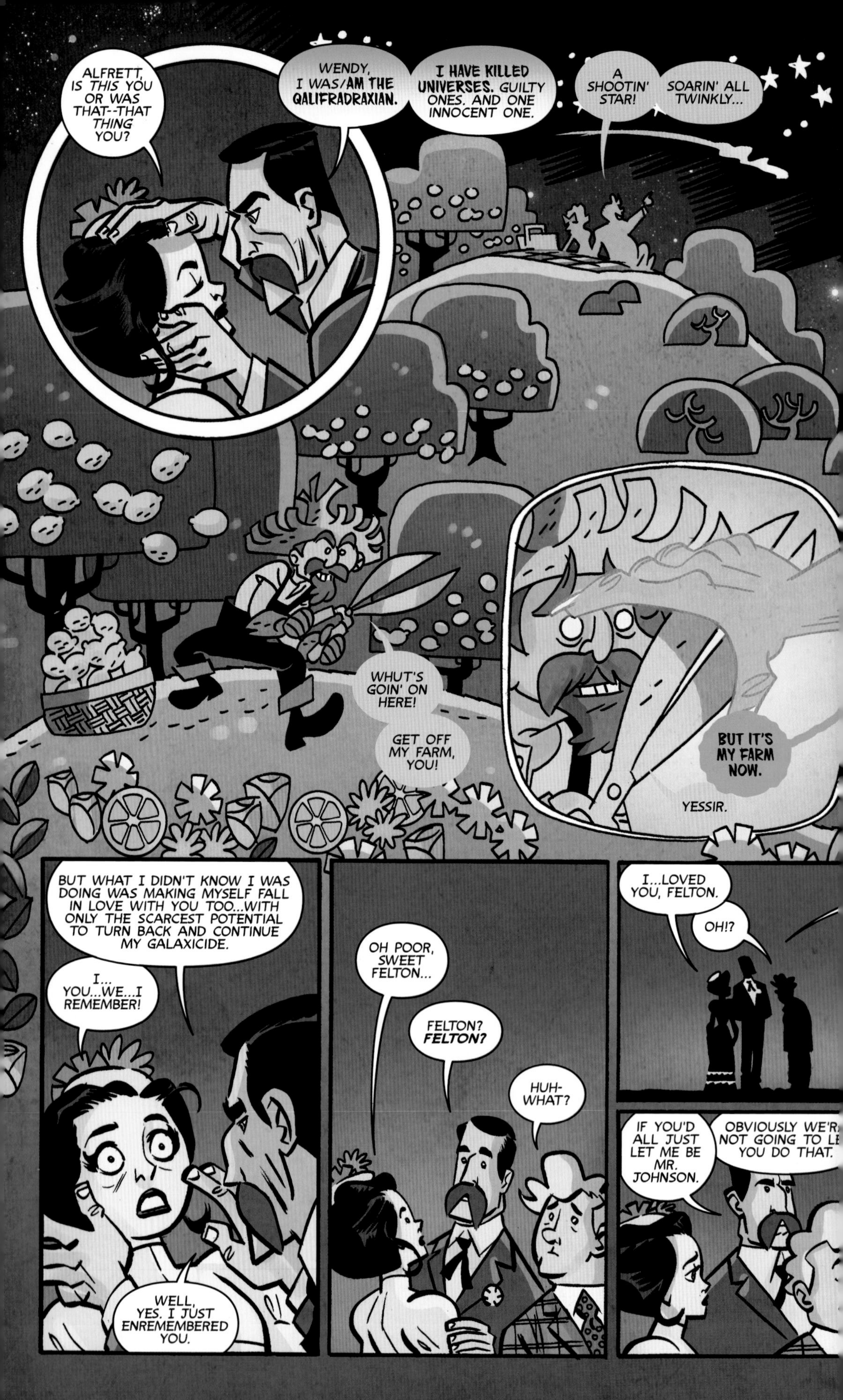

ALFRETT, IS THIS YOU OR WAS THAT--THAT THING YOU?
WENDY, I WAS/AM THE QALIFRADRAXIAN.
I HAVE KILLED UNIVERSES. GUILTY ONES, AND ONE INNOCENT ONE.
A SHOOTIN' STAR!
SOARIN' ALL TWINKLY...
WHUT'S GOIN' ON HERE!
GET OFF MY FARM, YOU!
BUT IT'S MY FARM NOW.
YESSIR.
BUT WHAT I DIDN'T KNOW I WAS DOING WAS MAKING MYSELF FALL IN LOVE WITH YOU TOO...WITH ONLY THE SCARCEST POTENTIAL TO TURN BACK AND CONTINUE MY GALAXICIDE.
I... YOU...WE...I REMEMBER!
WELL, YES. I JUST ENREMEMBERED YOU.
OH POOR, SWEET FELTON...
FELTON? FELTON?
HUH-WHAT?
I...LOVED YOU, FELTON.
OH!?
IF YOU'D ALL JUST LET ME BE MR. JOHNSON.
OBVIOUSLY WE'R
NOT GOING TO LE
YOU DO THAT.

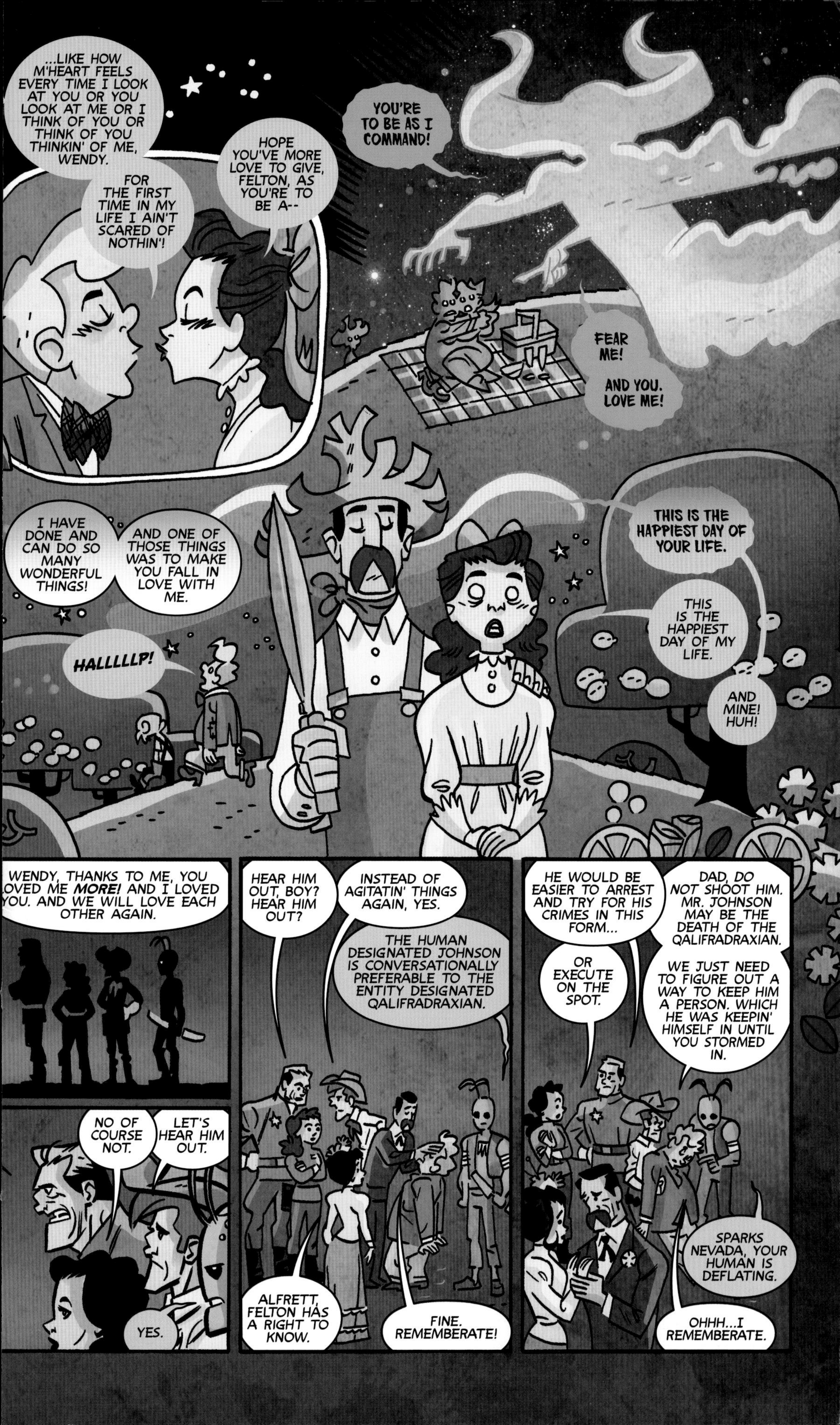
...LIKE HOW M'HEART FEELS EVERY TIME I LOOK AT YOU OR YOU LOOK AT ME OR I THINK OF YOU OR THINK OF YOU THINKIN' OF ME, WENDY.
FOR THE FIRST TIME IN MY LIFE I AIN'T SCARED OF NOTHIN'!
HOPE YOU'VE MORE LOVE TO GIVE, FELTON, AS YOU'RE TO BE A--
YOU'RE TO BE AS I COMMAND!
FEAR ME!
AND YOU. LOVE ME!
I HAVE DONE AND CAN DO SO MANY WONDERFUL THINGS!
AND ONE OF THOSE THINGS WAS TO MAKE YOU FALL IN LOVE WITH ME.
HALLLLLP!
THIS IS THE HAPPIEST DAY OF YOUR LIFE.
THIS IS THE HAPPIEST DAY OF MY LIFE.
AND MINE! HUH!
WENDY, THANKS TO ME, YOU LOVED ME *MORE!* AND I LOVED YOU. AND WE WILL LOVE EACH OTHER AGAIN.
NO OF COURSE NOT.
LET'S HEAR HIM OUT.
YES.
HEAR HIM OUT, BOY? HEAR HIM OUT?
INSTEAD OF AGITATIN' THINGS AGAIN, YES.
THE HUMAN DESIGNATED JOHNSON IS CONVERSATIONALLY PREFERABLE TO THE ENTITY DESIGNATED QALIFRADRAXIAN.
ALFRETT, FELTON HAS A RIGHT TO KNOW.
FINE. REMEMBERATE!
HE WOULD BE EASIER TO ARREST AND TRY FOR HIS CRIMES IN THIS FORM...
OR EXECUTE ON THE SPOT.
DAD, *DO* NOT SHOOT HIM. MR. JOHNSON MAY BE THE DEATH OF THE QALIFRADRAXIAN.
WE JUST NEED TO FIGURE OUT A WAY TO KEEP HIM A PERSON. WHICH HE WAS KEEPIN' HIMSELF IN UNTIL YOU STORMED IN.
SPARKS NEVADA, YOUR HUMAN IS DEFLATING.
OHHH...I REMEMBERATE.

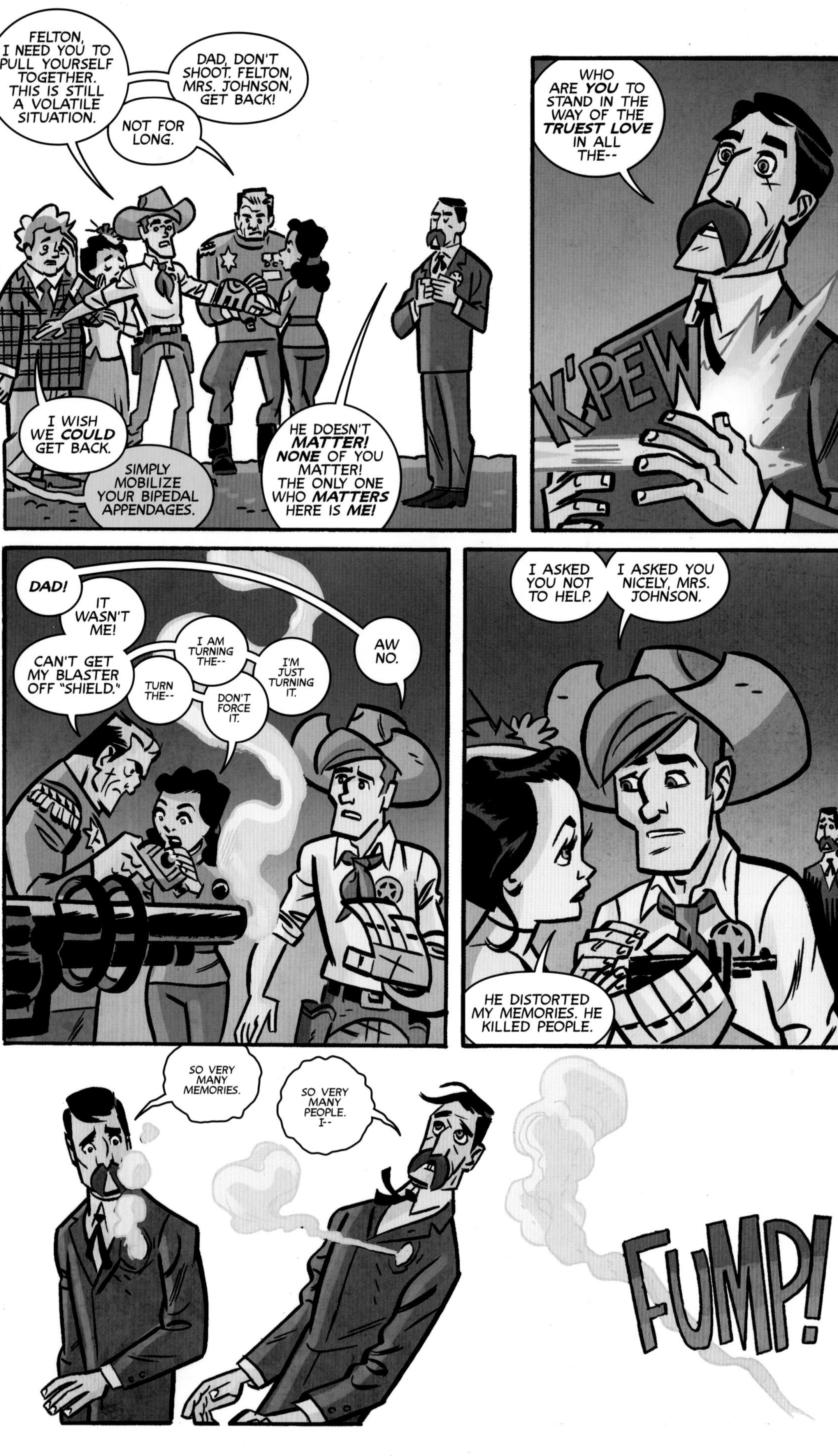
FELTON, I NEED YOU TO PULL YOURSELF TOGETHER. THIS IS STILL A VOLATILE SITUATION.
DAD, DON'T SHOOT. FELTON, MRS. JOHNSON, GET BACK!
NOT FOR LONG.
I WISH WE COULD GET BACK.
SIMPLY MOBILIZE YOUR BIPEDAL APPENDAGES.
HE DOESN'T MATTER! NONE OF YOU MATTER! THE ONLY ONE WHO MATTERS HERE IS ME!
WHO ARE YOU TO STAND IN THE WAY OF THE TRUEST LOVE IN ALL THE--
K'PEW
DAD!
IT WASN'T ME!
AW NO.
CAN'T GET MY BLASTER OFF "SHIELD."
I AM TURNING THE--
TURN THE--
DON'T FORCE IT.
I'M JUST TURNING IT.
I ASKED YOU NOT TO HELP.
I ASKED YOU NICELY, MRS. JOHNSON.
HE DISTORTED MY MEMORIES. HE KILLED PEOPLE.
SO VERY MANY MEMORIES.
SO VERY MANY PEOPLE. I--
FUMP!

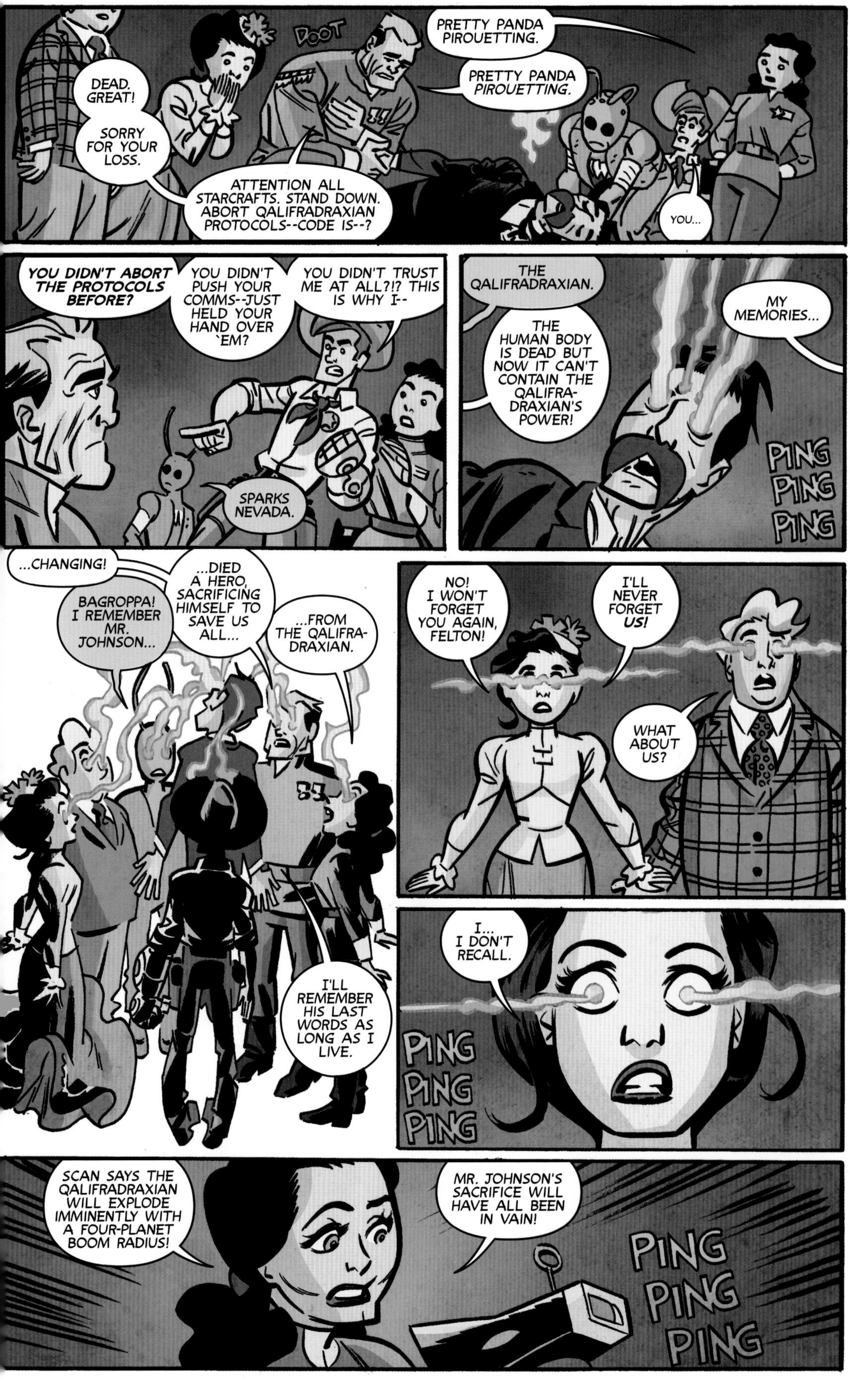
DOOT
PRETTY PANDA PIROUETTING.
PRETTY PANDA PIROUETTING.
DEAD. GREAT!
SORRY FOR YOUR LOSS.
ATTENTION ALL STARCRAFTS. STAND DOWN. ABORT QALIFRADRAXIAN PROTOCOLS--CODE IS--?
YOU...
YOU DIDN'T ABORT THE PROTOCOLS BEFORE?
YOU DIDN'T PUSH YOUR COMMS--JUST HELD YOUR HAND OVER `EM?
YOU DIDN'T TRUST ME AT ALL?!? THIS IS WHY I--
SPARKS NEVADA.
THE QALIFRADRAXIAN.
THE HUMAN BODY IS DEAD BUT NOW IT CAN'T CONTAIN THE QALIFRADRAXIAN'S POWER!
MY MEMORIES...
PING PING PING
...CHANGING!
BAGROPPA! I REMEMBER MR. JOHNSON...
...DIED A HERO, SACRIFICING HIMSELF TO SAVE US ALL...
...FROM THE QALIFRADRAXIAN.
I'LL REMEMBER HIS LAST WORDS AS LONG AS I LIVE.
NO! I WON'T FORGET YOU AGAIN, FELTON!
I'LL NEVER FORGET US!
WHAT ABOUT US?
I... I DON'T RECALL.
PING PING PING
SCAN SAYS THE QALIFRADRAXIAN WILL EXPLODE IMMINENTLY WITH A FOUR-PLANET BOOM RADIUS!
MR. JOHNSON'S SACRIFICE WILL HAVE ALL BEEN IN VAIN!
PING PING PING

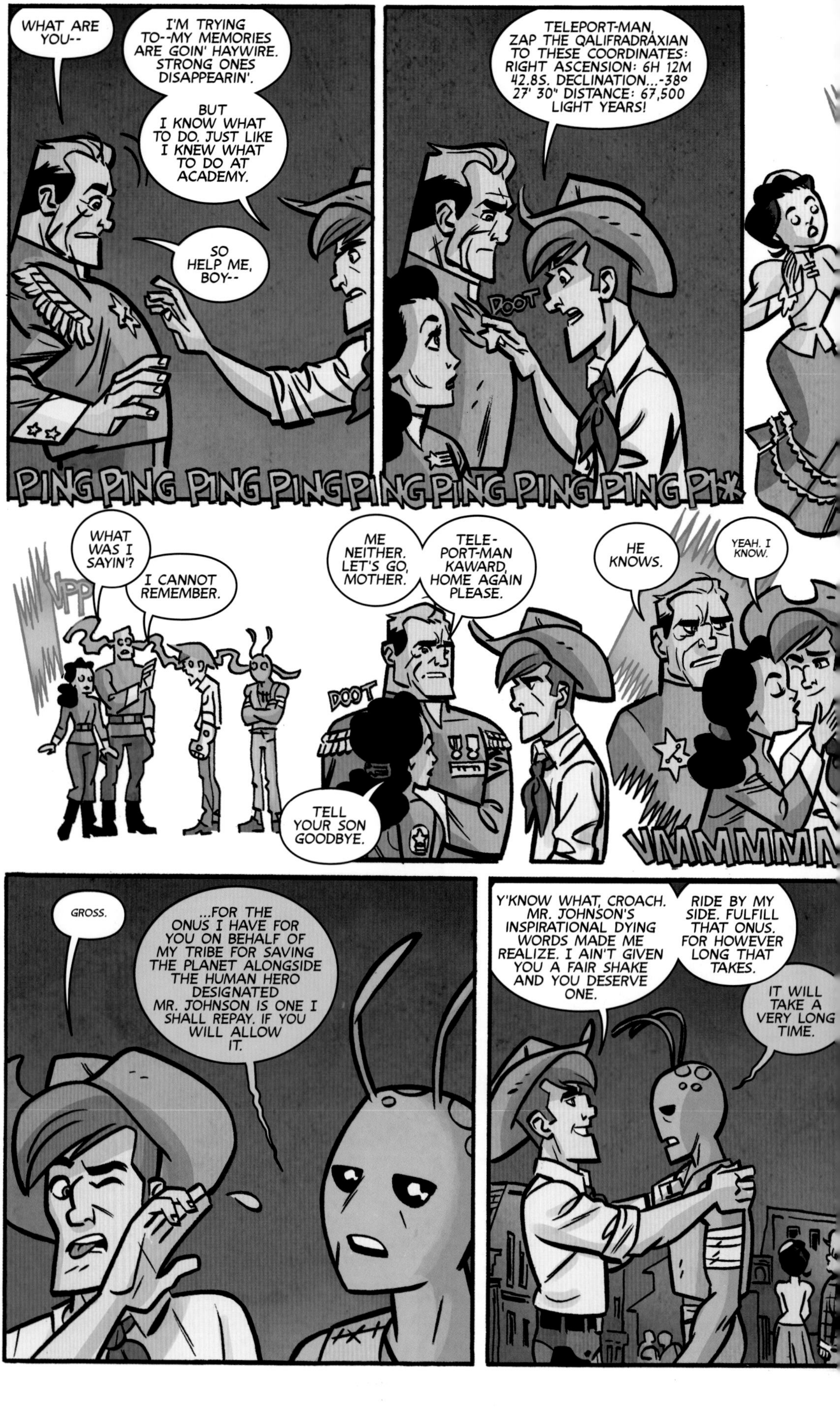
WHAT ARE YOU--
I'M TRYING TO--MY MEMORIES ARE GOIN' HAYWIRE. STRONG ONES DISAPPEARIN'.
BUT I KNOW WHAT TO DO. JUST LIKE I KNEW WHAT TO DO AT ACADEMY.
SO HELP ME, BOY--
TELEPORT-MAN, ZAP THE QALIFRADRAXIAN TO THESE COORDINATES: RIGHT ASCENSION: 6H 12M 42.8S. DECLINATION...-38° 27' 30" DISTANCE: 67,500 LIGHT YEARS!
DOOT
PING PING PING PING PING PING PING PING PI*
WHAT WAS I SAYIN'?
I CANNOT REMEMBER.
VPP
ME NEITHER. LET'S GO, MOTHER.
TELE-PORT-MAN KAWARD, HOME AGAIN PLEASE.
DOOT
TELL YOUR SON GOODBYE.
HE KNOWS.
YEAH. I KNOW.
VMMMMMM
GROSS.
...FOR THE ONUS I HAVE FOR YOU ON BEHALF OF MY TRIBE FOR SAVING THE PLANET ALONGSIDE THE HUMAN HERO DESIGNATED MR. JOHNSON IS ONE I SHALL REPAY. IF YOU WILL ALLOW IT.
Y'KNOW WHAT, CROACH. MR. JOHNSON'S INSPIRATIONAL DYING WORDS MADE ME REALIZE. I AIN'T GIVEN YOU A FAIR SHAKE AND YOU DESERVE ONE.
RIDE BY MY SIDE. FULFILL THAT ONUS. FOR HOWEVER LONG THAT TAKES.
IT WILL TAKE A VERY LONG TIME.

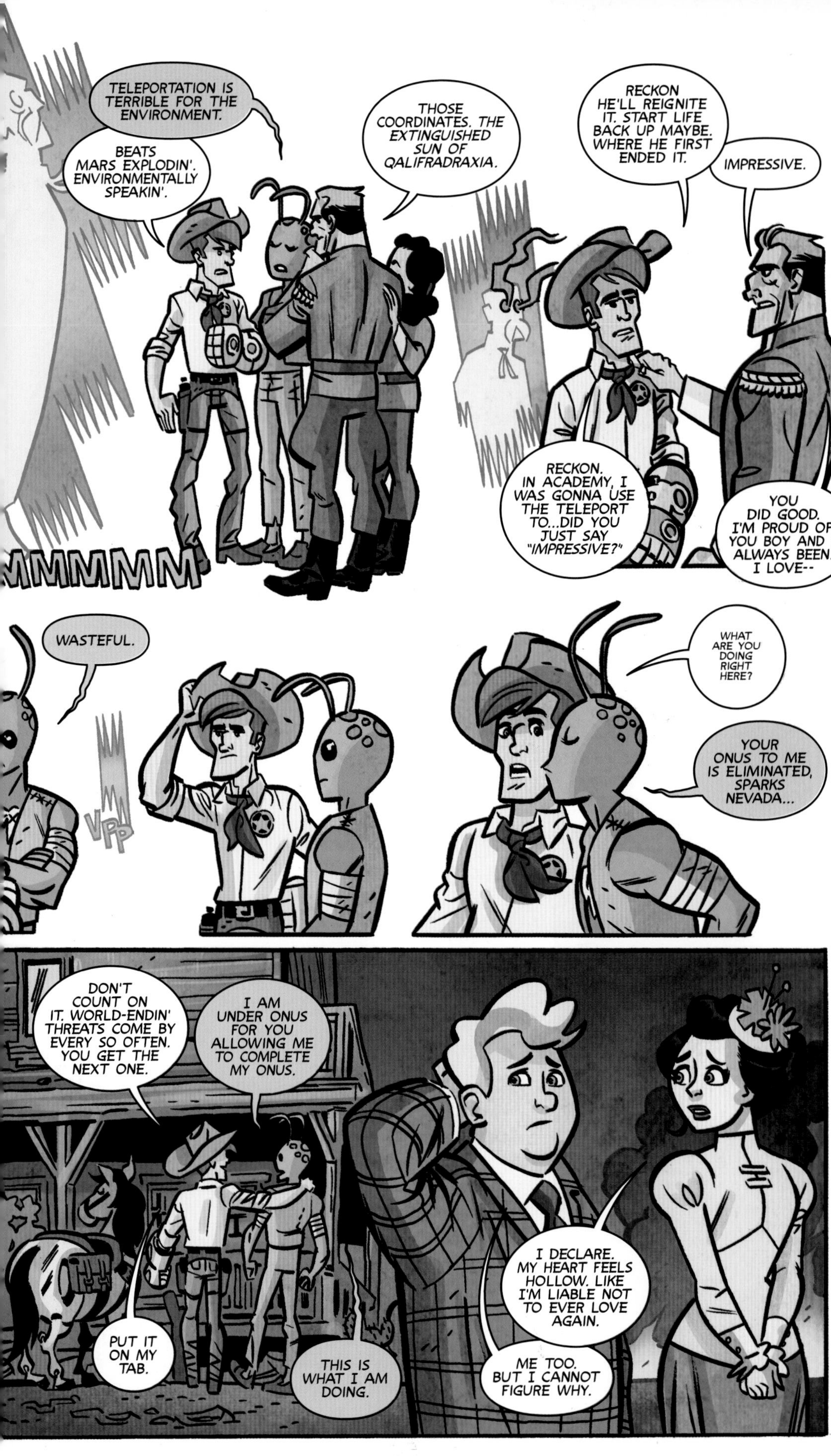
TELEPORTATION IS TERRIBLE FOR THE ENVIRONMENT.
BEATS MARS EXPLODIN'. ENVIRONMENTALLY SPEAKIN'.
THOSE COORDINATES. THE EXTINGUISHED SUN OF QALIFRADRAXIA.
MMMMMM
RECKON HE'LL REIGNITE IT. START LIFE BACK UP MAYBE. WHERE HE FIRST ENDED IT.
IMPRESSIVE.
RECKON. IN ACADEMY, I WAS GONNA USE THE TELEPORT TO...DID YOU JUST SAY "IMPRESSIVE?"
YOU DID GOOD. I'M PROUD OF YOU BOY AND I ALWAYS BEEN. I LOVE--
WASTEFUL.
VPP
WHAT ARE YOU DOING RIGHT HERE?
YOUR ONUS TO ME IS ELIMINATED, SPARKS NEVADA...
DON'T COUNT ON IT. WORLD-ENDIN' THREATS COME BY EVERY SO OFTEN. YOU GET THE NEXT ONE.
I AM UNDER ONUS FOR YOU ALLOWING ME TO COMPLETE MY ONUS.
PUT IT ON MY TAB.
THIS IS WHAT I AM DOING.
I DECLARE. MY HEART FEELS HOLLOW. LIKE I'M LIABLE NOT TO EVER LOVE AGAIN.
ME TOO. BUT I CANNOT FIGURE WHY.

BEHIND-THE-SCENES

A LOOK AT THE ORIGINAL SCRIPT FOR ISSUE #0 WITH COMMENTARY BY WRITERS BEN ACKER AND BEN BLACKER.

[1] *Acker: There was never any conversation about whether Sparks loves paperwork. The rule is, if the actor wears a bow tie, the character loves paperwork.*

[2] *Acker: I spent way too long trying to google the sound effect that Star Trek comics use for their doors. What is Star Trek trying to hide?*

[3] *Blacker: I'm pretty certain Felton was meant to be a throwaway character in the original stage show, sort of the voice of the townspeople whom Sparks serves. The way that Craig Cackowski voiced him endeared the character to us, and he became more circumloquacious with every episode in which he appeared. Not a great trait for comics, where space is limited.*

[4] *Blacker: "Whatever the bank is!" is a great line that I'd forgotten about.*

[5] *Blacker: "The whole! Durn! Town!" is SO in Cackowski's voice.*

[6] *Blacker: One of the great aspects of the language of comics is its ability to mimic certain cinematic tropes, especially as it pertains to pacing a story. Asking an artist for "Leone style" editing is demanding, but ultimately can really impact the feel of a book and amp up tension in what is, at its base, a static medium.*

PAGE ONE --
Panel 1
Establishing "when varmits need a catchin'" etc. One man rights the outlaw wrongs on Mars.

Panel 2
Sparks filling out paperwork at his desk in the Marshal station. [1]

> CAP (MARSHAL STATION AI): Marshal. A citizen requests "haaaaalp."
> SPARKS: Paperwork'll wait. Let him in.
> SFX: PWSHT-PWSHT! [2]
> CAP (MARSHAL STATION AI): The Marshal Station doors are open. The Marshal will see you.

Panel 3
Felton runs in.

> FELTON: MARSHAL HAAAALP! The town's bein'—she still ain't come back? [3]

Panel 4
Sparks up and ready to go.

> SPARKS: She ain't <u>comin'</u> back, Felton or she'd be back already. Now what's the town bein'?
> FELTON: ROBBED!

Panel 5
Split panel of saloon, feed, store, bank, gelato, stable being held up by gangs of robots, all in silhouette against the big windows with the names of the buildings written on them.

> FELTON: Every store and shop and whatever the bank is! [4] The whole! Durn! Town! [5]
> FELTON: Only place hain't bein' robbed is this here Marshal Station! Suspicious!

PAGE TWO --
Feel free to "Marvel Way" this page to give it even more of the feel of Leone style cutting. [6] *DEPUTYBOTS are clearly labeled as such. They are more basic than the robot outlaws they are currently running with. The Deputybots should be identical but with different numbers. The rest of the robots are outlaws with handkerchiefs and other cowboy accoutrements that mix and match being distinct pieces or metal and part of them.*

Panel 1

Establishing the thoroughfare outside the Marshal station (which is capable of liftoff and being a rocket), Sparks taps his badge like a Star Trek communicator. [7] Felton cowers in the doorway

    SPARKS: Attention Deputybots. Six 8.13s are in progress. Get online and stay there.
    SMALL CAP (MARSHAL STATION AI): The Marshal Station doors are open...
    SMALL SFX: PWSHT-PWSHT!

Panel 2

Over the shoulder shot of a shadowy DEPUTYBOT talking to Sparks.

    DEPUTYBOT: And who do you reckon organized them 8.13's?

Panel 3

Reverse shot, but instead of being over Sparks's shoulder, we're in a Sergio Leone shot of his hand hovering over his holster and beyond that, we've got Deputybot 3, guns drawn.

    DEPUTYBOT: I know what you're thinkin'...

Panel 4

Letterbox panel of Sparks's eyes, cool.

    DEPUTYBOT: "How'd y'all automatons get free will?"

Panel 5

Letterbox panel of Deputybot's mouth.

    DEPUTYBOT: Love changes a bot, Marshal. So does a birthday candle wish. So does peer pressure. And that's how your three Deputybots pinocchio'd our way to- [8]
    SFX: k'pew! [9]

Panel 6

Sparks has drawn his laser six-shooter. [10] The Deputybot is on the ground, a hole in him.

    SPARKS: One down.
    DEPUTYBOT 2: ...you to go.

PAGE THREE -
Nine panel grid!

Panel 1

Sparks shooting Deputybot 2.

    SPARKS: Not where I was goin' with that.
    SFX: k'pew!
    ANOTHER ROBOT: Can't shoot all of us, Marshal!

Panel 2

The panel is bisected diagonally left bottom to right top by the k'pew sound effect. On the left side of panel, DEPUTYBOT 2 is on the ground and ANOTHER ROBOT says his piece. On the right side of panel, he collapses on top of Deputybot 2!

    ANOTHER ROBOT: Not if you hope to -UNGH!
    SFX: k'pew!

Panel 3
YET ANOTHER ROBOT is shot.

    YET ANOTHER ROBOT: Can't shoot us all AND st-OW!
    SFX: k'pew!

Panel 4
THIS ROBOT NOW is shot.

    THIS ROBOT NOW: And stop the- DAG-GUMMIT!
    SFX: k'pew!

Panel 5
And THIS ONE too.

    THIS ONE: Gonna wanta hear this ...
    THIS ONE: ...there is a huge t-YOW!
    SFX: k'pew!

Panel 6
This ROBOT BUCKAROO talks and waves his hands in front of him all like "don't shoot me!"

    ROBOT BUCKAROO: Youcan'tshootusallandstopthefloodheadin'in
    ROBOT BUCKAROO: duetotheicecapMarswearsforahatbein'meltedbyLaserfaceLloyd
    ROBOT BUCKAROO: and-
    ROBOT BUCKAROO: and-

Panel 7
The robot buckaroo winces. Still alive.

    ROBOT BUCKAROO: And...what do you know about that?

Panel 8
Sparks is gone.

    ROBOT BUCKAROO: Where d'ya reckon he gone ta?

Panel 9
Robot Buckaroo shot. [11]

    ROBOT BUCKAROO: UNGH!

PAGE FOUR -
Panel 1
Sparks riding Mercury real fast towards panel-left but his arm's pointing panel-right, gun out, having just shot that robot buckaroo. He faces forward. Doesn't likes what he sees...

    SPARKS: Uh-oh.

SPARKS: Martian territoryti. [12]

Panel 2
Sparks spins his gun and kickstarts a rocket via the starter in the stirrup.

SFX: CHK-CHK!

Panel 3
Mercury ROCKETS over the Martian camp via rockets that come out of his rear flank chassis. Martians look up in awe and wonder. [13]

Panel 4
Mercury skids to a stop as the flood CHURNS past him. Sparks is pulling a block of glass out of the saddlebag.

PAGE FIVE -
Panel 1
Sparks and Mercury tear after the flood. We're far behind them watching them go, watching the flood go too, in the distance. [14]

In the foreground are cast-aside broken pieces of glass from a container formerly around the size of a cigar box.

On a larger piece we can easily read IN CASE OF FLOOD BREAK GLASS in official typeface. On a smaller piece we can see a post-it that reads "Marshal - keep this in your saddlebag AT ALL TIMES! - Doc 13."

Panels 2-4 are a flashback - let's give them a different palette.

Panel 2
Sparks and RED PLAINS RIDER in the Marshal station. Sparks is laughing, showing her the piece of glass. It contains a ring with clasps on it. Red is biting her lip, she's got something lousy to tell Sparks. Against the wall are the Deputybots, charging in charging stations.

SPARKS: ...then he says: "Step 1: Attach the wormhole generator to your lasso - the loop end, mind." Then he goes, "that is the the only step!"
SPARKS: You ain't laughin', Red. You notice that? [15]

Panel 3
Sparks is stoic, sure, but dying inside. Red is resolute. Back to him. Won't show Sparks this is tearing her up too.

RED: Reckon it's time I go back to the plains. They ain't gonna ride themselves.
SPARKS: But-
RED: I can't take the badge you offered me, Nevada. I just ain't the deputyin' type. Folks need me out there, where the law don't touch.

Panel 4
Sparks stares at the emergency glass in his hands as if he's in a short story and it's the symbol of something that means a whole lot to him. Over his shoulder, and subtle as f—, Deputybot #1 watches Sparks.

SPARKS (so small): Folks need you here.
CAP (MARSHAL STATION AI): The Marshal Station doors are open.
SFX: PWSHT-PWSHT!

[12] ***Blacker:*** *It was a good opportunity in the comics—from the original anthology to this collection—to get to show more of Mars. In the stage show and podcast, we liked to keep stories (generally) in town, as that's where all the beloved characters lived. And who cares, since there was no visual element anyway? Having the visuals really opened up the world and gives us an exciting new sandbox in which to create.*

[13] ***Acker:*** *I think this was the first time we got to show the rocket part of the rocket steed in action, an image that had been in our heads since the very beginning.*

[14] ***Acker:*** *We had a flood getting lasso'd with a wormhole in the original Sparks movie script we wrote back before we did the podcast.*

[15] ***Blacker:*** *I love any time we get to allude to Sparks and Red's romantic history. We did it a lot in the early days of the podcast, but we never really landed on what went wrong between them. Comics and other media always seemed a great place to explore that rich material. Also, they are so funny together, even in this scene, which isn't meant to be funny. You just root for them as a couple, I think. Which makes this scene sadder.*

[16] **Acker:** *We invented using "space" as a modifier. Don't look it up or anything. It's a fact. We did it first.*

[17] **Blacker:** *We went to the "space" well a lot in the early days of the show. It's an easy laugh that we could get away with before anyone knew who the characters were. Once the characters were more firmly established, most of the comedy came from their personalities playing off one another.*

I'm pretty sure the town on Mars has a "space-well."

[18] **Blacker:** *Catchphrase! I'm pleased to say that I don't think we ever overused this. And it was fun to fine the gradations of meaning for the catchphrase once it was well established. Sparks saying "I'm from Earth" sadly is one of the most heartbreaking moments of the show for me. Find it in the podcasts!*

[19] **Blacker:** *This is a scene that we originally wrote in 2003 or 2004 as part of the original Sparks feature movie. It's not a very good script, but all the pieces of the characters and what would become the Sparks canon and tropes were in there.*

[20] **Blacker:** *Classic Western movie cowboy move.*

[21] **Blacker:** *Boy did we wear some of these catchphrases into the ground in the live show and podcast. And yet, Marc Evan Jackson and Mark Gagliardi, who played Sparks and Croach, always always always made it funny.*

[22] **Blacker:** *This is another line ported over from the original feature script, and it always makes me laugh.*

Panel 5
Sparks solemnly ropes the flood.

PAGE SIX --
Panel 1
Sparks stands up in his stirrups. The flood disappears into the lasso.

> SPARKS: Buckin' like a space-bronco... [16]
> SPARKS: But... I'm! [17]

Panel 2
His arms out, his teeth clenched.

> SPARKS: From!

Panel 3
He yanks his arms back and gets the last of the flood.

> SPARKS: Earth! [18]

Panel 4
Sparks is down off Mercury, hitching the lasso to his belt.

> SPARKS: And not a drop touched the Martian camp. Tah-dah. Now to track down them robots before the Martians notice I been...

Panel 5
The Martians are all around him. Croach stands before him.

> SPARKS: ... here.

PAGE SEVEN --
Panel 1
Croach and Sparks stand awkwardly like it's their first date. The rest of the Martians are gone.

> CROACH: Holoba, Sparks-Nevada. I am Croach the Tracker. By locating your metal enemies, I shall fulfill the onus my tribe bears to you for containing the flood that would have devoured our overvillage. [19]

Panel 2
Sparks pushes his hat back a little by scratching his forehead to think it over. [20] Croach holds one hand to his head and points the other forward to the right.

> SPARKS: You really reckon you can find robots you ain't never seen that -
> CROACH: My tribe assigns descriptors without irony. [21] There is a metal being fifty units in that direction.

Panel 3
They ride, side by side.

> SPARKS: I don't put civilians in harm's way. You ride with me, it's trackin' only. Got me?
> LASSO: Marshal Nevada! Thank you for using the wormhole generator!
> CROACH: Your rope desires your attention. [22]

Panel 4

Sparks squints at his lasso.

LASSO: By now, you've either stopped a flood or died trying!
SPARKS: Gotta be a volume knob on here somewhere...

Panel 5

Croach reaches to turn the microscopic volume on the lasso on Sparks's belt. Sparks stares straight ahead, expressionless, but squaring his jaw like a Chuck Jones cartoon due to how Croach is being really rather forward, wouldn't you say?

CAP (DOC PRIME, getting smaller, disappearing by the end): Which of the following describes your experience with the wormhole generator? Very satisfied? Satisfied? Unsatisfied? Very unsatisfied?
CROACH: There. The rope's proclamations are relegated to the microspectrum.

Panel 6

Croach's antennae twitch. Croach looks as worried as a bug-eyed Spock like him can.

CROACH: Sparks-Nevada. Do you feel that?

PAGE EIGHT -
Panel 1

Sparks is still on Mercury, but not for much longer. His guns fly out of their holsters.

SPARKS: Whaaat?
CROACH: It is a disturbance in the magnetic equilibrium.

Panel 2

By a huge crater, among cactoids (low-flying balls of cactus), DEPUTYBOT 1 has souped himself up with upgrades. His head and torso are the same as the other Deputybots, but his arms and legs are amazing and advanced. Sparks's guns have flown into his hands. Behind him, the sun is just beginning to set.

DEPUTYBOT 1: That's right. I got upgrades. Magnets! [23] And others! So many deadly others! Reckon it's time you got killed by your very own deputy with your very own guns and on your very own - wait, no. That's it. I thought I had one more. [24] But I didn't. *And neither do you!*

Panel 3

We're behind Deputybot 1 as he shoots. Croach flies his saddle in front of Sparks to take the blast. Sparks is all like "No!"

SFX: k'pew! k'pew!
CROACH: Sparks-Nevada!

Panel 4

Croach sprawled on the ground. Sparks cradles his head. Croach's hoversaddle hovers nearby, Croach's leg is tangled in the stirrup. He looks messed UP! Please keep track of Mercury from here. He's not in this shot, but he's on the periphery of the action moving forward. We should see him in wide shots.

SPARKS: This is exactly what I told you to not do, Croach...
CROACH: That is not...
SPARKS: What is it?

[23] ***Blacker:*** *"Magnets" being a desirable upgrade for robots is another joke we hit a few times. It's just so silly. I love it.*

[24] ***Blacker:*** *I think this line is indicative of what we do as writers. Here is an insane circumstance and character—a newly sentient robot who wants to kill his old employer—but we make the characters talk like people with genuine feelings and foibles. This Deputybot is a braggart, but he also loses his train of thought. Sometimes those character moments take an extra beat—in any medium—but they are always worth it.*

CROACH: ...how you pronounce my signifier. [25]

Panel 5
Sparks walks towards Deputybot 1, putting on his robot fists.

DEPUTYBOT 1: What are you doin'? Walkin' towards your guns's barrels where the lasers live? You want to get shot by 'em by me? I'll oblige! I'll oblige you to death!

PAGE NINE -
Panel 1
Deputybot 1 pulls them triggers hard. Sparks leans into them.

SPARKS: They're out of laser bullets.
SFX: c'click c'click. [26]

Panel 2
Sparks punches this guy like the upwards version of when a super hero in a movie punches a car and it flies overtop of them. He puts his whole body into it and catches Deputybot 1 in the chin, already starting to send him flying.

SFX: POW!

Panel 3
Deputybot 1 landed on his back in a pile of cactoids. But he's smiling.

DEPUTYBOT 1: I can take anything you can dish out, Marshal! The upgrades I got, I cannot be beat. I can only beat! You!

Panel 4
We see Sparks's back in foreground. It's Deputybot 1's shot. They're squaring off, about to go at it. The background behind Deputybot is his memories: Sparks giving Red a badge, her leaving it, Sparks being sad. The Deputybot behind Sparks in the charging station. Yearning.

SPARKS (top left): But why? Why are we doin' this? Why'd you go rotten?
DEPUTYBOT 1 (bottom right): Wasn't no birthday wish! Wasn't no peer pressure!

Panel 5
On Sparks looking ahead at him like "tsk!"

SPARKS: Was it before or after you got magnets? Don't know why you robots keep gettin' magnets put it. They're as bad for your robot brains as water is to your robot bodies. [27]
CROACH (weakly, from off panel below): Water?

PAGE TEN -
Panel 1
Croach sturdies himself - near hand on Sparks's near shoulder, the other hand reaching all the way across both of 'em for the lasso on Sparks's hip. Sparks stares straight ahead at Deputybot 1 and does the thing with his chin again.

SPARKS: Yeah, water wrecks robots. You all right?
CROACH: I am sound, praise Nah Notek.
SPARKS: All... Right.

[25] **Blacker:** *It makes me smile that, in the final episode of the podcast, Croach finally accepts Sparks's pronunciation of his name. (I refuse to believe that Sparks actually got it right, just that Croach decided to be generous to his friend.)*

[26] **Blacker:** *We have never thought for any seconds about the physics or properties of the gun weapons in Sparks. Laser bullets. Sure. They can run out? Why not? This kind of stuff matters so little compared to the character stories that are going on and, as far as I know, this lack of consideration never bumped a listener.*

[27] **Blacker:** *See? Magnets. They're why the Joker went crazy too.*

Panel 2

With one hand, Croach holds the lasso loop out in front of him, pointed at Deputybot 1. With the other hand, he fiddles with the clasps. Sparks bends to look through the middle. The wormhole distorts his face a little.

CROACH: Help me hold it.
SPARKS: What are you doing?
CROACH: Ejecting the contents of the rope at your metal enemy. [28]
SPARKS: How do you know how to do that?
CROACH: The instructions were broadcast on the micro-spectrum.
SPARKS: All... Right.

Panel 3

PANEL BORDER is robot fists and Croach's hands holding the lasso loop together. Wide shot: Sparks behind Croach as they shoot a flood at Deputybot1 whose posture is pleading like John Turturro in Miller's Crossing. [29] He's sparking and malfunctioning.

DEPUTYBOT 1: I just want you zzzt!
DEPUTYBOT 1: ... to be able to see kzz it !
DEPUTYBOT 1: When!
DEPUTYBOT 1: you have... zzzk... a friend.
DEPUTYBOT 1(getting smaller to indicate dying): kzt! Right... in front of yoooooooou... [30]

Panel 4

Ride off towards camera, the sunset is behind them. Get it? They are riding off away from the sunset! Hilarious! Arguably hilarious. Croach rides a little in front of Sparks.

SPARKS: I didn't say your name right before?
CROACH: It is difficult to pronounce with a single human tongue.
SPARKS: Croach.
CROACH: Croach.
SPARKS: Croach?
CROACH: Croach.
SPARKS: Croach.
CROACH: No. [31]

[28] **Acker:** *This was the conclusion of that Sparks Nevada feature. Using the origin story for us telling Sparks stories in this Sparks and Croach origin story felt right to do.*

[29] **Blacker:** *A reference that, of course, everybody has.*

[30] **Acker:** *Oh man. Sparks really was emotionally unavailable at the start of things, wasn't he? Rebecca Rose Rushmore wasn't all wrong, was she?*

Blacker: *I feel like there's a whole series we could do that retells the entirety of the Sparks canon but they're reframed so that Sparks is the bad guy. Someone please do this.*

[31] **Blacker:** *Always. Hilarious.*

CREATORS

THE WOODS
JAMES TYNION IV • MICHAEL DIALYNAS
"The Woods is creepy, funny, charming, and mysterious. My favorite kind of comic, a deep mythology mixed with equally deep character work. Get in on the ground floor of something great!" –Jeff Lemire
VOL 1
THE ARROW

"The Spire is fantastic! My kind of genre free-for-all." –BRIAN K. VAUGHAN (Saga)
THE SPIRE
SIMON SPURRIER
JEFF STOKELY
ANDRÉ MAY
EISNER NOMINEE

MARK WAID • PETER KRAUSE
IRREDEEMABLE
AFTERWORD BY GRANT MORRISON

J.G. JONES
MARK WAID
STRANGE FRUIT
Foreword by
ELVIS MITCHELL

MICHAEL ALAN NELSON
DAN MORA
GABRIEL CASSATA
HEXED
THE HARLOT & THE THIEF VOLUME ONE

ABNETT & CULBARD
WILD'S END
FIRST LIGHT

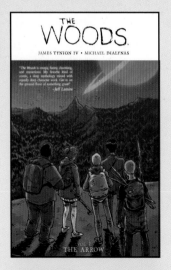

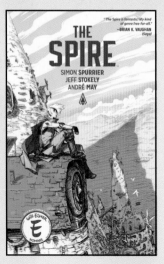

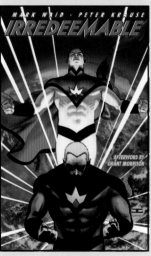

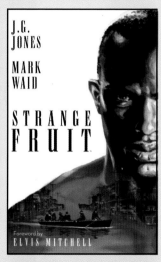

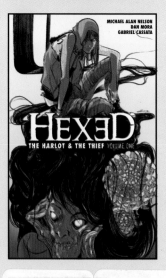

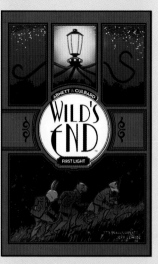

James Tynion IV
The Woods
Volume 1
ISBN: 978-1-60886-454-6 | $9.99 US
Volume 2
ISBN: 978-1-60886-495-9 | $14.99 US
Volume 3
ISBN: 978-1-60886-773-8 | $14.99 US

The Backstagers
Volume 1
ISBN: 978-1-60886-993-0 | $14.99 US

Simon Spurrier
Six-Gun Gorilla
ISBN: 978-1-60886-390-7 | $19.99 US

The Spire
ISBN: 978-1-60886-913-8 | $29.99 US

Weavers
ISBN: 978-1-60886-963-3 | $19.99 US

Mark Waid
Irredeemable
Volume 1
ISBN: 978-1-93450-690-5 | $16.99 US
Volume 2
ISBN: 978-1-60886-000-5 | $16.99 US

Incorruptible
Volume 1
ISBN: 978-1-60886-015-9 | $16.99 US
Volume 2
ISBN: 978-1-60886-028-9 | $16.99 US

Strange Fruit
ISBN: 978-1-60886-872-8 | $24.99 US

Michael Alan Nelson
Hexed The Harlot & The Thief
Volume 1
ISBN: 978-1-60886-718-9 | $14.99 US
Volume 2
ISBN: 978-1-60886-816-2 | $14.99 US

Day Men
Volume 1
ISBN: 978-1-60886-393-8 | $9.99 US
Volume 2
ISBN: 978-1-60886-852-0 | $9.99 US

Dan Abnett
Wild's End
Volume 1: First Light
ISBN: 978-1-60886-735-6 | $19.99 US
Volume 2: The Enemy Within
ISBN: 978-1-60886-877-3 | $19.99 US

Hypernaturals
Volume 1
ISBN: 978-1-60886-298-6 | $16.99 US
Volume 2
ISBN: 978-1-60886-319-8 | $19.99 US